BOOKS BY

MARIUS BEWLEY

MASKS & MIRRORS   *1970*
Essays in Criticism

THE ECCENTRIC DESIGN   *1959*
Form in the Classic American Novel

THE COMPLEX FATE   *1952*
Hawthorne, Henry James and Some Other American Writers

ANTHOLOGY

THE ENGLISH ROMANTIC POETS   *1970*
An Anthology with Commentaries

MASKS & MIRRORS

MARIUS BEWLEY

MASKS

&

MIRRORS

ESSAYS IN CRITICISM

NEW YORK   ATHENEUM   1974

Copyright © 1949, 1952, 1955, 1958, 1959, 1962, 1963, 1964, 1965,
1966, 1967, 1968, 1970 by Marius Bewley
All rights reserved
Library of Congress catalog card number 76-101396
ISBN 0-689-70512-3
Published simultaneously in Canada by McClelland and Stewart Ltd.
Manufactured in the United States of America by
The Murray Printing Company, Forge Village, Massachusetts
Designed by Harry Ford
First Atheneum Paperback Edition

FOR PEGGY GUGGENHEIM

ACKNOWLEDGMENTS

The Mask of John Donne. Part of this essay first appeared in THE KENYON REVIEW, Autumn, 1952; part was first published as the Introduction to *The Selected Poems of John Donne*, SIGNET CLASSICS, 1967; part of the material is new.

The Colloquial Byron is abridged somewhat from an article that first appeared in SCRUTINY, March, 1949. The Note on Lovelace's "La Bella Bona-Roba" is reprinted from SCRUTINY, September, 1949.

Several of the comments on Swift's poetry in *The Romantic Imagination and the Un-Romantic Byron* are taken from a review published in THE SPECTATOR, August 29, 1958.

Death and the James Family. THE NEW YORK REVIEW OF BOOKS, November 5, 1964.

Henry James's English Hours. Introduction to the edition of ENGLISH HOURS published by Horizon Press, 1968.

Two American Painters: Copley and Allston. PARTISAN REVIEW, February, 1949.

Mrs. Wharton's Mask. THE NEW YORK REVIEW OF BOOKS, September 24, 1964.

Scott Fitzgerald: The Apprentice Fiction. THE NEW YORK REVIEW OF BOOKS, September 16, 1965.

Longfellow. THE HUDSON REVIEW, Summer, 1963.

Sinclair Lewis. THE HUDSON REVIEW, Spring, 1962.

Mr. Clemens and Mark Twain. THE NEW YORK REVIEW OF BOOKS, September 8, 1966.

O Brave New World. THE NEW YORK REVIEW OF BOOKS, November 19, 1964.

Patriotic Gore, by Edmund Wilson. THE HUDSON REVIEW, Autumn, 1962.

The Heroic and the Romantic West. THE NEW YORK REVIEW OF BOOKS, April 8, 1965.

Wah-to-yah and the Taos Trail. THE NEW YORK REVIEW OF BOOKS, October 28, 1965.

James Fenimore Cooper: America's Mirror of Conscience. Adapted slightly from MAJOR WRITERS OF AMERICA Volume I, edited by Perry Miller, © 1962 by Harcourt, Brace & World, Inc., and reprinted with their permission.

The Land of Oz: America's Great Good Place. THE NEW YORK REVIEW OF BOOKS, December 3, 1964.

Wallace Stevens and Emerson. THE COMMONWEAL, September 23, 1955.

Eliot, Pound, and History. THE SOUTHERN REVIEW, Autumn, 1965.

Hart Crane's Last Poem. ACCENT, Spring, 1959.

A New Kind of Poetry? THE NEW YORK REVIEW OF BOOKS, January 20, 1966.

CONTENTS

Contents

IV

I

THE MASK OF JOHN DONNE

T HE REPUTATIONS of few English poets have undergone such extreme fluctuations as that of John Donne. In the present century—particularly in the period between the two World Wars—Donne's poetry has been rated immeasurably higher than at any time during the preceding two hundred years. Indeed, for a brief period his new rank seemed to threaten the preeminence of Milton in the seventeenth century. Even today, when the Donne fever of the 'twenties and 'thirties has considerably abated, to prefer Donne to Milton is to some extent the hallmark of the critical sensibility as contrasted with the scholarly and academic. But the point would not be pressed now with the old intensity of thirty years ago. While there may have been a shift in literary fashion, Donne's earlier popularity in this century will certainly have a lasting effect. The vast amount of Donne scholarship and criticism that was produced during the great Donne vogue—much of it sound and penetrating, some of it brilliant—has virtually guaranteed that one of the most important poets of the English literary tradition will never again be subjected to this sort of thing:

Donne is the most inharmonious of our versifiers, if he can be said to have deserved such a name by lines too rugged to seem metre. Of his earlier poems many are licentious; the later are chiefly devout. Few are good for much; the conceits have not even the merit of being intelligible; it would perhaps be difficult to select three passages that we should care to read again.

This undistinguished judgment is taken from the influential *Introduction to the Literature of Europe in the Fifteenth, Sixteenth, and Seventeenth Centuries* by Henry Hallam, the father of the gifted young man to whose memory Tennyson wrote *In Memoriam*. The third volume, in which Hallam speaks of Donne, appeared in 1839. Though more unhappily phrased, it repeats essentially the earlier judgment of Samuel Johnson in his "Life of Cowley" on the English metaphysical poets, of which "school" Donne may be counted the founding father:

The metaphysical poets [wrote Johnson] were men of learning, and to show their learning was their whole endeavour; but unluckily resolving to show it in rhyme, instead of writing poetry they only wrote verses, and very often such verses as stood the trial of the finger better than of the ear; for the modulation was so imperfect that they were only found to be verses by counting the syllables.

Although Donne published only three or four poems in his lifetime, manuscripts of his poems passed through the hands of a select coterie of intellectuals at the universities, the Inns of Court, and some of the most brilliant and promising young men of Elizabeth's and James's reigns. Ben Jonson, the most learned poet of his time, was Donne's friend—the only professional literary man Donne accepted in that role, for like Byron, and probably for somewhat similar reasons, Donne

4

preferred to seek his intimacies in a different sphere. But Jonson's genius, erudition, and intellectual influence in London made him an exception, as well no doubt as the admiration he felt for Donne's poetry. He told William Drummond of Hawthornden that he esteemed "John Donne the first poet of the world in some things." Donne was, in short, a leader of the avant garde in late Elizabethan and Jacobean London. His audience was deliberately restricted to the happy few whose education, background, and position equipped them to appreciate and esteem the most difficult poet of his day. Some snobbishness seems to have attached itself to the ability to do so. When his poems were first published as a volume in 1633, two years after his death, the printer introduced them with a note, not to the readers, but "To the Understanders." There was clearly a difference. The difficulty of Donne's poetry was the more dear to its admirers because it seemed to be so intimately associated with the genius of the English language. When Charles I, who was himself a great admirer of it, heard of a projected translation into Dutch, he expressed himself confident that no one "could acquit himself of that task with credit."

The influence of T. S. Eliot's poetry on the morale of the young literary intellectuals of the 'twenties and 'thirties must have resembled in certain respects the stimulus that Donne's poetry provided for an impatient generation long surfeited with Petrarchism and the poetic conventions of the earlier Elizabethans. Donne's influence on the metaphysical poets who came after him, and who are commonly regarded as his heirs, seems in fact to have been in the nature of a general stimulus, an infusion of new energy, rather than the imposition of a narrowly defined manner. His principal followers are not only very different among themselves, but extremely individual in the way each assimilated the master's influence. If we name here only the three most important and best poets in the Donne tradition, George Herbert, Richard Crashaw, and

Andrew Marvell, it becomes clear that his example was no straitjacket, but that the metaphysical style permitted the widest latitude and the most individual and personal assimilation of its tenets, however those might be defined. If in the cases of a few poets the elaborately drawn conceit (which Samuel Johnson took to be the defining characteristic of metaphysical poetry) was exaggerated beyond any possible functional or organic role within the poem, and became an interest and an end in itself, that was the abuse of a style rather than an intrinsic defect.

Donne's reputation and influence continued down through the early years of the Restoration. The first edition of his poems was followed by a second in 1635, and there were five more, this early series coming to an end with the edition of 1669. The next edition appeared only after the lapse of half a century, in 1719. Of the reasons one might adduce for this decline in Donne's reputation as a poet, perhaps the most important is related to the new taste for mathematical plainness in language fostered by the Royal Society. In his *History of the Royal Society*, 1667, Thomas Spratt commended its members for resisting extravagance of language introduced through the medium of poetry:

They have therefore been most rigorous in putting in execution the only Remedy that can be found for this *extravagance*, and that has been a constant Resolution to reject all amplifications, digressions, and swellings of style; to return back to the primitive purity and shortness, when men deliver'd so many *things* almost in an equal number of *words*. They have extracted from all their members a close, naked, natural way of speaking, positive expressions, clear senses, a native easiness, bringing all things as near the Mathematical plainness as they can, and preferring the language of Artizans, Countrymen, and Merchants, before that of Wits or Scholars.

Donne's poetry could not be expected to flourish in such a restrictive climate. By 1693 he was so out of favor that Dryden, associating the term "metaphysical" with his poetry for the first time and thus inadvertently christening the school, wrote of him:

> He affects the metaphysics, not only in his satires, but in his amorous verses, where nature only should reign, and perplexes the mind of the fair sex with nice speculations of philosophy, when he should engage their hearts, and entertain them with the softness of love.

After that, for nearly two hundred years Donne's reputation was in shadow, to the obscurity of which Dr. Johnson contributed by rejecting the whole school of poetry in his "Life of Cowley," from which I have already quoted. Johnson's essay squarely confronts the question of what constitutes the metaphysical character of poetry in the line of Donne. He found its essence to consist in "a kind of *discordia concors;* a combination of dissimilar images, or discovery of occult images in things apparently unlike. . . . The most heterogeneous ideas are yoked by violence together. . . ."

This is good enough in its way, but unfortunately it is a description which explains the failures of metaphysical poetry better than its achievements. It covers the poetry of John Cleveland or Edward Benlowes of perhaps even Cowley, but it leaves everything to be desired in the case of Donne or George Herbert or Marvell. There have been many attempts to define metaphysical poetry, or to describe its essential characteristics, in the present century. But the excellence of the best metaphysical poets cannot be captured in a formula. What is valuable in their poetry is exactly what will transcend the articles of any manifesto we may devise for them. It is probably best to begin by considering what metaphysical poetry is not.

Most of all, it is not philosophical poetry in any accurate sense of that term. It is studded with philosophical concepts and draws heavily on the technical vocabulary of metaphysics, but these are used with no design of presenting a comprehensive or coherent view of the universe and of man's place in it. This defect may appear to be supplied in some instances by the poet's reliance upon religious orthodoxy, or the appearance of it; but even here little attempt is made to expound doctrine, much less exhibit a theological system in its comprehensive consistency. The emphasis is invariably on the devotional, and the Metaphysicals end by being as remote from Dante as they are from Lucretius. It may be useful here to compare a passage of philosophical poetry by an Elizabethan poet with some verses from one of Donne's most famous poems which appears to be treating the same metaphysical problem, the nature of the relation between body and soul. Despite Donne's technical proficiency in dealing with the question of how spirit, an immaterial thing, can act upon matter, his interest in the poem is centered elsewhere than in the metaphysics.

The first passage is from a long poem by Sir John Davies, *Nosce Teipsum*, published in 1599. It expounds the nature of the soul, and it undertakes this task with a singleness of purpose and clarity of statement worthy of the most lucid expository prose. The verses quoted here are themselves only one step in an elaborately articulated argument plotted with logical care and precision:

But how shall we this union well express?
Naught ties the Soul: her subtilty is such,
She moves the Body, which she doth possess,
Yet no part toucheth but by Virtue's touch.

Then dwells she not therein as in a tent,
Nor as a pilot in his ship doth sit,
Nor as the spider in her web is pent,
Nor as the wax retains the print in it,

Nor as a vessel water doth contain,
Nor as one liquor in another shed,
Nor as the heat doth in the fire remain,
Nor as a voice throughout the air is spread:

But as the fair and cheerful morning light
Doth here and there her silver beams impart,
And in an instant doth herself unite
To the transparent air, in all and part:

Still resting whole when blows the air divide,
Abiding pure when the air is most corrupted,
Throughout the air, her beams dispersing wide,
And when the air is tost, not interrupted:

So doth the piercing Soul the body fill,
Being all in all, and all in part diffused;
Invisible, incorruptible still,
Not forced, encountered, troubled, or confused.

And as the sun above the light doth bring,
Though we behold it in the air below,
So from the Eternal Light the Soul doth spring,
Though in the body she her powers do show.

It is extraordinary how Davies has managed to sustain
page after page of this kind of verse at a level which consistently illuminates his argument without ever obtruding itself
as nonfunctional ornament or decoration. His images are
well-trained servants serving his meaning; never flatterers to
seduce it from its duty, nor yet again angelic messengers
bearing intimations of some higher Heaven of meaning than
the one Sir John wishes to enter. There is a kind of verbal
neatness and element of surprise in some of the images that
may momentarily remind one of metaphysical wit, but something much simpler is involved. These images are merely

illustrational, diagrammatic: they light up the meaning but do not contribute to its substance:

> *Water in conduit pipes can rise no higher*
> *Than the well-head from whence it first doth spring:*
> *Then sith to eternal God she doth aspire*
> *She cannot be but an eternal thing.*

With this straightforward exposition of the relation between body and soul we may contrast Donne's far different treatment of the same problem. Basically, the difference arises from the fact that Donne is not interested in the problem itself, but in something else: the relation of two lovers, or the nature of love itself. The meaning of "The Ecstasy," one of Donne's best-known poems, has been much debated. While it is possible to question Donne's final motive behind the poem, the argument *appears* to revolve around the proposition that love between the sexes is, or should be, a function of the total personality, not of the body alone. In Scholasticism man is a composite creature made up of body and soul, between which an intrinsic union exists, and man has his complete identity only in terms of this union. Soul and body together form one nature, and essentially human activity, including the emotions, proceeds from body and soul in conjunction. Sexual passion may degrade man to an animal level, but properly exercised in relation to his total personality it will be a function and fulfillment of his humanity. In contrast with some of his so-called "libertine" poems, Donne appears to be dramatizing this view in "The Ecstasy."

He presents his lovers to us in a spring landscape, implied rather than described in the opening stanza. The situation, both in setting and action, is thoroughly conventional, and had frequently been exploited by earlier Elizabethan poets. Donne's follower, Lord Herbert of Cherbury, would write a very similar poem in his "Ode upon a Question Moved, Whether Love Should Continue Forever," which should be read with "The Ecstasy" for purposes of comparison. Contemplating each other, the lovers fall into a trance, or more properly an ecstasy, for Donne is thinking of that term in mystical philosophy in which a knowledge or sense of God, short-circuiting the senses, is intuited directly. In the poem, however, not God, but each to the other, becomes the object of this exalted way of knowing. The following excerpt makes the poem's essential statement:

"The Ecstasy doth unperplex"
 (We said) "and tell us what we love;
We see by this, it was not sex;
 We see, we saw not what did move:

"But as all several souls contain
 Mixture of things, they know not what,
Love, these mix'd souls doth mix again,
 And makes both one, each this and that.

"A single violet transplant,
 The strength, the color, and the size,
(All which before was poor, and scant,)
 Redoubles still, and multiplies.

"When love, with one another so
 Interinanimates two souls,
That abler soul, which thence doth flow,
 Defects of loneliness controls.

"We then, who are this new soul, know,
 Of what we are compos'd, and made,
For, the atomies of which we grow,
 Are souls, whom no change can invade.

"But oh alas, so long, so far
 Our bodies why do we forbear?
They are ours, though they are not we; we are
 The intelligences, they the sphere.

11

* * *

"As our blood labors to beget
    Spirits, as like souls as it can,
Because such fingers need to knit
    That subtle knot, which makes us man:

"So must pure lovers' souls descend
    To affections, and to faculties,
Which sense may reach and apprehend,
    Else a great Prince in prison lies."

In their ecstatic state it is revealed to the lovers that their love for each other transcends sex, and is ultimately an activity of the soul. Their souls coming together in this love union are strengthened, the stronger supplying the weaknesses of the other. In this union they seem to themselves not two souls but one, and since this new soul knows that it is compounded of two separate souls which (according to Scholasticism) are simple principles unsusceptible to change of corruption, it has perfect self-knowledge of its own being. There is of course a contradiction here, since souls or spiritual principles are incapable by their nature of being compounded into something else, but had Donne been taking his metaphysics very seriously this poem would hardly have been written in the first place.

Although the lovers have discovered their love to be spiritual in essence, it can be consummated and fulfilled only if they resort to their bodies, for it is man's unique distinction that in the duality of his composition heaven and earth meet. This duality is explicitly introduced in the lines referring to the spirits of the blood that knit the subtle knot which makes us man. The Renaissance believed that subtle vapors or spirits were generated in the body and communicated the functions of life to it. There were several classes of these spirits, the most rarefied having their seat in the brain. Although material in nature, they were the middlemen, the messengers that leaped the hiatus between material body and immaterial soul, thus maintaining the indispensable bond of communication between the two aspects of man's nature.

The widely divergent treatments that a metaphysical problem has received at the hands of Davies and Donne should make it clear that however metaphysical poetry of Donne's school may be defined, it is not philosophical poetry in any real sense, although it uses the concepts and vocabulary of philosophy. Its use of them is invariably accompanied by a complex infusion of irony, and the poet has his eye on other things than the truth of the metaphysical propositions employed. He is "metaphysical" towards nonmetaphysical ends. During the seventeenth century Scholasticism continued to be taught at the two universities—greatly to the irritation and discomfort of the young Milton at Cambridge; but life had departed from it, and the intellectual temper of the time was that of Francis Bacon, not of the schoolmen. It is doubtful if metaphysical poetry like Donne's could have been written at all in a society that still commanded assent to the metaphysical system which the poet feels at liberty to treat with so free a hand. It is only because the terms and conceptions he takes over from metaphysics into his poems no longer express an activity of living thought in their proper sphere that he is able to divert them—or pervert them—to the surprising, even extraordinary, functions they perform in his poetry.

From the viewpoint of the malefactions Donne commits against the proprieties of metaphysical terminology, "The Ecstasy" is not an especially invidious example. Donne appears to be defining a kind of love to which his metaphysical images are relevant. But some years ago the French scholar Pierre Legouis persuasively argued that "The Ecstasy," like Marvell's "To His Coy Mistress," was a poem of seduction. If so, the deflection of the metaphysical vocabulary from its proper end is indeed startling. It is perhaps worth noting that the argument of "The Ecstasy," in which two

13

lovers' souls become one over-soul as a prelude to sexual union, is paralleled (or travestied) in "The Flea," which is overtly a poem of seduction. The flea, which has sucked blood from the veins of both lovers, becomes the symbol of their transcendent union and identity:

> *This flea is you and I, and this*
> *Our marriage bed, and marriage temple is;*
> *Though parents grudge, and you, we're met,*
> *And cloistered in these living walls of jet.*

The flea, being their marriage temple by virtue of their commingled blood in its body, acquires a special sanctity so that it becomes a sacrilege to kill it. The more one reads Donne the more difficult it is to believe he was really more "metaphysically" serious in "The Ecstasy" than in the latter poem. A certain doubt about Donne's motives sooner or later crosses the minds of many of his critics. T. S. Eliot, who was one of his early modern champions, a few years after his famous essay of 1921, "The Metaphysical Poets," was led to express a revised opinion. "In making some quite commonplace investigations of the 'thought' of Donne," he wrote, "I found it quite impossible to come to the conclusion that Donne believed anything. It seemed as if, at that time, the world was filled with the broken fragments of systems, and that a man like Donne merely picked up, like a magpie, various shining fragments."

Expressing a somewhat similar opinion from a different point of view, C. S. Lewis wrote in an essay on Donne's love poetry: "Paradoxical as it may seem, Donne's poetry is too simple to satisfy. Its complexity is all on the surface—an intellectual and fully conscious complexity that we soon come to the end of. Beneath this we find nothing but a limited series of 'passions'—explicit, mutually exclusive passions which can be instantly labeled as such—things which can be readily talked about, and indeed must be talked about, because in silence they begin to lose their hard outlines and overlap, to betray themselves as partly fictitious."

But if Donne's poetry, with Eliot's help, was over-acclaimed for a few years in this century, such animadversions as these are unfair despite an undoubted element of truth. Eliot is probably thinking of Donne's personal religious settlement, which was certainly a complex one, and we shall discuss it presently. But metaphysical (and theological) conviction and consistency presented peculiar difficulties in those days of religious transition that have been paralleled in ours only on the political level, and even there, only during comparatively brief intervals of intensified suspicion and witch-hunting. The sense of metaphysical insecurity that Donne's poetry finally leaves one with is, from one point of view, an added element of drama and tension. C. S. Lewis's criticism is perhaps the more damaging because it is aimed directly at the quality of the experience celebrated. The undeniable cynicism of much of Donne's love poetry is not in itself Lewis's target, but a certain emotional superficiality which appears to be related to it. Both critics seem to be condemning Donne for a lapse of sincerity, or a failure of candor. Although he does not say so, one feels that Eliot as a devout High Churchman is a little outraged by a note of latitudinarianism that no reader can fail to miss in *Satyre III* and some of the religious poetry, whereas Lewis is frankly desiring something that Donne was not prepared to offer: the seventeenth-century equivalent (one almost suspects) of Keats's sonnets to Fanny Brawne.

The answer to these objections must come from a fuller consideration of Donne's personality and background, but at this point we may anticipate the illumination of biography by taking a summary look at the poems. During the long period in which Donne's reputation was obscured, he found an able advocate in Coleridge. In *Biographia Literaria* Coleridge makes a highly perceptive remark about Donne. True, Coleridge is also talking about Dryden, but the application to Donne is particularly significant. "The vividness of the descriptions or declamations in Donne," he writes, ". . . is as much and as often derived from the force and fervor of the describer, as from the reflections, forms or incidents which constitute his subject and materials. The wheels take fire from the mere rapidity of their motion."

Coleridge recognized what Donne's contemporary admirers recognized: that his achievement as a poet was not in his treatment of a particular subject matter, but in the creation of a style, the revitalization of a language that was on the point of growing tired. His poetry did not illuminate ideas as such, but brought a new freshness to the language and renewed its energy. The elegies by Donne's admirers that were included in the posthumously published edition of his poems were mostly agreed on this. The best of the elegies was by Thomas Carew, gentleman of the Privy Chamber, royal sewer or taster to the King, and an excellent poet. Although he does not of course use the word *originality* in describing Donne's poetry, that is what his critical assessment of it amounts to. Donne, he says, has purged English poetry of "pedantique weeds"; he has replaced "servile imitation" with "fresh invention"; he has opened up new resources for the creative imagination ("pregnant phansie"), and he has done this by introducing a new austerity into his verse line. What other critics would refer to as his metrical roughness or hardness, Carew more aptly calls "masculine expression." He means by this phrase a strenuous encounter between language and meaning in which the two components, like Donne's recurrent lovers, are strengthened and renewed by merging in a common intensified identity. As Carew puts it:

> . . . *to the awe of thy imperious wit*
> *Our stubborn language bends, made only fit*
> *With her tough-thick-ribbed hoops to gird about*

Thy giant phansie which had prov'd too stout
For their soft melting phrases.

The antecedent of "which" in the fourth line is not
Donne's "giant phansie" but "our stubborn language,"
which requires a masculine and imperious imagination like
Donne's to dominate it and extract the meaning it is so
reluctant to yield. The "soft melting phrases" of the last line
belong to the earlier Elizabethans, with their smoothly flowing, richly ornamented verses. The central ground for praise
in the elegy seems to be that in Donne's writing there is a
harmony and interdependence of parts, of words, emotions,
and thoughts. Later in the elegy, although he is referring to
the sermons rather than the poetry, he speaks of "thy brave
soul, that shot such heat and light,/ As burnt our earth, and
made our darkness bright." Heat stands for Donne's emotion,
light for his thought. Yet these are indivisible aspects of *one*
fire—in this case, Donne's creative imagination expressing
itself through language. Carew would appear to have anticipated in certain respects Eliot's attribution to Donne in his
1921 essay of a unified sensibility. That famous but belea-
guered phrase, however its application and interpretation
may have been distorted by later scholars and critics, would
not have been totally unintelligible to Donne's contemporaries
and immediate followers.

But as we have seen, Eliot, who had announced that
Donne's thought and feeling were harmoniously one in a
unified or associated sensibility, later came to question the
quality and consistency of Donne's thought. Now the quality
of a poet's *thinking* is certain to affect the quality of his
poetry, but whether one approves or disapproves of *what* is
thought is not especially relevant from a literary-critical point
of view. It is difficult not to suspect that it was Donne's
thought rather than his thinking that troubled Eliot after his
first enthusiasm had waned. It is not at all to the discredit of

17

Donne's intelligence and erudition to say that for a man living in the twentieth century his thought may well seem negligible. The poetry neither presents original ideas (as paraphrasable entities) nor develops old ones. Nevertheless, it is among the most intelligent, nervously alert poetry in English. What it does do supremely well is to develop a complexly poised attitude toward experience. Donne was not only a man of unusual intelligence and learning, but, despite the fact that his motives have often been suspected, he was morally and spiritually sensitive beyond most of his contemporaries. Since he was at the same time ambitious and worldly, his greatest problem was to reconcile these two contradictory aspects of his character. Deeper than the intellectual and moral inconsistency sensed by Eliot, or the emotional superficiality that repelled Lewis, his poetry possesses a strong pragmatic purpose, which is to bring the poet himself and his talents into line with the demands made by his political society on an Elizabethan who seeks to make his way in the world, without at the same time betraying his conscience and integrity more than absolutely necessary. The world being what it was in those days, this was a tall order. The astonishing thing is not that Donne sometimes appears to have failed, but that on the whole he succeeded so well.

II

DONNE was ordained a priest of the Church of England on January 23, 1615. He was already forty-three—late in the day to begin such a career. It is certain that Donne, whose prospects of secular advancement had once appeared so bright, would have welcomed an alternative course, but he was virtually pushed to the altar. In view of the distinction and dedicated devotion of Donne's subsequent career, the

Anglican faithful might well see a directing Providence in the pattern of events that brought about his ordination, but from a more secular point of view it was that royal source of bounty, King James I, who did the pushing.

King James was familiar with Donne's intellectual gifts through a polemical book Donne had written, and which appeared in 1610, defending the oath of allegiance which attested the King's supremacy as head of the Anglican Church. The general argument of the book is revealed in its full title: *Pseudo-Martyr, wherein out of certain Propositions and Gradations, This Conclusion is evicted. That Those which are of the Romane Religion in this Kingdome, may and ought to take the Oath of Allegeance.* After that, James would hear of no advancement for Donne outside the Church. Although it was certainly to the King's advantage to have such a man working for him *inside* the Anglican fabric, it is no small tribute to his perspicacity and intelligence that he saw Donne so clearly in the role of churchman almost from the first. When pressured by his favorite, Robert Ker, Earl of Somerset, to confer political advancement on Donne, according to Donne's friend and first biographer, Izaak Walton, "the King gave a positive denial to all requests and, having a discerning spirit, replied, 'I know Mr. Donne is a learned man, has the abilities of a learned divine, and will prove a powerful preacher. And my desire is to prefer him in that way, and in that way I will deny you nothing for him.' " With these words in his ears, Donne submitted to the inevitable, but he did so with good grace. After a young manhood that may have been blemished, but was probably only fashionably unedifying, Donne became the most popular, and one of the greatest, preachers of his Church in a century renowned for its pulpit eloquence. So Donne, who had been described by an early friend as "a great visitor of ladies, a great frequenter of plays," in the words of Walton "became *crucified to the world*, and all those vanities, those imaginary

pleasures that are daily enacted on that restless stage; and
they were as perfectly crucified to him."

Undoubtedly Walton exaggerates: it is difficult for us to
think of Donne as a saint, even though many of his contemporaries did so. However that may be, enough advancement was
accorded Donne in the Church to satisfy at least in part the
desire for influence, place, and fortune he had always felt
while still in the world. He was made a chaplain to the King,
and he held the important appointment of Reader in Divinity
to the Benchers of Lincoln's Inn, where he had studied much
earlier. In 1621 he was elected Dean of St. Paul's, the
cathedral church of the Bishop of London, and had he lived a
little longer he would have died a bishop himself, for Charles
I admired Dr. Donne no less than his father had.

By the time Donne ascended the altar steps, the poems that
make up *Songs and Sonnets* had almost certainly all been
written. On the eve of his ordination Donne, who had been
content for his poems to be circulated in manuscript, suddenly had a desire to publish them. But his friends dissuaded
him. The Anglican Church of those days could point to many
men of wit and secular sophistication who wrote verses, and
even published them. But many of the love poems of Donne's
youth were hardly the sort to appear with propriety under the
name of a clergyman of forty-three, especially one who was
not averse to getting ahead in the Church. While the dates of
the Divine Poems are very uncertain, some of them at least
were still to be written, but they do not raise the same kind of
problems or excite speculation in the way the earlier poems
do. The Donne whose poetry and enigmatic personality have
attracted the twentieth century so strongly is the cynical
young poet of the last decade of Elizabeth's reign, and the
financially distressed young husband and father of the early
years of James's. It is here rather than in the priestly years
that one must look for suggestions and clues that may help us
towards a better understanding of Donne. Eliot, the erstwhile

champion turned Devil's advocate, in the act of sacrificing Donne to Lancelot Andrewes, wrote: "About Donne there hangs the shadow of the impure motive." But it is not difficult to be severe about impure motives when an invitation to martyrdom is not lying on one's own hall table, and when one does not have a large and growing family of children who are vulgarly susceptible to hunger and cold. Critics in general would probably agree that Donne's motives (like most men's) were not perfectly undevious. Therefore let us consider here what those motives may have been, and how his poetry was affected by them.

Donne was born and educated a Catholic at a time when adherence to the ancient faith was attended by the heaviest penalties and liabilities. In attempting to understand the complexity of his personality, it would be difficult to exaggerate the importance of this fact. His great grandmother had been the sister of St. Thomas More, Chancellor of England, who had been beheaded in 1535 for refusing the oath of supremacy—that same oath which Donne was to defend in *Pseudo-Martyr*. But St. Thomas More had been only the first of a long line of heroic Catholics in Donne's family who were willing to suffer exile and death for their faith. His own brother Henry, his younger by a year, died in the Clink prison to which he had been sent for concealing a Roman priest. Donne's father, a wealthy London ironmonger, was apparently a more aggressive businessman than Catholic, but his mother was devout, and her brothers Elias and Jasper Heywood were among the first English members of the Society of Jesus. Jasper indeed was Superior or Prefect to the Jesuit Mission in England. Donne knew his learned and (by all reports) arrogant uncle Jasper in his childhood, and one suspects from the violent animus of Donne's later references to the Jesuits that Jasper may have impressed his nephew not only powerfully but unfavorably. His prose satire, *Ignatius His Conclave*, published in 1611, in which the founder of the Jesuits outplays Machiavelli on his own ground and even overawes Lucifer, was, to say the least, an unusual performance to come from the nephew of the Jesuit Prefect.

Still earlier there had been his maternal grandfather, John Heywood, whose interludes mark an important step in the development of the English secular drama. John Heywood died in banishment for his faith—only one among the many in Donne's family whose talents went unrewarded because of their attachment to Rome. This family is still capable of touching the imagination after three centuries, and it is reasonable to think that its effect on Donne must have been profound. The intellectual distinction that it represented was of a kind that naturally appealed to him, while its magnificent example of sacrifice and worldly loss was one he was ambitious enough to fear with all his heart. For a young man of Donne's secular ambitions, dissociation from his religious background was an imperative necessity; yet for a young man of Donne's Jesuit-trained and disciplined conscience, dissociation—if it were not to appear as apostasy—would be a long and arduous process, requiring all the subtlety of intelligence his scholastic training could draw upon.

Even Phillip II was shocked by the incredible ineptitude of the Papal Bull *Regnans in Excelsis*, which in 1570 declared Elizabeth deposed and released her subjects from their allegiance. From that moment the Queen's government had little alternative but to regard Catholics as traitors. It was Pope St. Pius V far more than the excellent and forbearing Queen who was responsible for the English martyrs. Magnificent they may have been, but Donne was determined not to join them. A more serious question for the brilliant young worldling was the question of a career. In Elizabethan England virtually all public careers were closed to Catholics. They were not even welcome at the two universities. As degrees were conferred by Oxford and Cambridge only after the candidate had taken the oath of supremacy, Catholics were excluded from academic honors though they might study at one of the colleges. In 1584, at the age of twelve, Donne was matriculated at Oxford, where he remained for three years, after which, according to Walton, he studied at Cambridge for a similar period. But not taking the loyalty oath, he left both universities without a degree. Later, after his conversion to Anglicanism, he received an honorary Master of Arts degree from Oxford for having written *Pseudo-Martyr*, and after his ordination he received a Doctor of Divinity degree from Cambridge by King James's royal mandate.

From the universities Donne proceeded to study law in London, first at Thavies Inn and then at Lincoln's Inn, where many years later he was to become Reader in Divinity. At some uncertain period during this decade—probably between 1594 and 1596—he traveled abroad in Spain and in Italy, where he mastered the languages. In 1596 he joined the famous expedition against Cadiz under the joint command of the Earl of Essex and the now elderly Lord Admiral Howard, who had defeated the Spanish Armada eight years earlier. The following year Donne joined the Islands Voyage, also under the command of Essex, which planned to intercept the Spanish treasure ships off the Azores. Out of his experience on this expedition he wrote "The Storm" and "The Calm," the second poem being a favorite with Ben Jonson.

It is to this decade that most of the cynical and libertine love poems belong. It was also during this period that Donne was converted to Anglicanism. Izaak Walton assigns the conversion to the period during which Donne was at Lincoln's Inn:

About the nineteenth year of his age, he, being then unresolv'd what Religion to adhere to, and considering how much it concern'd his soul to choose the most Orthodox, did therefore (though his youth and health promised him a long life) to rectifie all scruples that might

23

concern that, presently lay aside all study of the Law: and, of all other Sciences that might give him a denomination; and begun seriously to survey, and consider the Body of Divinity, as it was then controverted betwixt the *Reformed* and the *Roman Church.*

The poetry which coincides with this decade during which Donne's inward struggle must have been most intense, and which in a sense leads up to *The Anniversaries,* which we shall consider in some detail, is the *Songs and Sonnets.* The chronology of Donne's life and writings is often quite uncertain, but one is fairly safe in surmising that while the young Donne was wrestling with his theological doubts, and annotating Cardinal Bellarmine's *Disputations concerning the Controversies of the Faith against the Heretics of this Present Time,* he was either writing or *would* write within the next few years most of his "libertine" love poems. This fact suggests a curious psychological tension or ambivalence and invites a closer inspection of the more blatantly sexual poems. J. B. Leishman in his book on Donne, *The Monarch of Wit,* writes of him: "Must he not often have asked himself . . . whether the differences between the Roman and the Anglican churches were of such fundamental importance as to make it necessary for him to continue to endure the disabilities imposed on Catholics, which had already prevented him from taking a university degree, and which would deny him all possibility of public employment? . . . And may one not, without being cynical, suggest that he reached the conclusion he subconsciously wanted to reach . . . ?"

It seems very possible to me that the "libertine" poems may have been written, not as a celebration of sexual experience, but as a subconscious strategy to assist Donne in prying himself free of Rome. It is the kind of thing that might occur subconsciously to any Jesuit-trained young man in Donne's position. In the *Songs and Sonnets* he not only generates a mood of cynicism in sexual matters, a cynicism that will prove as destructive when directed against faith as when exercised on its immediate object; even when he appears to be most serious in his love poems, a sense of the hopelessness or feebleness of the experience frequently causes him to magnify it, as in "The Canonization," by expressing it in terms that are properly reserved for religious usage. D. W. Harding, in his essay "Coherence of Theme in Donne's Poetry," has written of a concealed fear in Donne: "It seems reasonable to think that Donne's elaborate building up towards an experience was associated with some anxiety about the worth of the event when it finally came or about the adequacy of his response to it." The more one reads the early poems the more difficult it is to believe that Donne's insistence on sexual experience at this period was not subconsciously a facet of his more compelling drive to escape from Rome. That restless, almost feverish, drive towards sex, with which he so rarely seems satisfied ("Only let me love none, no, not the sport," he had cried in "Love's Usury"), requires explanation. In the nature of the case, any explanation must be suggestive rather than final; but to examine *Songs and Sonnets* from this point of view provides an insight into their motives which adds greatly to the interest of their organization. The religious imagery, the Scholastic terminology and logic in which he regularly speaks of erotic experience, serves to build up imaginatively the incomplete actuality, to endow it with some of the emotional satisfaction which the lapsing Catholic in him stood in need of, and some of the spiritual substance, at least in appearance, which he missed. More importantly, it would simultaneously have served to accelerate the disintegration of his faith, especially insofar as that faith could have been expressed in a philosophical vocabulary. *Songs and Sonnets* is a protracted exercise in how to blunt the precision of a philosophically exact language and make it unfit for its original purpose. Donne's love poems, including the "outrageous" ones, represent a highly complicated mixture of elements and attitudes that are difficult to isolate; but the essential thing about these poems is how little interested Donne seems to be in the experience *for its own sake*. The following lines from "Love's Usury" provide an interesting insight into the situation that, as far as the "outrageous" poems go, may be taken as representative:

> *Till then, Love, let my body reign, and let*
> *Me travel, sojourn, snatch, plot, have, forget,*
> *Resume my last year's relict: think that yet*
> > *We'd never met.*

Donne's mask of impersonality is always so well maintained that it is difficult ever to penetrate it. And these lines are in Donne's characteristic style, with its clutching insistence on verbs, both in number and placing. Yet the strong imperative voice of the command has a persuasive force; the "travel" sounds autobiographic in Donne's case; and there is a kind of hot-breathed, almost repellent, intimacy in that triad, "snatch, plot, have," that manages to get under the skin of impersonality. I should say that Donne was personally involved in these lines—as personally as the emphatic placing of "Me" suggests. But while the urgency behind them is expressed in sexual terms, the force is not concentrated there. There is some insistence on the verbs of motion, and Donne seems to be moving away from, quite as much as towards, such experiences. The triad of verbs which, supposedly, represent possession are the weakest. They do not possess the object as much as they claw at it. They are sick verbs—too sick to enact the bold program Donne outlines for them. Unconsciously, Donne knows it, for "forget" in the context of the poem does not represent the carefree, untroubled spendthrift of his passions; *forgetting* is merely a process that will enable him lamely to "resume last year's relict." Without enthusiasm for it, the game he is playing seems to be a way of

26

easing some deeper restlessness. The very words in which he describes the experience betray his disgust and his sense of frustration. One is tempted to conclude that the real vigor of this poem arises from feelings that are ultimately beyond the realm of sex.

III

SATYRE III, one of Donne's finest poems, may have been written as late as 1597, although it probably belongs to an earlier year. The poem is not so much an examination of the representative claims of the Roman, Anglican, and Genevan Churches as a statement of the necessity for conducting such an examination. Characteristically, Donne arrives at no conclusion except that man must search unceasingly for the truth. But in the course of the poem he gives us some unforgettable pictures of types of Elizabethan Christians. The energetic quality of Donne's thinking is strikingly reflected in the strenuous rhythm of these often-quoted lines which dramatize the labor and effort exerted by the poet in his search. It is easy enough to falsify the motives of conversion to oneself and others, but it is impossible to fake conviction in poetry like this:

> *On a huge hill,*
> *Cragged, and steep, Truth stands, and he that will*
> *Reach her, about must, and about must go;*
> *And what the hill's suddenness resists, win so;*
> *Yet strive so, that before age, death's twilight,*
> *Thy soul rest, for none can work in that night.*

Whatever the date of *Satyre III*, we know that Donne had been ordained several years when he wrote Holy Sonnet XVIII. The theological argument of this sonnet is much the same as that of the earlier satire:

27

Show me, dear Christ, Thy spouse so bright and clear.
What! is it She, which on the other shore
Goes richly painted? or which robb'd and tore
Laments and mourns in Germany and here?
Sleeps she a thousand, then peeps up one year?
Is she self-truth and errs? now new, now outwore?
Doth she, and did she, and shall she evermore
On one, on seven, or on no hill appear?
Dwells she with us, or like adventuring knights
First travel we to seek and then make love?
Betray kind husband Thy spouse to our sights,
And let mine amorous soul court Thy mild dove,
Who is most true, and pleasing to Thee, then
When she is embrac'd and open to most men.

The scarcely submerged comparison of the Church, the Bride of Christ, with a prostitute is surely one of the more startling images in English poetry, and the devout reverence with which Donne brings it off may be taken as a measure of his genius.

Donne appears not so much to have been converted *to* the Church of England as he was converted *away from* the Church of Rome. The result is that his later theological convictions are broadly tolerant. In leaving Rome he appears not so much to have acquired new beliefs as to have discarded old ones. But in 1601 Donne wrote a curious poem that makes one wonder if, even in his twenty-ninth year, his sympathies were not still deeply, if secretly, with the ancient Church. This poem, like *The Second Anniversary* of 1612, is titled *The Progress of the Soul*. It is a mere fragment, for although we possess fifty-two ten-line stanzas, the argument has barely got under way when Donne breaks off. That argument is an extraordinary one based on the Pythagorean doctrine of metempsychosis or reincarnation. It sets out to show us the progress of the soul of heresy from its vegetable

form in the apple which Eve ate in Eden, and through which
original sin came into the world, through successive reincarnations in all the great heretics of history—Mahomet, Luther,
Calvin—to its final abode in the reigning Queen of England,
the supreme authority in the Anglican Church. Donne
sketches in his argument for the poem very early on:

VII

For the great soul which here amongst us now
Doth dwell, and moves that hand, and tongue, and brow,
Which, as the Moon the sea, moves us; to hear
Whose story, with long patience you will long;
(For 'tis the crown, and last strain of my song)
This soul to whom Luther, *and* Mahomet *were*
Prisons of flesh; this soul which oft did tear,
And mend th'wracks of th'Empire, and late Rome,
And liv'd when every great change did come,
  Had first in paradise, a low, but fatal room.

VIII

Yet no low room, nor than the greatest, less,
If (as devout and sharp men fitly guess)
That Cross, our joy, and grief, where nails did tie
That All, which always was all, every where;
Which could not sin, and yet all sins did bear;
Which could not die, yet could not choose but die;
Stood in the self same room in Calvary,
Where first grew the forbidden learned tree,
For on that tree hung in security
  This Soul, made by the Maker's will from pulling
  free.

IX

Prince of the orchard, fair as dawning morn,
Fenc'd with the law, and ripe as soon as born

That apple grew, which this Soul did enlive,
Till the then climbing serpent, that now creeps
For that offence, for which all mankind weeps,
Took it, and t'her whom the first man did wive
(Whom and her race, only forbiddings drive)
He gave it, she, t'her husband, both did eat;
So perished the eaters, and the meat:
  And we (for treason taints the blood) thence die and
  sweat.

In Stanza VIII Donne says that the cross on which Christ
was crucified was made from wood of the same tree on which
the original apple grew—a polite and devious way of suggesting that Christ is crucified anew in the religious policy of the
Crown. If this interpretation seems, at this point, premature,
I am presuming on the extraneous support—if it is needed—
which *The Anniversaries* will lend. The boldness of this
poem is in some respects even greater than that which we find
in *The Anniversaries*. Since it is one of the least regarded of
Donne's poems, it is worth pointing out that the verse is
sometimes very good and characteristic Donne indeed. F. R.
Leavis, in his essay "T. S. Eliot and the Life of English
Literature," has written of Donne: "Donne brought into
non-dramatic poetry the Shakespearian use of English—the
living spoken language, the speaking voice, and the attendant
sensitive command of rhythm, tone and inflexion." While the
three stanzas I have quoted are not among the most notable in
the poem in this respect, the terse, idiomatic syntax, which
reproduces the rhythms of spoken rather than of written
speech, are confirmatory of Leavis's observation.

But are we certain that in 1601 Donne was a professed
Anglican? Izaak Walton, as we have seen, implies that his
conversion was much earlier. Donne had been secretary to Sir
Thomas Egerton since 1598, and Egerton was Elizabeth's
Attorney General, Lord Keeper of the Great Seal, and a

member of the Privy Council. His official position opposed him to Catholics, and probably his temperament as well. He had prosecuted the Jesuit martyr Edmund Campion, who had been hanged, drawn, and quartered in 1581, and his zeal in the interests of the state Church continued well into the next reign. He would certainly not have taken Donne into his household if his religious position had been suspect. Sir Herbert Grierson and others have suggested that the hostility to Elizabeth reflected in this poem is to be associated with the Queen's unpopularity that followed upon the execution of the Earl of Essex in 1601. Donne certainly admired Essex, had served under him in the Cadiz and Azores expeditions, and had seen him at closer quarters when Elizabeth committed him as a state prisoner into Egerton's keeping in 1599 after he had fled from Ireland without her permission. But however Donne may have sympathized with Essex, the hostility to Elizabeth in this poem is specifically theological in character. She is to be presented as the great heresiarch of history, in direct line of descent through Luther and Mahomet back to the Edenic apple that brought evil into the world.

The Progress of the Soul has never been one of Donne's more popular or widely read poems, but it is a brilliant poem at times, and it gives us a vivid insight into Donne's deeply disturbed state of mind in 1601. It makes one thing quite clear: his transition to Anglicanism was not an easy one. The poem breaks off as the soul, having passed through various lower forms of life, enters its first human being, Themech, sister and wife to Cain. The last three lines indicate in what a spirit of skepticism Donne must have written the poem:

> *There's nothing simply good, nor ill alone,*
> *Of every quality comparison*
> *The only measure is, and judge, opinion.*

The year in which Donne wrote *The Progress of the Soul* was also the year of his marriage. Anne More was Lady Eger-

ton's niece, and during most of the period Donne was employed as the Lord Keeper's secretary, Anne was living at Sir
Thomas's house in London, where she must frequently have
been in Donne's company. The two fell in love, Anne being
then only sixteen, Donne twenty-eight. They were secretly
married in London in December, 1601. Anne's father, Sir
George More, did not see Donne as a suitable son-in-law, and
on being informed of the match he was sufficiently outraged
to persuade Sir Thomas Egerton (who was reluctant) to
dismiss his secretary. For a brief period Donne was even
committed to the Fleet prison while Sir George vainly endeav-
ored to secure an annulment. Donne's once-brilliant prospects
vanished overnight. The patrimony he had inherited years
before had long since been dissipated on his travels abroad;
he was in debt, had lost his position with Sir Thomas for
good, and although his father-in-law came to accept the marriage, he was not yet willing to give the couple financial
assistance. The next years were impoverished and difficult,
and matters were not helped by the rapid succession of children who were born to them. Among the expedients to which
Donne resorted in this crisis, he became what would now be
called a research assistant to Dr. Thomas Morton, who later
became Bishop of Durham. Morton was considered a highly
successful controversialist against the Catholics, and Donne
was employed in collecting material from the Church Fathers
and from canon law for his use. Inexorably, circumstances
drove Donne, as we have seen, in the direction of the Anglican priesthood; but he resisted as long as could, and continued to seek advancement through the customary channel of
patronage.

It was in pursuit of patronage that Donne wrote and published two puzzling poems, *The First Anniversary*, 1611, and
The Second Anniversary, 1612. These poems were written to
commemorate the death of Elizabeth Drury, who had died in
1610, just short of her fifteenth birthday. It is not clear if

Donne had known Sir Robert before he sent him the first commemoration of his daughter's death, but it is certain that he had never seen the girl. Sir Robert Drury was a courtier of large fortune and larger ambition. Sir Henry Wotton gives an amusing picture of him in a letter to Sir Robert's own brother-in-law, Sir Edmund Bacon: "Sir R. Drury runneth at the ring, corbeteth his horse before the King's window, haunteth my Lord of Rochester's chamber, even when himself is not there, and in secret divideth his observances between him and the house of Suffolk: and all this (they say) to be ambassador at Bruxels." Sir Robert was clearly a vain and ambitious man, and his hope that his young daughter would some day be Queen of England was a little absurd; but if any further proof were wanting, the fact that he was able to get down without difficulty the praises that Donne addressed to his deceased daughter—one of the few men either in his time or since who have been able to do so—should clinch the matter. He gave Donne and his wife quarters in a house adjacent to his great mansion in Drury Lane, and late in 1611 Donne accompanied Sir Robert and Lady Drury to the Continent on a trip extending over ten months. *The Second Anniversary* was written in 1612 while Donne was in France.

The Elizabethans and the seventeenth century were able to take hyperbolic praise and fulsome flattery in stride, but even Donne's contemporaries were shocked by *The Anniversaries*. Ben Jonson declared "that Donne's Anniversarie was profane and full of blasphemies; that he told Mr. Donne, if it had been written of the Virgin Marie it had been something; to which he answered that he described the Idea of a Woman, and not as she was." Donne soon came to regret having allowed the two poems to be published, but a good deal of modern criticism has responded more warmly. Their apparent extravagance is of the same order as Shelley's apotheosis of Emilia Viviani in *Epipsychidion*, but in Donne's case it seems to conceal a deeper and more complexly elaborate meaning behind the ostensible subject. *The Anniversaries* irresistibly invite exegesis and interpretation.

From a modern point of view *The First and Second Anniversaries* suggest the private joke, but not the innocent and trivial private joke that contemporary readers have grown accustomed to in the early poetry of Auden. It has something in it of those malignant jokes of the Elizabethan or Jacobean playwrights—Volpone, for example, and his sinister bag of tricks. If I am correct in reading the poems in this way, they are one of the most successfully *private* jokes ever perpetrated, for Donne has still not been found out.

One of the several things that *The Anniversaries* are simultaneously celebrating is Donne's departure from the Roman Catholic Church. The disturbing aspect of the two poems partly arises from the fact that the concealed eulogy Donne addresses to the ancient Church is seriously intended, and in view of this sincerity the grotesque deflection of the praises to an object so improper transcends cynicism, and enters an almost malevolent realm of feeling. The Anglican no less than the Catholic might be shocked by the performance, and it is understandable that Donne kept the joke as private as possible. Perhaps in the rarefied tenuosities of his own brain, where he had stabled so many paradoxes for so many years, he partially succeeded in sequestering the joke from his fullest consciousness. But certain passages, once the tip is taken, become so explicit that it is difficult to believe that Donne did not know perfectly well the fullest implications of his performance.

Critics have commonly granted that Elizabeth Drury is a symbol for something transcending anything Donne connected with the dead child herself, but at this point most of the discussions become vague. "Elizabeth Drury had become nothing less than a symbol of pure spirit, of immortal beauty, harmony, and innocence," writes a critic whose view may be taken as representative. This will not do. There are at least three significations which the symbol of Elizabeth Drury carries, and each qualifies and conditions the others. But it is Elizabeth Drury in her own identity who provides the ironical commentary on the other two aspects of the symbolism. The presence of the child in the poem, as Donne presents her, may work towards irreverence, or something worse; but once Donne's drift has been taken, it is never an irrelevance.

But what precisely *does* the girl-symbol of *The Anniversaries* taken under its larger aspects mean? Putting the child in her own identity aside for the moment, we may say that, in a general way, Donne has presented us with a cosmic metaphor, alive and growing in every line—a metaphor so vast that it stands for the whole of creation taken in its religious meaning, and yet capable of such particularity that it stands simultaneously for the possibilities of the individual soul when it is fully alive and in spiritual health. The opening lines of *The First Anniversary* make it clear that what we have to deal with is not a particular person, but an abstraction —a symbol of what at one moment appears to be the soul's interior awareness of its own spiritual possibilities, and a moment later the objectification of those possibilities in terms of a theology:

> *When that rich Soul which to her heaven is gone,*
> *Whom all do celebrate, who know they have one,*
> *(For who is sure he hath a soul, unless*
> *It see, and judge, and follow worthiness,*
> *And by deeds praise it? he who doth not this,*
> *May lodge an inmate soul, but 'tis not his.)*
> *When that Queen ended here her progress time,*
> *And, as to her standing house, to heaven did climb,*
> *Where loath to make the saints attend her long,*
> *She's now a part both of the choir, and song,*
> *This world, in that great earthquake languishèd.*

In these opening lines the problems presented by Elizabeth Drury have not yet arisen for the reader. Not being acquainted with her yet, he would have little difficulty in interpreting "that rich Soul which to her heaven is gone" as true religion in banishment. Expelled from earth, Heaven becomes true religion's native home. If, incarnated in the person of the young girl, religion is part of the choir of saints, the theological truth which is her essence is at the same time the subject of the saints' song of praise and the object of their contemplation. Back on the earth, from which true religion has been banished, most men are now spiritually dead; but a few still recognize a living spiritual principle or soul within themselves. Anticipating the concealed argument of the poem here, we may say that those "who know they have one" are the persecuted but faithful Catholics, and it is only they who continue to celebrate true religion in her banishment.

Elizabeth Drury becomes, in Donne's description, a symbol of the Church, the Bride of Christ:

> *She, of whom the Ancients seem'd to prophesy,*
> *When they call'd virtues by the name of she;*
> *She in whom virtue was so much refin'd,*
> *That for alloy unto so pure a mind*
> *She took the weaker sex; she that could drive*
> *The poisonous tincture, and the stain of Eve,*
> *Out of her thoughts, and deeds; and purify*
> *All, by a true religious alchemy;*
> *She, she is dead; she's dead: when thou know'st this,*
> *Thou know'st how poor a trifling thing man is.*
> *And learn thus much by our anatomy,*
> *The heart being perish'd, no part can be free.*
> *And that except thou feed (not banquet) on*
> *The supernatural food, religion,*
> *Thy better growth grows witherèd, and scant.*

Donne here links the girl-symbol with those prophecies in the Old Testament that foretold the coming of Christ and His Church. If Elizabeth Drury is associated with Mary in this passage, the emphatic identification is made, not with the

Virgin, but with the Church. The "true religious alchemy" by which Elizabeth Drury overcomes original sin ("The poisonous tincture, and the stain of Eve") seems a clear reference to the Catholic Sacramental system—to baptism certainly, but "true religious alchemy" is an almost perfect description of the very heart of Catholic doctrine: transubstantiation and the Mass. Although the Anglican Church had copied the Catholic sacraments to some extent, Donne is referring to the original here and not to the copy, for he insists on the fact that Elizabeth Drury is dead. With the death of true religion, man also withers. In the last three lines of this passage Donne makes a curious distinction between "feeding" and "banqueting" on religion. To "feed" on supernatural food clearly enough means to take spiritual nourishment. Is it perhaps possible that by "banqueting" on religion, which Donne apparently condemns, he was making an ironic reference to the confiscation of Catholic ecclesiastical properties and endowments on which the Tudors had grown fat?

The following passage from *The First Anniversary* enforces the interpretation that Donne regarded the Anglican Church at this time as an inadequate copy of the Roman original:

For there's a kind of world remaining still,
Though she which did inanimate and fill
The world, be gone, yet in this last long night,
Her ghost doth walk; that is, a glimmering light,
A faint weak love of virtue, and of good,
Reflects from her, on them which understood
Her worth; and though she have shut in all day,
The twilight of her memory doth stay;
Which, from the carcass of the old world, free,
Creates a new world, and new creatures be
Produc'd: the matter and the stuff of this,
Her virtue, and the form our practice is.

We recall what Donne, ten years before in *The Progress of the Soul*, had appeared to think of Elizabeth's Anglican Establishment. In this passage there is a hidden, and yet unmistakable, comparison between the Catholic and the Anglican Churches, almost in the manner of *The Hind and the Panther*. Donne is here in the process of making a very qualified intellectual acceptance of the new Church, but all his prejudices still seem markedly in favor of Rome. The meaning of these lines, once the theological dimension of the girl-symbol is accepted, is that the true Church is the life and the soul of the world, but the true Church has entered its "last long night." Elizabeth Drury alive, Donne seems to be saying, symbolizes the Catholic Church; but she is dead, and he turns to contemplate the consequences of her death for the world. All is not hopeless, for her ghost still walks abroad, and in her ghost—or the image of Elizabeth Drury dead—we have the image of Anglicanism. There is, Donne appears to say, a real relation between the Roman and the Anglican Churches, just as there is a real relation between Elizabeth Drury and her ghost; but the new world which is created by this ghost is not the brave new world of Shakespeare. It is founded on death, and there is something spurious about the life it shows. Near the beginning of *The Second Anniversary*, still lamenting the lifelessness of the world since the death of Sir Robert's daughter, Donne has these lines:

> *Or as sometimes in a beheaded man,*
> *Though at those two red seas, which freely ran,*
> *One from the trunk, another from the head,*
> *His soul be sail'd to her eternal bed,*
> *His eyes will twinkle, and his tongue will roll,*
> *As though he beck'ned and call'd back his soul,*
> *He grasps his hands, and he pulls up his feet,*
> *And seems to reach, and to step forth to meet*
> *His soul; when all these motions which we saw,*

Are but as ice, which crackles at a thaw:
Or as a lute, which in moist weather rings
Her knell alone by cracking of her strings:
So struggles this dead world, now she is gone;
For there is motion in corruption.

A recent biographer conjectures that Donne may have seen
the beheading of the Earl of Essex, which the headsman
badly bungled, and recalled it when he wrote this vivid
description. Perhaps: but it also seems likely to me that a
number of concealed implications lurk behind that vividness.
It is easy to read the image of the beheaded man as a
reference to the substitution of royal for papal supremacy,
just as the lute with the broken string may refer to the
suppression of monasticism in the same way as Shakespeare's
"bare ruined choirs where late the sweet birds sang." At any
rate, if Elizabeth Drury alive signifies true religion, or the
ancient Church, the picture of the life that remains after her
death is not a very reassuring one, although Donne tries to
make the best of it:

> *. . . though she have shut in all day,*
> *The twilight of her memory doth stay.*

Donne's concealed contention appears to be that the theological content and the liturgy of Anglicanism are actually
newly created out of the doctrine and the liturgy of Rome.
The figure of Elizabeth Drury, then, is a symbol of both the
Roman and the Anglican Churches; and the disparity between Elizabeth Drury alive and Elizabeth Drury dead may
be taken as a measure of the interior conflict that Donne
suffered during the long protracted spiritual crisis that seems,
in its intensest form, to have followed rather than preceded
his conversion. To revert to C. S. Lewis's charge once more
that Donne's passions end up by being "partly fictitious," it
is this uncertain ambivalence in Donne's attitudes to the two

Churches that simultaneously gives depth to his irony, and serves to conceal it from a recognition that would have been dangerous at the time.

It is an accidental felicity that both the dead child and the old Queen who had so largely shaped the Anglican fabric were named Elizabeth; but there is surely nothing of accident in the following passage, which comes near the opening of *The First Anniversary*, and which established the tone and the method of procedure followed throughout. Donne is directly addressing the "sick world" which is in a lethargy since the death of Elizabeth Drury:

> *Her death did wound and tame thee then, and then*
> *Thou might'st have better spar'd the sun, or man.*
> *That wound was deep, but 'tis more misery,*
> *That thou hast lost thy sense and memory.*
> *'Twas heavy then to hear thy voice of moan,*
> *But this is worse, that thou art speechless grown.*
> *Thou hast forgot thy name, thou hadst; thou wast*
> *Nothing but she, and her thou hast o'erpast.*
> *For as a child kept from the Font, until*
> *A Prince, expected long, come to fulfill*
> *The ceremonies, thou unnam'd hadst laid,*
> *Had not her coming, thee her palace made:*
> *Her name defin'd thee, gave thee form, and frame,*
> *And thou forget'st to celebrate thy name.*
> *Some months she hath been dead (but being dead,*
> *Measures of time are all determinèd)*
> *But long she hath been away, but long, long, yet none*
> *Offers to tell us who it is that's gone.*
> *But as in states doubtful of future heirs,*
> *When sickness without remedy impairs,*
> *The present Prince, they're loath it should be said,*
> *The Prince doth languish, or the Prince is dead:*
> *So mankind feeling now a general thaw,*

A strong example gone, equal to law,
The cement which did faithfully compact,
And glue all virues, now resolv'd, and slack'd,
Thought it some blasphemy to say she was dead,
Or that our weakness was discoverèd
In that confession; therefore spoke no more
Than tongues, the soul being gone, the loss deplore.

We know that Donne could pun on his own name with remarkable effectiveness, but that is nothing to the fantastic (but implicit) punning on the name of Elizabeth in these lines, which center, appropriately enough, in a christening. In these lines the praises offered to Elizabeth Drury are metamorphosed into an encomium of the dead Queen Elizabeth, whom Donne had attacked so violently just ten years before in *The Progress of the Soul.* To a considerable extent the encomium is intended ironically—but such was Donne's position relative to the Anglican Church at that time, the encomium becomes a statement of practical policy as well. It is of Queen Elizabeth as Head of the Established Church that Donne is speaking here. The royal supremacy is, in fact, the defining doctrine of Anglicanism. Although Elizabeth's father had been the actual founder of the state Church, it took its real form under Elizabeth, and it is, therefore, literally true to say that Elizabeth was the expected Prince who bestowed her name upon it—who gave it form and frame in the Elizabethan Settlement. And as Head of the Church it is natural that the Queen might be said to inhabit it as a palace —if indeed another ironical reference is not intended to the number of ecclesiastical establishments that had passed to the use of the Crown. The reference to "states doubtful of future heirs" is an explicit allusion to the end of Elizabeth's reign, when there was a general uncertainty about the succession, and especially about the religious policy of James. Elizabeth's example, Donne says, was "equal to law," and in that phrase he recognizes the essentially legalistic nature of the state Church, as well as the necessity—if such a *legal* structure were to endure—of enforcing the law. After the strong religious policy of the Queen, James's accession must have done a good deal towards revealing weaknesses in the organization. The Stuarts, perhaps because of certain of their virtues, were incapable of cementing the religious extremists of the Kingdom into an effective *via media*, and although Donne's insights may seem a little ahead of history in this passage, it is not astonishing that a man who, from his first youth, had been immersed in the religious problems of the age, and whose ambitious, practical nature compelled him to study the contemporary religious scene with an astute eye, should have seen more deeply than his associates.

But if expediency persuaded Donne to deal differently with the Head of the English Church, even in disguised or camouflaged statement, than he had done with the royal heresiarch some years earlier in *The Progress of the Soul*, a decade had not changed his private attitude so completely that strong traces of the earlier disposition are not present in the form of irony. I have already insisted that Elizabeth Drury also symbolizes the pre-Reformation Church at many points in these poems. What the pre-Reformation Church eventually came to signify in Donne's mind after he had taken Anglican Orders and become Dean of St. Paul's is not my concern here. To the younger Donne the pre-Reformation Church inevitably meant the Roman Church, and although the Donne of *The Anniversaries* had already (for whatever reasons) rejected the Roman Church, it is still the Church that he looks back to nostalgically, and with more than a little faith. There are a number of lines in the above passage which may be read in a double, or even a triple, sense:

Her death did wound and tame thee then, and then
Thou might'st have better spared the sun, or man.

42

That wound was deep, but 'tis more misery,
That thou hast lost thy sense and memory.
'Twas heavy then to hear thy voice of moan,
But this is worse, that thou art speechless grown.
Thou hast forgot thy name, thou hadst; thou wast
Nothing but she, and her thou hast o'erpast.

If it is Elizabeth Drury's death Donne is speaking of here, the passage deserves those strictures that Jonson and many other critics have directed against *The Anniversaries*. But if the death is that of Queen Elizabeth, whose living presence had given viability and organization to the Kingdom's ecclesiastical structure, the passage takes on greater depth and significance, and loses much of its extravagance. But it acquires the richest and most complex meaning of all if we interpret the death of the girl-symbol as referring to the suppression of the Catholic Church. The passage of course has reference to all three levels at once. There is a recurrent refrain through *The Anniversaries*: "She, she is dead; she's dead." The cumulative effect of this refrain as it is repeated so often is that of a lamentation for the banished Church, and the spiritual health it brought with it:

She to whom this world must itself refer,
As suburbs, or the microcosm of her,
She, she is dead; she's dead: when thou know'st this,
Thou know'st how lame a cripple this world is.
And learn'st thus much by our anatomy,
That this world's general sickness doth not lie
In any humour, or one certain part;
But as thou saw'st it rotten at the heart,
Thou seest a hectic fever hath got hold
Of the whole substance, not to be controlled,
And that thou hast but one way, not to admit
The world's infection, to be none of it.

The earlier world took its life and form from the presence in it of the ancient Church, the true religion, represented by the *living* Elizabeth Drury. But the contemporary world of Donne has forgotten the beauty of its first phase under the royal domination of the second: "Thou hast forgot thy name, thou hadst; thou wast / Nothing but she, and her thou hast o'erpast." These lines are taken up again a little further down the page:

> *Her name defin'd thee, gave thee form, and frame,*
> *And thou forget'st to celebrate thy name.*

I have already said this refers to Queen Elizabeth; but it *also* refers to Donne's deeper nostalgic meaning—his regret for the banished Church of his forebears, and it should, I think, be read partly as a hidden reference to the prohibited Roman ceremonies. The paradox is, of course, that the Anglican Church, newly christened by Queen Elizabeth in her capacity of Head of the Church, is prevented by that very fact from celebrating those holy mysteries—especially the Mass— which had been the identity and life of the ancient Church in England. And Donne, it will be recalled from the long passage quoted earlier, follows this up with, "yet none / Offers to tell us who it is that's gone." This may refer to the new Anglican hierarchy and clergy, who preach against Catholic theology; and it may also be a reference to the underground Catholic Church in England, whose clergy was prevented by Elizabethan penal laws from preaching Catholic doctrine publicly. But the whole passage we have been discussing is so filled with ambiguities of this nature that they must be left to the reader's private attention.

One of the more important aspects of the passage has still to be considered. Elizabeth Drury in her own identity as Sir Robert's daughter is brought forward here, for Donne is determined that the concealed argument of the poems will not usurp their ostensible subject. "Some months she hath been dead" refers directly to Elizabeth Drury. But it is noteworthy how Donne uses the passage for an internal adjustment of the symbol under all its aspects, making it self-consistent chronologically:

> . . . *but being dead,*
> *Measures of time are all determinèd.*

Applied to Elizabeth Drury, this is egregious flattery; to Queen Elizabeth, it carries an historical significance; to the pre-Reformation Church, its connotation is cosmological. But the three interpretations sink their differences for a moment, and the poem moves smoothly on under the pretense of praising the little girl. Donne does three things here more or less simultaneously: (1) he celebrates and declares himself (by implication at least) for the Anglican Church; (2) he mourns the suppression of the pre-Reformation Church and its effect on the world; (3) he accuses the world of participating in that suppression by her present forgetfulness, and he then dramatizes his own forgetfulness by demoting the whole argument to that level at which, as he cynically confesses at the end of both *Anniversaries*, he pays his yearly rent to Sir Robert for his lodgings in Drury Lane. What in effect Donne does here is to transpose the profoundly serious theological problem to the level of a time-serving courtier's outrageous flattery. It appears to be a deliberate underlining of the unsavory aspects of Donne's situation, a cryptic indictment of the motives Donne had gradually been compelled to act on in his search for worldly advancement.

Toward the end of *The Second Anniversary* Donne appears to accept the idea of the state Church more wholeheartedly than at any earlier point. These lines applied to Elizabeth Drury are merely embarrassing; applied to the dead Queen, they immediately take on weight and a new historical dimension:

She, who being to herself a State, enjoy'd
All royalties which any State employ'd;
For she made wars, and triumph'd; reason still
Did not o'erthrow, but rectify her will:
And she made peace, for no peace is like this,
That beauty, and chastity together kiss:
She did high justice, for she crucified
Every first motion of rebellious pride:
And she gave pardons, and was liberal,
For, only herself except, she pardon'd all:
She coin'd, in this, that her impressions gave
To all our actions all the worth they have:
She gave protections; the thoughts of her breast
Satan's rude officers could ne'er arrest.
As these prerogatives being met in one,
Made her a sovereign State, religion
Made her a Church; and these two made her all.

If Donne's words mean anything, there can be little doubt that he is talking here about the old Queen, who had embodied in her own person both the state and the Church. There are still ambiguities present in Donne's attitude to the Queen, but on the whole the tone of the passage strongly suggests that Donne had become, or was becoming, resigned at last to the Established Church, and *The Second Anniversary* ends with a conventional attack on Catholics, especially in France, where Donne was living when he wrote the lines.[1]

Such an interpretation as the one offered here of *The Anniversaries* must necessarily remain conjectural, although passage by passage the poems support it with unusual consistency. But even the reader who finds such an interpretation convincing must bear in mind that the three levels of meaning

1. The identification of the Elizabeth of *The Anniversaries* with Queen Elizabeth has also been argued very persuasively by Marjorie Hope Nicolson in *The Breaking of the Circle*, 1950.

covered by the girl-symbol, Elizabeth, do not exist in the poems as three distinct layers, consistently built in according to an elaborately structured plan. They make their appearances, these three levels of meaning, and they retire—only to come forward again on some later page. There is an element of the casual, of the accidental, in these successive "appearances." It could scarcely be otherwise in poems in which Donne wished to conceal his meaning rather than reveal it. If my interpretation is, in the main, correct, Donne would have had good reason to conceal his meaning. It was not a day for indiscretions and revelations. How little Donne courted any kind of martyrdom is indicated perhaps by the almost sinister cleverness with which he hid, or disguised, so much of what he had to say. The ambiguously multiple images and landscapes of some of Dali's paintings seem utterly primitive and simple-minded by comparison. Nor does it seem particularly strange, when one has studied Donne's personality in his life and works, that he might have felt an overpowering compulsion to make such a concealed confession of his views about the world he lived in, and his relations with it. There are elements of the tortured, the theatrical, and the perversely sincere in such a performance that correspond closely to the conception of Donne's character that has been presented here. And Donne would have been capable of taking ironic pleasure in the fact that these poems that carry such concealed criticisms and judgments on the world he lived in were, on the surface and to all intents and purposes, the egregious flattery of a courtier seeking advancement and place.

Donne died in 1631 in the odor of sanctity and the theater, which is as it should have been. Walton gives us this vividly memorable picture of Donne's last performance:

> A Monument being resolved upon, Dr. Donne sent for a Carver to make for him in wood the figure of an Urn, giving him directions for the compass and height of it;

and to bring with it a board of the just height of his body. These being got: then without delay a choice Painter was got to be in a readiness to draw his Picture, which was taken as followeth;—Several Charcole-fires being first made in his large Study, he brought with him into that place his winding-sheet in his hand, and had this sheet put on him, and so tied with knots at his head and feet, and his hands so placed, as dead bodies are usually fitted to be shrouded and put into their Coffin, or grave. Upon this Urn he thus stood with his eyes shut, and with so much of the sheet turned aside as might show his lean, pale, death-like face, which was purposely turned towards East, from whence he expected the second coming of his and our Saviour Jesus. In this posture he was drawn at his just height; and when the picture was fully finished, he caused it to be set by his bed-side, where it continued, and became his hourly object till his death.

Donne had been an enthusiastic playgoer in his youth in the most brilliant days of the English drama. One of the greatest figures of the theater was his lifelong friend, and although the pulpit was Donne's stage, perhaps the single most characteristic quality of his poetry is its dramatic impact. I have already quoted F. R. Leavis on the Shakespearean affinities of Donne's verse. Over and over again there is an immediate dramatic projection in his poems, coming as soon as the poet speaks. The language seems to grow directly from the dramatic situation or tension that underprops each poem. It is perhaps this dramatization of feelings very like our own that helps us to experience his poetry with an intimacy offered us by none of his contemporaries among the nondramatic poets. Donne has been called both a medieval and a modern, but he deserves the second epithet far more richly than the first, which he may not deserve at all. The ability to use a Scholastic terminology, even more seriously than Donne, is by no means unknown in the twentieth century, and it does not necessarily imply that the user belongs in the Middle Ages. The conflicts in Donne's personality, reflected so perfectly in his art, his perplexities of faith and doubt, the tortured ambiguity one senses so strongly in his motives, his cynicism and his capacity for affection, the ironical quality of his self-knowledge and his psychological curiosity—all these have a familiar look in our day. And yet in a curious way we have remained a little uncertain about the exact place Donne ought to occupy among the great English poets. Commenting on this fact on the tercentenary of Donne's death, Allen Tate pointed to a quality in him that most readers must continue to feel: "The uncertainty of these critics about Donne's place," he said, "is remarkable in the case of a poet three hundred years dead. The uncertainty comes of Donne's being still alive."

THE COLLOQUIAL BYRON

I T W O U L D B E conceded by most critics that the poems in which Byron made his most substantial contribution to literature are *Beppo*, *The Vision of Judgment*, and *Don Juan*. All three shared a tone that, first struck in *Beppo*, charmed Byron's readers at once. Francis Jeffrey did an excellent job of isolating this tone in his review of *Beppo* in *The Edinburgh Review* for February, 1818. Remarking enthusiastically on the style, he says that its ease and gaiety imply

> the existence of certain habits of dissipation, derision, and intelligence in general society. . . . It is perfectly distinct from the witty, epigrammatic and satirical vein, in which Pope will never be surpassed—or equalled; and from the burlesque, humourous and distorted style which attained its greatest height in *Hudibras*. . . . The style of which we are speaking is, no doubt, occasionally satirical and witty and humourous—but it is on the whole more gay than poignant, and it is characterized, exactly as good conversation is, rather by its constant ease and amenity, than by any traits either of

extraordinary brilliancy, or of strong and ludicrous effect. . . . The great charm is in the simplicity and naturalness of the language—the free but guarded use of all polite idioms, and even of all phrases of temporary currency that have the stamp of good company on them. . . .

This is excellent criticism from a man whose merits are sometimes obscured, and it is criticism that Ronald Bottrall (who seems to have been unacquainted with the Jeffrey review), writing in *The Criterion* in 1938, could do little more than substantiate and enlarge in his essay "Byron and the Colloquial Tradition in English Poetry." The author of *Beppo* (Byron had published it anonymously) has presented us, Jeffrey had said, with "about one hundred stanzas of good verse, entirely composed of common words in their common places; never presenting us with one sprig of what is called poetical diction, or even making use of a single inversion, either to raise the style or assist the rhyme—but running on in an inexhaustible series of good, easy colloquial phrases, and finding them fall into verse by some unaccountable and happy fatality." To Jeffrey the tone of *Beppo* had seemed a complete innovation ("unique we rather think in our language"), and the nearest approach to it he could think of was Prior, Peter Pindar, or Moore in the facetious vein.

It is an unusual thing about much Byron criticism that, having isolated predominant virtues in the poetry (sometimes with a great deal of sensitivity, as in the Jeffrey review), critics have had a tendency to look upon these qualities as an anomaly in the English tradition. Byron's apparent intractability is partly owing to the impact of his personality on the somewhat narrow imagination of much traditional criticism rather than to the impact of his actual poetry on a responsive sensibility. Despite what the vaunters of the Italian influence may say to the contrary, his poetry is intensely English; but a shock like that felt by Scrope Davies and Byron's estimable friend John Cam Hobhouse, when the first cantos of *Don Juan* reached England (a shock that was to be widely and deeply shared), seems somehow to have implanted the persistent idea that there is something slightly alien about Byron's modes of feeling. Even Matthew Arnold's admirable estimate is influenced when he sees Byron so largely against a background of Continental evaluations, and sets him off as so largely the opponent of British Philistinism. With Arnold on Byron I should not wish to quarrel, but his emphasis does underline the situation. And Eliot is in the tradition (but, on the whole, less amiably) when he writes in his essay on Byron: "He was right in making the hero of his house-party a Spaniard, for what he understands and dislikes about English society is very much what an intelligent foreigner in the same position would understand and dislike also." Yes: but surely an intelligent Englishman also. If this remark is enlightening from several points of view, it also suggests that Byron doesn't quite belong.

What occurs in Byron criticism occurs also in much Byron scholarship. Claude Fuess in his *Lord Byron as a Satirist in Verse* is typical when he writes that Beppo may be taken as marking the turning point between the old era of Augustan influence and the new one to come. "It is significant," he continues, "that this poem is written, not in the characteristically English heroic couplet, but in the thoroughly foreign ottava rima. Responsive to an altered and agreeable environment, Byron found in Italy and its literature an inspiration which affected him more profoundly than it had Goethe only a few decades before. The results of this influence, shown to some extent in his dramas though more decidedly in his satires, justify terming the years from 1817 until his death his Italian period. A mere mention of its contribution to satire indicates its importance: it produced *Beppo*, *The Vision of Judgment*, and *Don Juan*." But Fuess then rather disarmingly admits: "we may feel convinced that Byron drew from the Italian satirists something of their general tone, and yet be unable to clarify our general reasons for this belief or to frame them into an effective argument. Of such a sort, indeed, is much of the influence which Pulci, Berni, and Casti had on Byron. It is vague and evasive. . . ."

In line with the Italian influence, one other may be mentioned, and it must be confessed that Byron himself is largely responsible. In 1817 he wrote to his publisher Murray: "Mr. Whistlecraft has no greater admirer than myself. I have written a story in 89 stanzas, in imitation of him, called Beppo." The poem in question was, of course, John Hookham Frere's *Prospectus and Specimen of an Intended National Work*, purportedly written by the brothers Whistlecraft. Since Frere was a student of the Italian burlesque writers, this admiration has been seized on by a number of Byron scholars for anything they can make of it, with the result that Byron's greatest works are coupled in print with a poem that only obfuscates their real merits and hides their real intentions. This is not to say that Frere's work—his use of ottava rima for example—may not have been suggestive, but his usefulness was mechanical and it has been critically misleading.

Against this background, Bottrall's attempt to insist on the traditional English quality in Byron must evoke warm sympathy. But Jeffrey, in noting the sharp distinction between Byron and Pope, had been perfectly right. It is therefore unfortunate that Bottrall, in setting up what he calls a "colloquial tradition" for the purpose of securing Byron firmly to native bedrock, runs the tradition from Dryden through Pope. He makes the best of the case by emphasizing *not* Byron's couplet poems, where the evidence would be weakest, but the later, richly colloquial, poems. "The eighteenth century element in him," F. R. Leavis has written of Byron, "is essential to his success, and yet has at the same time the effect of bringing out how completely the Augustan order has disintegrated."

I wish to go a little further and suggest that Byron not only represents the deterioration of the Augustan order, but that his colloquialism really sidesteps the Augustans and refers back to certain Caroline poets. One may as well begin by admitting that had Dryden and Pope never written we might not have *Beppo* and *Don Juan*. But that would not be because Byron was using effects taught him by the Augustans. Pope was a powerful stimulant on Byron's imagination, but the two men belong to different orders. Despite superficial similarities between the Augustan Age and the Regency, their respective social styles were operated by very different mechanisms. Byron ended by writing a kind of poetry with which Pope's manner could never have consorted with ease.

If Dryden and Pope had not written we might not have *Beppo* and *Don Juan:* but the language had already arrived somewhat earlier than Dryden at a stage of sophistication equal to achieving effects that we recognize as characteristically Byronic in those two poems. Any language can be perfectly equated only with the contemporary life for which it speaks, but the advances in language which *Don Juan* represents over these Carolinian poems of which I am thinking should be accounted a specifically personal achievement on Byron's part: for what Dryden and Pope added to increase the resonance of those particular colloquial effects the earlier poets had invented, so far as Byron was concerned, was of a general nature—a broad deepening of the resources of language. Almost certainly without knowing it, Byron was in touch with a remoter vein than he supposed; and so, if one cannot altogether agree with Bottrall's "colloquial tradition," one need not thereby suppose that the peculiar success of *Don Juan* is an anomaly, except insofar as that term is applicable to every work of art. It may just be possible to show that, after all, Byron *does* belong.

II

B u t h e r e I should like to take out several pages paren-
thetically for general comment. Bottrall's use of the phrase
"colloquial tradition" engenders a moment of hesitation and
doubt. When he mentions early in his essay that Langland,
Skelton, Chaucer, Dunbar, Henryson, Donne, Herbert, Dryden, Pope, Hopkins, Eliot, and Pound are, in *some* of their
poetry, colloquial, one certainly agrees—but hastens to question if the phrase does not embody a paralyzing inclusiveness
insofar as its value to literary criticism is concerned. By
appearing more exact and narrow than it is, it might easily
prove misleading: and one reflects that Bottrall himself has
constructed a line (Dryden, Pope, Byron) on the strength of
what seem superficial colloquial resemblances.

Whenever a language achieves a high degree of sophistication in a particular mode, an ease and assurance in saying
those things which the civilization it speaks for thinks most
worth saying, that language has a centrifugal tendency to fly
outward towards colloquialism and freedom. But there are as
many different kinds of colloquialisms or freedoms as there
are different kinds of language. Colloquialism isolated from
the conventional language structure over which it plays has
little interest or vitality. Its value lies in the peculiar illumination, the subtlety of emphasis, it brings to the forms and
tropes of language at any given time, and the colloquial tone
is continuously redefined through a span of time by changes
in these conventions. For if the colloquial character has certain principles that remain more or less constant, there is
ceaseless change going on within the structures of language,
in reaction to which colloquialism has its being. It might be
objected that this is partly a verbal difficulty. Possibly: for I

do not think that Bottrall's term is useless, but dangerous. My objection does not center on the word "colloquial," but on "tradition." A colloquial tone or rhythm always has specific reference to *the particular state of the language* (and the vast theater that phrase implies) with which it is taking liberties. Its reference to its own continuous tradition is only a glancing one. The moment of operation for the colloquial mode is an insistent present with very little of the past inheritable *under its own name*.

The best way to see how particular restraints and the particular freedoms generated by them produce entirely *new* colloquial overtones is to examine some one poem in which the process can be observed. I have chosen Richard Lovelace's beautiful and unusual "La Bella Bona-Roba" for that purpose here, but I am alive to some objections that might be raised against the choice. For example, it follows the rhythm of the thinking rather than of the speaking voice. However, I am not convinced that this distinction cuts deep, and it may be disregarded for the present purpose:

I cannot tell who loves the skeleton
Of a poor marmoset, naught but bone, bone:
Give me a nakedness with her clothes on.

Such whose white-satin upper coat of skin
Cut upon velvet rich incarnidin,
Has yet a body (and of flesh) within.

Sure it is meant good husbandry in men,
Who do incorporate with aery lean,
T'repair their sides, and get their rib again.

Hard hap unto that huntsman that decrees
Fat joys for all his sweat, whenas he sees
After his 'say, naught but his keeper's fees.

Then, Love, I beg, when next thou takst thy bow,
Thy angry shafts, and dost heart-hunting go,
Pass rascal deer, strike me the largest doe.

There is a curiously modern flavor about some of the above stanzas, and possibly *only* when one recognizes this does it become clear how essentially different in structure, and consequently in the quality of delight offered, this poem is from anything that could be written today. Its deceptive modernity is based on the movement of thought through the words in such a way that there is an intimate familiarity bred between thought and speech convention. But these conventions mold the form of the familiarity, the intimacy, what one dares call the "colloquialism," to a countenance that is not at all modern.

Consider the reflective repetition of "bone" in the first stanza. The slight elevation of tone in the opening line is at once brought into intimate touch with the thought as that reflective repetition reproduces the pattern of the thought's operation. The singularity of the opening figure, "skeleton of a poor marmoset," has a strangeness that is acceptable at once because it is so profoundly personal. But Lovelace's figure is not devised, either in our decadent modern sense or in the Elizabethan sense of a *made* thing showing craft. It is organic in the poem as a whole, for it is in this opening figure that one feels the whole poem has its origin. In the second, third, and fourth stanzas the rhythm continues to mirror the activity of the working mind with considerable subtlety, and the terse directness, the "colloquial" spareness, of many of the words is effective. Several of the figures are of a rather homely variety, but woven with sureness into the courtly fabric. Thus, "Fat joys for all his sweat," "T'repair their sides," and "keeper's fees" look back to the characteristic imagery of Jacobean dramatic writing. These middle stanzas are certainly colloquial if one is permitted to define "col-

loquial" as an effective, familiarly free gallantry of language
with its own syntactical and decorous properties. But with
Stanza V the real reason for taking this poem as a good
example of the point we wish to make becomes apparent.
The fifth stanza represents a decided shift in imagery and
tone. The sinuosities of personal thought are here ironed out
in a highly conventional development. But the second stanza,
one now recognizes, had represented an anticipation of this
conventional resolution, and in Stanza V one retrospectively
recognizes that the change in tone has been prepared for. The
new tone looks backward across the preceding stanzas until it
locks hands with Stanza II, and so exerts its authority, hum-
bling the intervening colloquialism to a different and new cast
or expression. The transitions (and effective colloquialism is
largely a matter of transition from constraint to freedom)
have a perfect understanding of the whole situation. The
conventional "white-satin upper coat of skin" and the conventional clothes images have been precursors of the exquisite
double pun in "heart-hunting" and "rascal deer"—exquisite
of course only in this context. For the elaborately artificial
pun of the last stanza has been approached in a colloquial
mood that, now focusing on the deftly introduced "rascal," [1]
transforms this closing device, so uncolloquial in itself, into
something intimately felt.

Even if one should be inclined to question the application
of "colloquial" to this poem, preserving the term for verse in
a less courtly manner, the pattern of restraint and freedom
that lies at the heart of colloquialism is very evident here, and
it may become apparent later that certain other Caroline
writers, by coarsening this mode and using it to encompass
other intentions, wrote verse that sounds very much like
Byron.[2]

1. Formerly a rascal deer signified an ill-conditioned animal in the
herd.
2. For a fuller discussion of "La Bella Bona-Roba" than can be
incorporated here, see pages 68–76.

III

WHO WERE these "pre-cursors"? Saintsbury gives us a hint. Writing on the minor Caroline poets in the *Cambridge History of English Literature* he came to treat of that almost forgotten poet, Sir Francis Kynaston, who died in 1642 shortly after publishing his heroic (in parts mock-heroic) poem, *Leoline and Sydanis*. Speaking of this poem, Saintsbury offers it qualified approval and remarks that it "presents an early, a fairly original, and a very interesting anticipation of 'Whistlecraft' and *Don Juan*." Turning to it in the second volume of Saintsbury's *Minor Caroline Poets*, one finds a poem in which the colloquial manner is much closer to the style that Byron would develop in his late poems than anything that can be found in Dryden or Pope. The colloquialism has a certain raffishness that never moves with a sense of corrective point, and its brand of negligence is more easy and more disreputable than was common with Dryden (except for the comedies) and Pope. The poem has 3,381 lines written in rhyme royal, and while it presents a sustained performance, the tone throughout is not always consistent with remarks that I shall make about the passages quoted. And even when it seems to anticipate *Don Juan* most closely it does little more than provide a substantial base on which the greatest Byronic colloquial effects in verse could be achieved. If these finest effects of Byron's poetry could be explained in terms of other writers they would hardly be worth discussing at all. In his essay on Byron, T. S. Eliot quotes as "first-rate" the following stanza from *Don Juan:*

> *He from the world had cut off a great man*
> *Who in his time had made heroic bustle.*
> *Who in a row like Tom could lead the van,*

Booze in the ken, or at the spellkin bustle?
Who queer a flat? Who (spite of Bow-Street's ban)
On the high toby-spice so flash the muzzle?
Who on a lark with black-eyed Sal (his blowing)
So prime, so swell, so nutty, and so knowing?

Eliot rightly calls this something new in English verse; but
the following stanzas from *Leoline and Sydanis* sound very
much like Byron's manner in the earlier cantos, where he has
been writing at somewhat lower pressure:

XXIII

But to the matter shortly now to go,
That day the Prince did wed his beauteous bride,
As then the custom was, he did bestow
Rich scarfs, and points, and many things beside,
Which in fine curious knots were knit and tied;
And as his royal favours, worn by those
Whom he to grace his royal nupitals chose.

XXIV

Favours are oft, unhappily, by chance
Bestow'd; for 'mongst those courtiers that did wear
The Prince's points, a Marquess was of France,
Who for some heinous fact he had done there,
Hang'd in effigie, fled from France for fear,
And so for refuge to Carleon came,
Monsieur Marquis Jean Foutre *was his name.*

XXV

Who though he had a farinee face,
Thereto a bedstaff leg, and a splay foot,
By angry nature made in man's disgrace,
Which no long slop, nor any ruffled boot
Could mend, or hide, for why they could not do't,

60

*Though his mouth were a wide world without **end**,*
His shape so ugly as no art could mend—

XXVI

Although his weatherwise autumnal joints,
As if they wanted Nature's ligaments,
Did hang together, as if tied by points,
Though most deformed were his lineaments;
Yet fouler was his mind, and base intents,
His matchless impudence, which appeared in this,
That he made love to beauteous Sydanis.

XXVII

So by the canker-worm the fragrant rose
Is tainted: so the serene wholesome air
By black contagion, pestilential grows,
As she by this base wretch, who thought to impair
The chastity of one so matchless fair;
But his foul base intents being once detected,
Were with all scorn and just disdain rejected.

XXVIII

In dire revenge thereof, that day the bands
Were made between Prince Leoline and his bride;
As the Arch-flaman joined had their hands,
And made them one, which no man ought divide,
Upon the Prince's point this caitiff tied
A magic knot, and muttered a spell
Which had an energetic force from hell.

XXIX

For by it was he maleficiated,
And quite depriv'd of all ability
To use a woman, as shall be related,
For Nature felt an imbecility,

Extinguishing in him virility:
The sad events whereof to set before ye,
Is as the dire Praeludium to our story.

It will not, perhaps, be necessary to set a parallel passage
from *Don Juan* beside Kynaston at this point, for the resemblances are fairly insistent. There is, for example, the explicit
impatience of the opening line; the familiar easy references to
images of fashion and dress; the casually introduced morality,
which the speaker pretends to take seriously ("Who for some
heinous fact," "Yet fouler was his mind and base intents,"
etc.); the impertinent descriptions ("bedstaff leg," "Did
hang together as if tied by points," and others); the affected
gravity ("In dire revenge thereof"); the double rhymes with
their impudent emphases; the burlesque quality of the action
and tone; the feigned and overstated veneration for young
females, resulting (when viewed in a larger context than the
present quotation) in a cynicism towards romantic love; the
ribaldry that masquerades as a sense of decorum. All these
things add up to other more broadly significant resemblances.
There is the vigorous sweep of the narrative, its jaunty
rhythm that recognizes no obstacles in the telling. Going
back to Jeffrey's comment on *Beppo*, one finds that his description of that poem applies almost equally well to this
passage from *Leoline and Sydanis*.

Despite these resemblances, however, the tone of the colloquialism is Carolinian. If the writing here is broader, the
intentions coarser than in Lovelace's poem, the free speech
rhythms and the courtly conventions nevertheless interact in
somewhat the same way as in "La Bella Bona-Roba." Stanza
XXVII is a good place to examine this interaction.

The first two lines of the stanza are good in their own
right. "The serene wholesome air" recalls one of Kynaston's
best short poems which begins:

Do not conceal thy radiant eyes,
The starlight of serenest skies. . . .

62

But if for a moment in the first two lines of Stanza XXVII Kynaston wishes to sound a note that is seriously effective in the Carolinian lyric convention, it is for the purpose of achieving a quite other effect in the stanza as a whole. From the third line there is a growing Spenserian heaviness in the imagery which is clearly conscious and deliberate. One passes through "black contagion," "pestilential," and "base wretch," the beauty of the Carolinian voice in the first two lines becoming gradually coarsened and progressively vulnerable to the burlesqued tone in the closing couplet in which, had it been written by Byron, some might have detected an eighteenth-century influence.

Probably *Leoline and Sydanis* would not seem very inviting reading today, except in patches. Douglas Bush, in his *English Literature in the Earlier Seventeenth Century*, says that it recalls the plots of Shakespeare's comedy and Shakespeare's sources. That is certainly true; but it also manages to suggest, by the recurrent colloquialism of its style and rhythm, specifically contemporary concerns. In a stanza by stanza commentary that Kynaston wrote on *Troilus and Criseyde* (and which from a few extracts I have seen printed in a bookseller's announcement in 1796 appears to have a good deal of critical interest) he observed: "Some do not improbably conjecture that Chaucer, in writing the loves and lives of Troilus and Criseyde, did rather glance at some private persons, as one of King Edward the third's sons, and a lady of the court, his paramour; than follow Homer, Dares Phrygius, or any author writing the history of those times. . . ." It is impossible not to suppose, the tone of Kynaston's own poem being what it is, that he did not have Charles's court steadily in view.

Although the poem was published in 1642 it may have been written several years before. As esquire of the body to Charles I, Kynaston would have been in the midst of talk and curiosity about the fashionable Platonic love that the Queen had introduced from France. Davenant had written his play

The Platonic Lovers in 1635, and literary repercussions were general, as the most casual acquaintance with the writers of the day will indicate. One of the main themes in the action of *Leoline and Sydanis* was introduced in Stanzas XXVIII and XXIX, and this theme is obviously intended as a broad burlesque on the court fashion. For example, Leoline, having failed to consummate his marriage, kneels by the nupital bed and addresses Sydanis in verses that are virtually an anatomy of Platonic love:

XLV

Or you a goddess are, whose Deity
Till now I knew not; as Diana chaste,
Whose sacred heavenly sweets, without impiety,
By no man can be wantonly embrac't;
And therefore a just punishment is cast
On my presumption, which was so much more,
To touch you, whom I rather should adore.

XLVI

And therefore by your bed, as by a shrine,
I'll kneel, as penitent for my offense,
In my affecting of a thing divine,
Since you an object are, whose excellence
Is so exalted above human sense,
As like the Sun, it rather doth destroy
Sensation, than permit me to enjoy.

XLVII

Which though I do not, yet you still shall find,
There is no want of love in me, no more
Than want of beauty in your heavenly mind,
Which I religiously shall still adore:
And though I as a husband lov'd before,

I'll turn Platonic lover, and admire
Your virtue's height, to which none can aspire.

But Kynaston was not the only writer of his day in whom
colloquial freedom produced overtones that suggest the Carolinian use of language could be like Byron's. Nathaniel Whiting is the most abused among the romantic epic writers of his
day, but yet his kind of colloquialism has something like the
interest one finds in Kynaston's poem. Saintsbury called his
poetry "uncouth jargon," and argued that *The Pleasing History of Albino and Bellama* was "graceless and slatternly,"
but this is excessive dispraise. The intonation we are looking
for may be a little more than fugitively glimpsed in the
following stanzas. Bellama is telling her father why she will
not marry the wealthy but objectionable Don Fuco:

Bellama with a look fraught with disdain
(Though hatred did not make her anger bold)
Says, "Sir, I'm sorry you do entertain
Such high conceits of folly hemmed with gold:
    Think you no marriage good if equal lands
    Be not matchmakers and do join their hands?

"Don Fuco has ten thousand pounds a year,
With weighty titles would o'erload a mule,
A piece of arras finely wrought and dear;
But does he square his life to virtue's rule?
    With vice as wealth, to countless sums he thrives,
    But is, in virtue, full as poor as wives.

"He knows to steer an horse and hollo hounds,
But not to guide his actions, less his tongue;
He speaks in state, but ev'ry sentence sounds
Of comic fragments or some tavern song.
    And shall I him, hail'd by unworthy pelf,
    Take to rule me, who cannot rule himself?

"Shall I see other female vessels thrive
  With mine own nectar, and they fee'd with money,
Whilst I like careful bee do keep my hive,
  And work the comb for them to suck the honey?
    No, I'll no sharers have in my delight,
    I'll have it one and only, else good night."

There are no specific similarities between Whiting's verse and *Don Juan* of the kind that *Leoline and Sydanis* presents. Nevertheless, there are likenesses of a general character that we become aware of immediately when we place, beside such verses as those quoted above, stanzas like these from Canto I in which Julia is berating her husband for jealousy:

"Yes, Don Alfonso! husband now no more,
  If ever you indeed deserved the name,
Is't worthy of your years?—you have three-score—
  Fifty or sixty, it is all the same—
Is't wise or fitting, causeless to explore
  For facts against a virtuous woman's fame?
Ungrateful, perjured, barbarous Don Alfonso,
How dare you think your lady would go on so?
"Is it for this I have disdained to hold
  The common privileges of my sex?
That I have chosen a confessor so old
  And deaf that any other it would vex,
And never once he has had chance to scold,
  But found my very innocence perplex
So much, he always doubted I was married—
How sorry you will be when I've miscarried!"

IV

SOME general remarks and conclusions should be offered here. Whiting, although of some small interest to the argument of this essay, is not a court poet. He was an Anglican clergyman from Queens' College, Cambridge, who defaulted to Puritanism. Sir Francis Kynaston, however, occupies an unusual position. He was so conscious of the elegant requirements of aristocratic life that in 1635 he founded a kind of college for young nobles called the Museum Minervae, to which Charles I contributed £100 from the treasury. While the Museum was intent on keeping in touch with the latest developments in science and logic, emphasis was placed on the more elegant arts, and the young cavaliers were taught behavior, music, riding, and dancing, as well as modern languages, coins, heraldry, and antiquities. The full course required seven years, but doubtless a great deal of refined leisure was involved in the studies.

In short, Kynaston very consciously belonged to an aristocratic society that anticipated features of the Regency world of Byron, and no doubt some of the similarity that one notes between the poetry of the two men arises from a similarity in aristocratic styles. But there may be another explanation as well. The Carolinians possessed a highly formal language, rich with rhetorical conventions and devices. The skill with which they used this language was suggested in the discussion of Lovelace's fine poem. The formality of their language, and the definition which the Court provided for their attitudes, enabled them to maintain a certain distance between themselves and their feelings—a distance which allowed various shades of detachment and cynicism to circulate freely around their verbal statements. The effects that are achieved in this mode may cover a wide range of feeling, but they are always distinct from effects in any mode in which the poet identifies himself with what he is feeling. These conventions were not formally accessible to Byron as a Regency writer, but he had built up a rhetoric of his own, beginning with *Childe Harold*. Even in the first two cantos of that poem he was well on his way towards achieving a detachment that, when his state of mind radically changed during his self-imposed exile, could be utilized in *Beppo* and *Don Juan* with entirely different effects. "Childe Harold at a little distance stood," begins one of the stanzas in his early poem. It was that fine little distance between the word and its open-faced meaning that Byron managed to keep free in *Don Juan* for the ironic intention. And this was something the Carolinians had known how to do two hundred years earlier.

Note:
Lovelace's "La Bella Bona–Roba"

RICHARD LOVELACE'S "La Bella Bona-Roba" is so difficult a poem in some respects that the necessity for compressing my treatment of it in an essay devoted to another poet left too many things unsaid and made for some obscurity. Shortly after this essay originally appeared in *Scrutiny* in 1949, Donald Davie in a penetrating and courteous letter of comment raised several objections to certain of my claims for it. In those days the late Rosamond Tuve had recently published her influential book, *Elizabethan and Metaphysical Imagery*. Davie began by quoting the following passage from it:

> This recognition of author's *interpretation* as controlling subject must be distinguished from the modern author's portrayal of his own *process* of interpreting or feeling, of "the very movement of thought in a living mind," the "interplay of perception and reflection"

(these phrases come from F. O. Matthiessen's and Edmund Wilson's essays on Eliot). The earlier authors' subject was different, however similar his stuff; his subject was still "his meaning," not "himself seeing it." One finds the choice of images made upon different grounds, and their structural function differently affecting their nature, if one reads first Eliot's "Prufrock" and then even a difficult borderline case like Donne's "Elegy XI, Upon the losse of his Mistresses Chaine, for which he made satisfaction." Eliot shows us a man having a thought. Donne arranges the thoughts a man had, upon losing his mistress' property, into a carefully logical and hence wantonly witty exposition of the "bitter" and disproportionate cost of ladies.

Davie goes on to comment on certain of my statements in the light of this passage:

Of Stanza V, Mr. Bewley remarks that "The sinuosities of personal thought are here ironed out in a highly conventional development." But from those "sinuosities," from the rhythm which "continues to mirror the activity of the working mind," from the repetition which "accurately reproduces the pattern of the thought's operation," it is plain that this critic treats Lovelace as showing "a man having a thought," not as arranging "the thoughts a man had." Miss Tuve, one gathers, would have to take issue with Mr. Bewley and argue for the poem as "artificial . . . in the Elizabethan sense of a made thing showing craft."

Most of the remainder of Davie's letter is devoted to a lucid exposition of the conventional element present in "La Bella Bona-Roba," part of which I quote here:

To begin with, it seems that the opening figure is not so "strange," because not so "profoundly personal," as

Mr. Bewley asserts or as it appears upon first sight. From the notes to the Oxford edition of Lovelace (ed. C. H. Wilkinson, 1930) it appears that the series of images, "monkey-ape-baboon-marmoset," was in common parlance connected with the courtesan, just as "Bona-Roba" was an accepted euphuism for the same. . . . The figure "clothes-flesh" was conventional in Lovelace's period and continually recurrent in his own work. . . . This blunting of the gratuitous element in the first figure leads me to question whether the repetition of "bone," in the second line, is indeed "reflective." It now seems, I think, less novel and interesting, sheerly emphatic, not "bone, yes, bone," but "bone upon bone." The notes, giving the precise meanings from venery, of "assay," of "keeper's fees," of "rascal deer," give the impression that the third and fourth stanzas are logical stages in an ordered and logical argument. Here, says Mr. Bewley, "the rhythm continues to mirror the activity of the working mind with considerable subtlety." But it seems to me that between the activity and the mirroring of the activity has occurred a stage in which the activity has been pruned and arranged as strict argument. For the "Sure" of the third stanza ("Sure it is meant good husbandry in men") carries the sense of "It is true, I grant you . . ."; and before the fourth stanza we are to supply, as it seems to me, a "Yet," or a "But"—"On the other hand. . . ." [1]

The kind of colloquialism I was trying to isolate in "La Bella Bona-Roba" was of a particular kind—one whose freedoms were bred of a reaction to the restraints and conventions existing in the language of educated men in the poet's own time. So far from ignoring or minimizing the conventional

1. The full text of Davie's letter, together with my reply, will be found in *Scrutiny*, September, 1949, pp. 234–41.

element, my analysis of the poem depended on its presence, but for the sake of brevity I had to speak of the conventional content of the poem in general terms, assuming its existence rather than offering a detailed exposition. The following is an excerpt from my fuller analysis of the poem which Davie's letter made possible.

*　　*　　*

In taking "La Bella Bona-Roba" as an example of a convention-filled Carolinian poem, chosen to illustrate a quite other point in a different argument, I did not think it necessary to discuss its logical construction in any detail. Davie is, of course, perfectly correct in saying the middle stanzas exhibit an argument, and that " 'Sure' of the third stanza carries the sense of 'It is true, I grant you. . . .' " But we were aware of this from its most famous use as a logical nexus in Hamlet's soliloquy, "How all occasions do inform against me." And I would point to this soliloquy as a good example of how, in the seventeenth century, the "sinuosities of personal thought" could find a natural mode of expression through a logical order that was native to them but alien to us.

Turning now to Davie's particular objections to my reading, I think I had better present a detailed analysis of what the poem seems to mean, for I am convinced that unless we read it, from one point of view, as the poem of a man *having a thought* we shall not be able, despite its elaborate logic, to know what thought the man has had; and this I believe is an index of its profoundly personal character. . . . It appears that the question "Can a poet's image simultaneously participate in a common conventional currency and the personal feeling of the poet?" would be answered in different ways by Davie and myself. Before considering the marmoset image I think one might, with the effect of greater detachment, glance at an analogous image. I suppose that Davie would grant that the cormorant was an even more widely used image in seventeenth-century poetry than the 'monkey-ape-baboon-marmoset" series of images. A typical instance of its use occurs in Dryden's *Conquest of Granada*, Part I:

> *You like some greedy cormorant devour*
> *All my whole life can give you in an hour.*

No one would maintain that this is distinguished poetry, or that Dryden drew very deeply on his sensibility in making such an image. Yet Marvell could write something strangely similar, exhibiting quite as high a conventional content, and make it exquisitely personal:

> *Now let us sport us while we may;*
> *And now, like am'rous birds of prey,*
> *Rather at once in our Time devour,*
> *Than languish in his slow-chapt power.*

I find Marvell's image everything Dryden's is not: immediate, personally urgent, and sensuously vivid: not, indeed, for any one sense, but in the imagination where all the senses merge in a composite unity. This is not, of course, personal in the way some Romantic poetry is, but I should be most inclined to take issue with Mr. Davie when he invokes the terms "gratuitous" and "arbitrary" as significant notes of the personal.

"La Bella Bona-Roba" seems to be a radical criticism of the conventionally wanton ethics of love that prevailed at the earlier Stuart Court, and which reached full flowering later in writers like Sir George Etherege and the Earl of Rochester. We only possess the outlines of Lovelace's career, but we know well enough that his experience of the milieu was immediate and protracted. The sentiments of most of his verse are representative of the fashion, but this poem is an occasion on which he seems to have had a strong personal reaction. The first stanza begins by falling back on the seventeenth-century concern with death and progressive decay. The current belief that the world was in a cycle of deterioration, moving from a remote Golden Age towards an impending dissolution, was an implicit assumption behind a poem like Lovelace's "Love Made in the First Age," where the theme is stated with conventional wantonness, and love and decay are joined. The conjunction is not unusual for the time, but I still find the opening image of "La Bella Bona-Roba" strange and personal, for the image of illicit erotic experience (the marmoset) is instantaneously transformed into a *memento mori* (the skeleton). Since a *memento mori* is meant to serve as an object of penitential meditation, it still seems to me that the repeated "bone" of the first stanza is meant to be a reflective repetition. There is a meditative withdrawal and shudder on the poet's part reflected in that repetition, and it is emphasized by his knowledge that he is almost alone in his reaction. The opening, "I cannot tell who loves the skeleton/ Of a poor marmoset," probably means "I cannot measure or count the multitude." It may even mean, "I cannot talk about the following sentiments to my usual type of companion." In such a reading the unusual verbal compression, by no means typical practice in the time, causes the thought and phrasing to impinge with great directness on each other. If we were to read the sentence as a simple confession of unperspicacious ignorance it would be a very unconventional performance for a Carolinian courtier indeed. In the third line Lovelace begins to dissociate himself from the popular attitude. "Give me a nakedness with her clothes on" has an immediacy in no way blunted by the fact that skin-clothes images were common in the seventeenth century. The immediacy resides in the near-personification of "a nakedness," a quality divorced from its subject and standing up in its own right, a self-existent entity. This immediacy is pressed home when one realizes the economy with which Lovelace is making an unusually complex statement in a minimum of words, and using conventional images for his own personal meaning. No contrast is intended between clothes and skin, for they are plainly identical. What Lovelace is asking for is a "nakedness" (physical love) that doesn't end with decay and death—that has no skeleton within, but which offers profounder fulfillment, which he symbolizes in the image of an interior "nakedness" replacing the skeleton, and hence triumphing over the *memento mori* of the opening figure. The second stanza relates to the enlarged physical appetites and capacities that characterized the men of the Golden Age, which Lovelace describes in "Love Made in the First Age." One might almost wonder if Lovelace were not simply regretting his own physical and sensual limitations. But the appetites of the Golden Age were the reward of incorruption, and the third stanza of "La Bella Bona-Roba" presents the desired fulfillment in terms of marriage which it contrasts with the wasteful illicit love of Stanzas I and IV. The man who establishes himself in marriage, consorting with a single love (aery lean) rather than with a flock of loves, repairs the damage inflicted on him in Eden when Eve was fashioned from his rib. His own flesh rejoins him, and he is a complete man again. But the rake has none of these satisfactions, and is left with expenses and penalties as his reward. In the closing stanza the "rascal deer," or lean deer that the hunter must pass over, relate to the skeleton of the opening line, and "the largest doe" relates to the fleshly ideal body of the second stanza, which carries no *memento mori* hidden within itself.

This seems to me the correct interpretation, but the meaning (*the thought Lovelace had*) is clear only because it is possible to arrive at it by watching Lovelace *have the thought*, in the process of which we sense the deeply personal feeling that is involved. It is possible to read this poem—perhaps easier to do so—in an exactly opposite sense from the one I have given here. In such a reading the successive "nakednesses" in the second stanza would be read as a salute to carnal pleasure only. The "Sure it is meant . . ." of the third stanza would be read with an ironic inflection, and "aery lean" would then be interpreted, not as an aery with a single bird, but as an impoverished nest. Stanza IV would become a description of the man foolish enough to have married, and so placed himself at the mercy of a gamekeeper able to exact penalties for random poaching. Instead of making a serious moral judgment on the manners of his time, in such an interpretation Lovelace would be making a severe indictment of marriage.

It seems to me that both of these readings take due cognizance of seventeenth century poetic and logical conventions. But while elaborately extensive ambiguity of this kind is present in a few poems of the time, it is not a common practice by any means, and in any case the poem in either reading does not have the air of playing this kind of trick. I think, then, that the only guide we have to which of the two interpretations Lovelace intended will lie in discovering on which side the personal quality of his images and rhythm seems most intense and interesting, on which side the movement of the argument seems most intimately and sinuously to reflect the movement of his own mind as he develops that argument; and the reader can prove for himself how the quality changes on successive readings as he passes from one interpretation to the other. He can prove for himself how the quality deteriorates when he reads the poem with the second meaning in mind. The first interpretation, aligning itself rather loosely with seventeenth century melancholy, imparts a seriousness and subtle complexity to the whole poem which it loses entirely in the conventional cynicism of the second reading. For example, consider Stanza IV. According to the first interpretation, the huntsman is a striking symbol of metaphysical restlessness and unease. The keeper, suggesting a Divine Judge, will impose formidable sanctions for his transgressions. In the second reading the huntsman is a rather contemptible figure, not wily enough to remain unde-tected in his amorous adventures, and the keeper becomes his shrew of a wife. This reading desensitizes the rhythm, for since the flexible colloquial line enforces the deeper personal meaning, one must, in the second reading, try to ignore the rhythm and concentrate on the static presence of rhetorical conventions in the poem, which then loses its distinction and sinks down to the level of mediocrity.

I have no quarrel whatever with the distinction which Davie takes over from Miss Tuve's work, but when one is dealing with a poem of high value I do not think it can be enlarged into a critical principle of deep or inflexible validity. The distinction is obviously valuable and true up to a point, and it should also be rather obvious. But in applying it to particular poems of first-rate quality, a great deal of tact and restraint seem to me to be called for. Seventeenth-century poetic conventions and logical structure are certainly present in this poem, but it is the remarkably free and personal way that Lovelace dominates them that makes "La Bella Bona-Roba" one of the finer short poems of his time.

THE ROMANTIC IMAGINATION AND THE UNROMANTIC BYRON

I T I S O F some interest that Byron, who has been accepted as the embodiment and symbol of Romanticism—perhaps in Europe more than in England—should be the one major English Romantic poet whose modes of thought and feeling cannot be reconciled easily with those of his principal contemporaries. Wordsworth, Coleridge, Shelley, and Keats inhabit a different world of feeling, and they face Byron across a gulf that is not readily passable. Except for Shelley, Byron wasted little admiration on the poetry of his compeers. When we examine Byron's poetry we discover that its most Romantic characteristics are ones that criticism today would consider somewhat peripheral to the heart of Romantic experience.

Except for a brief period in 1816, when Shelley, while rowing Byron around Lake Geneva, almost persuaded him that he admired Wordsworth, Byron makes little attempt to find consolation or spiritual release through Nature. At the conclusion of a tour of the Alps he made in 1816, he recorded in a journal he was keeping for his sister:

I am a lover of Nature and an admirer of Beauty. I can bear fatigue and welcome privation, and have seen some of the noblest views in the world. But in all this—the recollections of bitterness, and more especially of recent and more home desolation, which must accompany me through life, have preyed upon me here; and neither the music of the Shepherd, the crashing of the Avalanche, nor the torrent, the mountain, the Glacier, the Forest, nor the Cloud, have for one moment lightened the weight upon my heart, nor enabled me to lose my own wretched identity in the majesty, and the power, and the Glory, around, above, beneath me.

With the exception of the several "Wordsworthian" stanzas in Canto III of *Childe Harold*, Byron's verse attests to this incapacity plainly enough, and it makes him unique among English Romantic poets. Among the "Romantic" characteristics in his verse we might count as most important his Titanism, and especially the cult of personality which his poetry encourages. But Titanism is by no means exclusive to Romantic literature. It flourished in Marlowe, and even in Dryden's heroic tragedies. As for the cult of personality, it develops in Byron's poetry in a direction hardly characteristic of the Romantics. As the Earth was at the very center of the universe with all the planets and stars revolving around it in the Ptolemaic system, so the Romantic poet made his own ego the hub of a creation which appeared to emanate from the poet in the act of perceiving. Virtually all contemporary critics of Romanticism have tended to see this as the most important identifying factor in the Romantic vision. Albert S. Gerard has put it quite simply: "If one impulse can be singled out as central to the Romantic imagination, it is the *Sehnsucht*, the yearning toward the absolute, the aspiration to oneness and wholeness and organic unity, the dream of perfection." A whole metaphysic is implicit in this conception of the ego as the creative heart and center of reality. A few years ago, René Wellek, more technically, defined Romanticism as "that attempt . . . to reconcile man and nature, consciousness and unconsciousness, by poetry which is 'the first and last knowledge.' "

This attempt of the poet to make his imagination and external reality a continuum in which each reshapes and alters the other is common to all the major Romantics in England *except* Byron. There is nothing at all in Byron's poetry of this exalted conception of the creative faculty, of the Romantic imagination, as a surrogate for God making the universe anew in the image of the poet's individual personality. At its worst in Byron, the cut of personality is little more than the cult of the glamorized celebrity whose every move is attended by the eyes of a bewitched continent, while at its best it is only the same conception held a little in check, and going under the name of "the Byronic hero."

Byron was the last of the great English satirists. This fact alone would make him an anomaly in the Romantic age, which—apart from Byron—was virtually incapable of producing distinguished satire. It is not difficult to understand why. The satiric mode demands the existence of a world and a social order that are independent of the poet's perception. If the perceiving subject and the object perceived tend to become identified in Romantic poetry and theory, as Wellek and nearly all modern critics maintain, then the castigation of satire becomes not a mode of social correction but a form of perversely indulged masochism. Nor does the Egotistical Sublime, which is the superb name Keats gave to Wordsworth's mode of seeing and knowing, permit irony to flourish, either at the expense of the self or others. Where so little distance is permitted between the perceiver and the perceived, there is no room for irony to circulate, and where the self or the ego is invested with almost God-like attributes, self-irony, were it possible, would approach blasphemy. But it is not possible because the Egotistical Sublime and self-irony are irreconcilable modes and cannot exist together. Hence it is that true satiric genius is at odds with the Romantic sensibility.

Byron, who is a great English poet because he is a great English satirist, can be called a Romantic only if we allow the secondary characteristics of Romanticism to take over from the primary characteristics altogether in his poetry. By the secondary, or superficial, characteristics of Romanticism is meant its taste for exoticism and far places, mystery, supernaturalism, theatricality, and a dozen other such qualities. Of these things we have more than enough in Byron. But of essential Romantic "philosophy," if we may call it so, we have very little. Apart from the few memorably faked moments in *Childe Harold*, Canto III, when Byron tried to merge with Nature, most of his energy goes into keeping his identity compact and inviolate. To form a continuum with a transcendental reality outside himself is the last thing he wants. It is of course quite possible to read Byron's insistence on the inviolability and self-sufficiency of his own selfhood as in itself Romantic. A key passage would be the closing scene of *Manfred*, in which Manfred sends the Demons who have come to claim him back to their element:

> *Back to thy hell!*
> *Thou hast no power upon me*, that *I feel;*
> *Thou never shalt possess me*, that *I know:*
> *What I have done is done; I bear within*
> *A torture which could nothing gain from thine:*
> *The mind which is immortal makes itself*
> *Requital for its good or evil thoughts,—*
> *Is its own origin of ill and end—*
> *And its own place and time: its innate sense,*
> *When stripped of this mortality, derives*
> *No colour from the fleeting things without,*

But is absorbed in sufferance or in joy,
Born from the knowledge of its own desert.

As I have said, it is quite possible to read this as an expression of the Romantic view of things. Samuel Chew as long ago as 1915 called *Manfred* "more than any other single English poem . . . typical of the Romantic period." But to me the most significant thing about Manfred's conception of his own ego here is that it is not open-ended, but utterly closed. There is no flowing outward from its own center, nor does anything flow in upon it. It almost seems to look forward to A. C. Bradley's conception of the personality as a finite center held incommunicado in the opaque shell of its own encircling experiences. And as none of the characters in the play, natural or supernatural, ever really get through to Manfred, nor he to them, the action seems to support such an interpretation.

Shelley's interpretation of personal identity in his brief prose essay "On Life" is an extreme instance, but it is more representative of that version of reality and the selfhood out of which Romantic poetry was written than anything in Byron:

> Nothing exists but as it is perceived. The difference is merely nominal between those two classes of thought, which are vulgarly distinguished by the names of ideas and external objects. Pursuing the same thread of reasoning, the existence of distinct individual minds, similar to that which is now employed in questioning its own nature, is likewise found to be a delusion. The words *I*, *you*, *they*, are not signs of any actual difference subsisting between the assemblage of thoughts thus indicated, but are merely marks employed to denote the different modifications of the one mind.

> Let it not be supposed that this doctrine conducts to the monstrous presumption that I, the person who now

write and think, am that one mind. I am but a portion of
it. The words *I*, and *you*, and *they*, are grammatical
devices invented simply for arrangement, and totally
devoid of the intense and exclusive sense usually attached to them.

In important and central respects Byron is quite different
from his contemporaries in the Romantic age. He writes his
poetry in the belief that his own ego does not merge with, but
confronts, Nature, the world, and society. At times, particularly in the earlier work, Byron may seem to himself lonely
and isolated—alienated, to use a much overused word of our
own day. But this "alienation" is in itself an implicit recognition that there is an inhabited world outside himself—a world
of material things, of men and women—that claims an existence entirely objective and essentially unmodified by his own
processes of perceiving. Blake wrote: "I assert for My Self
that I do not behold the outward Creation & that to me it is
hindrance and not Action; it is as the dirt upon my feet, No
part of Me." This would have been inexplicable to Byron.
His descriptions of Nature and society always begin with the
fact that material *things*, animate or inanimate, are very
palpably in front of him, and he is always interested in them.
In his descriptive poetry he does not always observe the world
of men and Nature very freshly or originally, but the reader
never doubts that Byron is convinced that it is *there*. On this
point, he is as much the commonsensical Englishman as
Samuel Johnson refuting Bishop Berkeley by kicking the
stone in his pathway. This implicit faith in material creation
was so little an assumption of the other Romantics that its
presence throughout Byron's poetry differentiates it sharply
from most of the major poetry of his time.

Blake was, and Shelley appears to have become, a complete idealist, educing the visible world of matter from their
own minds. Coleridge and, especially, Wordsworth did not

go so far—but for them also the imagination reshaped the visible world until man became a reduced mirror image of God in the act of creating the universe. "The primary IMAGINATION," Coleridge had written in his famous formulation in *Biographia Literaria*, "I hold to be the living Power and prime Agent of all human Perception, and as a repetition in the finite mind of the eternal act of creation in the infinite I AM." Every man's primary imagination created the world he saw, touched, smelled, and heard, by the act of perceiving it, and so, by analogy, he became like God bringing the universe into existence. Similarly, the poet who writes a true poem (drawing here upon his secondary imagination) is also analogous to God, for the true work of art is a created universe in little.

In Romantic poetry almost as much as in twentieth-century poetry, the creative process itself, the act of writing a poem, becomes the favorite subject matter of the poet because he can conceive of no higher act, nothing that elevates man so near to the divine, as creating, or re-creating, the universe by means of his imagination in a literary work of art. Much of the best poetry of Keats, Shelley, Coleridge, and Wordsworth is, in one way or another—often in a disguised way—devoted to this subject. Here are only a few of the great poems of the Romantic age that can be read with complete plausibility and logical consistency (just as all of Wallace Stevens' poems can be) as commentaries on the imagination and the creative process: "The Ancient Mariner," "Kubla Khan," "Dejection," "Alastor," "I Stood Tip-Toe," "Sleep and Poetry," *Endymion*, "The Eve of St. Agnes," "Lamia," "La Belle Dame sans Merci," "The Fall of Hyperion." Finally, all of Wordsworth's great poems concerned with memory, the recovery of the past and its reconstitution in the context of the present, are really dealing with artistic creation. Most of all there is *The Prelude*, which as an intellectual or spiritual autobiography purports to trace the development of a poet's mind and sensibility through all the slow gradations of growing up and maturing until at last this creative power, this splendor of the imagination, has been achieved.

In the concluding book of *The Prelude*, as the young Wordsworth makes his night ascent of Mount Snowdon, the moon suddenly emerges, metamorphosing and shedding a glory on the mountain landscape. It is one of Wordsworth's great passages. The moonlight in its unifying and transfiguring power becomes a symbol of the imagination:

> *The power, which all*
> *Acknowledge when thus moved, which Nature thus*
> *To bodily sense exhibits, is the express*
> *Resemblance of that glorious faculty*
> *That higher minds bear with them as their own.*
> *This is the very spirit in which they deal*
> *With the whole compass of the universe:*
> *They from their native selves can send abroad*
> *Kindred mutations; for themselves create*
> *A like existence.*

The Romantic poet who viewed the landscape of the natural world in this "philosophic" perspective was bound to see the world illuminated and transfigured—re-created, as it were —by this power of the imagination. This was especially true for Keats in his earlier poetry. The moon in its mythological embodiment as Cynthia or Diana frequently symbolized the visionary imagination for him, and in the myth of Cynthia and Endymion, the young Shepherd-King as frequently represented the man of creative vision and power—in short, the poet. Near the close of his early poem "I Stood Tip-Toe," Keats describes the bridal night of the goddess and the Shepherd-King. Their physical union represented for Keats at this point in his career—and as late as *Endymion*—the entry of the poet into the full and complete possession of his vision and imaginative powers. Whenever this occurs, the world appears to undergo transfiguration. Here is Keats's description of the physical world re-created through the efficacy of poetic power or energy:

Oh for three words of honey that I might
Tell but one wonder of thy bridal night!
Where distant ships do seem to show their keels,
Phoebus awhile delay'd his mighty wheels,
And turn'd to smile upon thy bashful eyes,
Ere he his unseen pomp would solemnize.
The evening weather was so bright and clear,
That men of health were of unusual cheer;
Stepping like Homer at the trumpet's call,
Or young Apollo on the pedestal:
And lovely women were as fair and warm,
As Venus looking sideways in alarm.
The breezes were ethereal, and pure,
And crept through half-closed lattices to cure
The languid sick; it cool'd their fever'd sleep,
And soothed them into slumbers full and deep.
Soon they awoke clear eyed: nor burnt with thirsting,
Nor with hot fingers, nor with temples bursting:
And springing up, they met the wond'ring sight
Of their dear friends, nigh foolish with delight;
Who feel their arms, and breasts, and kiss and stare,
And on their placid foreheads part the hair.
Young men, and maidens at each other gaz'd
With hands held back, and motionless, amaz'd
To see the brightness in each other's eyes;
And so they stood, fill'd with a sweet surprise,
Until their tongues were loosed in poesy.
Therefore no lover did of anguish die:
But the soft numbers, in that moment spoken,
Made silken ties, that never may be broken.

Cynthia! I cannot tell the greater blisses,
That follow'd thine, and thy dear shepherd's kisses:
Was there a poet born?—but now no more,
My wand'ring spirit must no further soar.

This is very early Keats, written when he was still much under Leigh Hunt's influence, and one has to love Keats a great deal to find it more than tolerable verse. But the extravagant claims Keats is making here for poetry and the redemptive powers of the poetic imagination have great interest for anyone concerned with Romanticism. In this passage he is making a veiled or allegoric "philosophic" statement about the ability of the Romantic imagination to *regenerate* the world—and in Keats's passage the regeneration is so complete that it almost amounts to a new creation. Later, in "Lamia," he was to question this view radically which he brings forward here; and in "The Fall of Hyperion," his last important poem, he virtually retracts it. But "I Stood Tip-Toe" remains a central document for those who wish to know what the possibilities for poetry appeared to be in the eyes of the young Romantics who were practicing their art in the opening years of the nineteenth century. And I think today that most of us would be inclined to bring a loving forbearance to this verse for the sake of a young poet's faith in his art that, in the end, proved to be as vulnerable as it was beautiful.

Matthew Arnold thought that Wordsworth was the greatest of the Romantic poets—the greatest, indeed, of all English poets after Shakespeare and Milton. I see no reason to question his judgment today. Certainly Wordsworth was the Romantic poet who had the power, beyond any of the others, to present us immediately and directly with a world that had undergone transfiguration. He does not tell us about it, as Keats does in the early passage we have just discussed: he gives it to us, places us in the midst of it. We experience it in our senses; we breathe it; we take it into our hearts. It is a world of luminous, unearthly beauty that is as real to the man who is capable of reading Wordsworth today as the world outside his window: yet finally it is not a *real* world, but a country of the mind—of a mind that is forever transmuting reality to a higher state. That Wordsworth was able to achieve this astonishing thing over and over again impresses me as one of the incomparable feats of English poetry.

He was of course one of the most gifted technicians in the English literary tradition, and this gift was the more powerful because he seems to have exercised it almost involuntarily. I do not mean that Wordsworth shirked revisions, or that he failed to think deeply about his craft. The 1815 Preface alone would be enough to refute a statement so absurd. But Wordsworth, I fancy, struggled with his poetry as saints are sometimes said to struggle with God. To struggle so, to search in the face of all hardships and denials for the ultimate perfection that so often seemed out of reach, was the very condition of his mind's existence. We know that Wordsworth was a stubborn and a determined man, but will had little to do with his triumph. It was, in the end, a matter of love—love of his language, of his countryside, of his medium and art. But inseparable from that there was the love of something else— something else that only his poetry can give us a hint of: something towards which only the discipline of his art and his soul's dedication to it was capable of leading him. To attempt to define the vision that his art discovered for him in an essay like this would be to kill it. But it is *there* in all of his greater poetry—a pervasive life, a redeeming factor, a healing power.

I have suggested that Wordsworth is the poet of "transfiguration," of the world seen with redeemed eyes, of man glorified in the absolving medium of imagination. As an obvious example of what I mean, there is the well-known passage from Book IV of *The Prelude* in which the young Wordsworth, coming back to Hawkshead for his summer

vacation after his first year at Cambridge, returns home in
the early dawn after having danced all night:

> *The memory of one particular hour*
> *Doth here rise up against me. 'Mid a throng*
> *Of maids and youths, old men, and matrons staid,*
> *A medley of all tempers, I had passed*
> *The night in dancing, gaiety, and mirth,*
> *With din of instruments and shuffling feet,*
> *And glancing forms, and tapers glittering,*
> *And unaimed prattle flying up and down;*
> *Spirits upon the stretch, and here and there*
> *Slight shocks of young love-liking interspersed,*
> *Whose transient pleasure mounted to the head,*
> *And tingled through the veins. Ere we retired,*
> *The cock had crowed, and now the eastern sky*
> *Was kindling, nor unseen, from humble copse*
> *And open field, through which the pathway wound,*
> *And homeward led my steps. Magnificent*
> *The morning rose, in memorable pomp,*
> *Glorious as e'er I had beheld—in front,*
> *The sea lay laughing at a distance; near,*
> *The solid mountains shone, bright as the clouds,*
> *Grain-tinctured, drenched in empyrean light;*
> *And in the meadows and the lower grounds*
> *Was all the sweetness of a common dawn—*
> *Dews, vapours, and the melody of birds,*
> *And labourers going forth to till the fields.*
> *Ah! need I say, dear Friend! that to the brim*
> *My heart was full; I made no vows, but vows*
> *Were then made for me; bond unknown to me*
> *Was given, that I should be, else sinning greatly,*
> *A dedicated Spirit. On I walked*
> *In thankful blessedness, which yet survives.*

It has been necessary to quote this passage at some length
because the opening fifteen lines, which are very good verse

but somewhat pedestrian poetry, are required to establish the rather fatigued and complacent tone which is suddenly shattered by the fanfare, "Magnificent/ The morning rose in memorable pomp." This rural world of staid matrons, old men, frolicsome youths and maids, crowing cocks, and field laborers is, in effect, confronted apocalyptically by the Royal Procession of the dawn. But Wordsworth sustains the suggestion of trumpets and kettledrums only for the length of one line. In view of the intense subjective revelation that the boy experienced on that occasion, nothing less than a flaunting of purple, crimson, and gold is called for here, but it must be for a moment only: otherwise the essential nature of the experience would be falsified. The tone changes immediately. It is still elevated but spiritualized. There is an authentic note of spiritual vision in the way Wordsworth is able to suggest so convincingly that the mountains have been dematerialized, and have become shapes of golden light. With the introduction of phrases like "grain-tinctured" and "empyrean light," we feel as if we had entered the world of one of Samuel Palmer's water colors. We are uncertain whether the "labourers going forth to till the fields" are really field hands, or angels descended among men.

This is a fine passage, but by no means one of Wordsworth's greatest. I have discussed it here because it clarifies to some extent the nature of Wordsworth's transfiguring vision. It is clear that in Wordsworth the Romantic imagination has certain affinities with religious experience. But I should like to look at another of his poems—what is probably his greatest sonnet—and attempt to see how he is able to observe a scene (in this case, an urban scene and not a landscape) and bring about a complete transfiguration by means of words alone.

Wordsworth's sonnet "Composed upon Westminster Bridge, September 3, 1802" is one of the unquestioned triumphs of the Romantic age in England. While it does not exhibit the stock paraphernalia of conventional Romantic poetry, it throws a strong white light on the Romantic method of proceeding when Romanticism is living at its highest level. Here is the sonnet:

Earth has not anything to show more fair:
Dull would he be of soul who could pass by
A sight so touching in its majesty:
This City now doth, like a garment, wear
The beauty of the morning; silent, bare,
Ships, towers, domes, theatres, and temples lie
Open unto the fields, and to the sky;
All bright and glittering in the smokeless air.
Never did sun more beautifully steep
In his first splendour, valley, rock, or hill;
Ne'er saw I, never felt, a calm so deep!
The river glideth at his own sweet will:
Dear God! the very houses seem asleep;
And all that mighty heart is lying still.

This was written when Wordsworth and his sister were on their way to Calais. He was to meet and take his leave for the last time of Annette Vallon, by whom he had had a daughter ten years before whom he had never seen. Dorothy has described the occasion of the sonnet in her *Journal:*

We left London on Saturday morning at half past five or six. . . . We mounted the Dover coach at Charing Cross. It was a beautiful morning. The city, St. Paul's, with the river, and a multitude of little boats, made a most beautiful sight as we crossed Westminster Bridge. The houses were not overhung by their cloud of smoke, and they were spread out endlessly, yet the sun shone so brightly, with such a fierce light, that there was something like the purity of one of nature's own grand spectacles.

Wordsworth was not fond of the city, and his attitude towards it was that which he expressed in Book VII of *The Prelude*, or in his short poem "The Reverie of Poor Susan," which is built on a contrast between the pernicious city and redeeming nature. This sonnet records the surprised shock with which Wordsworth, from the coach, suddenly recognizes the beauty before him. But it is the city seen from a very particular point of view—a city which, under the conditions of that early hour, becomes a symbol of solitude and contemplation. It relates, in Wordsworth's imagination, to those wonderful *lonely places* which had for so long figured conspicuously among the fountainheads of his poetic power. It is the *absence* of humanity that makes it beautiful, and that *absence* is realized as a positive presence in the poem.

"Ships, towers, domes, theatres, and temples," are all associated with scenes of crowded life and bustling activity. But now, silent and deserted, they become symbols of stillness no less eloquently than the lonely mountain landscapes he loves to describe. "Open unto the fields and to the sky," they are assimilated into nature itself, and the sonnet's imagery insists on this. The stillness is emphasized by the remarkable vividness with which Wordsworth creates the crystalline purity of light and air that bathes the city. They almost become things that we can see and touch, for the city wears them "like a garment." Smoke might, in a sense, be described as visible air. By describing *this* air as "smokeless," Wordsworth not only sets it apart, in a pure and holy hour, from the industrial day that is about to begin, but has not yet begun: but in a curious way some of the materiality we connect with smoke fuses in our minds with the purity of the air and light so that they seem to have an almost ponderable quality, and this impression is strengthened by conjoining the adjective "glittering," which we instinctively associate with diamonds or other jewels, with the adjective "smokeless."

Having virtually made light and air into tangible elements, Wordsworth provides them with a substantial function to perform. They "steep" the city in "splendour." "Steep" means to soak in liquid for the purpose of altering qualities, softening, or cleansing. So the light and air are here changing the city into something quite different from what it habitually is, and this process is described in almost chemical terms. This pure and glittering atmosphere performs a symbolic function very similar to that of the moonlight, representing the imagination, which Wordsworth described in Book XIV of *The Prelude*, where he recounts his night ascent of Mount Snowdon.

Despite the silence and emptiness of the city, we are not given a static picture. Wordsworth communicates a profound impression of life—motionless and suspended, it is true—but the more intense and concentrated for that:

> *Dear God! the very houses seem asleep;*
> *And all that mighty heart is lying still!*

This is not the stillness of death, but of intenser life: a moment of intuitive vision such as he had described a few years before in "Tintern Abbey":

> *. . . that serene and blessed mood*
> *In which the affections gently lead us on,—*
> *Until, the breath of this corporeal frame*
> *Almost suspended, we are laid asleep*
> *In body, and become a living soul:*
> *While with an eye made quiet by the power*
> *Of harmony, and the deep power of joy,*
> *We see into the life of things.*

The sense of hidden, but quietly pulsing, life that is contained in the line

> *And all that mighty heart is lying still*

92

has been prepared for two lines earlier by the description of the Thames,

> *The river glideth at its own sweet will.*

It is only in this contemplative silence, this light and air of quiet joy, that man is aware of the flowing river, and the rhythm of nature and life that it embodies. With the activities of the day, the river's commercial traffic and the cries of the boatmen, it will be forgotten again. The sonnet, in short, is saying something like Eliot said in *The Dry Salvages:*

> . . . *the river*
> *Is a strong brown god—sullen, untamed and intractable,*
> *Patient to some degree, at first recognized as a frontier;*
> *Useful, untrustworthy, as a conveyor of commerce;*
> *Then only a problem confronting the builder of bridges.*
> *The problem once solved, the brown god is almost*
> *   forgotten*
> *By the dwellers in cities—ever, however, implacable,*
> *Keeping his seasons and rages, destroyer, reminder*
> *Of what men choose to forget.*

I shall come back to the "transfiguring" power of Wordsworth's vision as we encounter it in this sonnet later: but here one may say that this power, which is the essence of Wordsworth's Romanticism, has no counterpart in Byron's poetry. Byron has a good many successful and vivid descriptions of landscape and seascape, but they tend to be built around conventional conceptions of the picturesque, like a Salvator Rosa, or in the case of *Childe Harold*, Canto IV, perhaps a set of Piranesis. Such descriptions usually end as so many set pieces more or less detachable from context. But by the time Byron has fully developed his late satiric style, in which his greatness lives, we recognize in his descriptions a new infusion of power. In a sense, such passages as I am thinking of are scarcely descriptions at all, and yet they evoke the visible scene with memorable immediacy, and they become hieroglyphs for spelling out an attitude, a vision, as unlike Wordsworth's as possible, yet as deeply felt, as comprehensive in scope, and as pointed in intention. We begin by noting two things about this "new vision" of Byron's. It is the antithesis of the Wordsworthian Romantic vision, and it is not exactly new. In fact it contains some very traditional elements.

In *Don Juan*, near the end of Canto X and the beginning of Canto XI, young Juan, sent on a mission to England by the Empress Catherine, arrives on the outskirts of London, which he surveys from Shooter's Hill. Byron gives us the London scene at sunset, whereas Wordsworth gave it to us in the early morning; but *physically* it is virtually the same scene that both describe. The following stanzas from Cantos X and XI are not consecutive:

A mighty mass of brick, and smoke, and shipping,
   Dirty and dusky, but as wide as eye
Could reach, with here and there a sail just skipping
   In sight, then lost amidst the forestry
Of masts; a wilderness of steeples peeping
   On tiptoe through their sea-coal canopy;
A huge dim cupola, like a foolscap crown
On a fool's head—and there is London Town.

Don Juan had got out on Shooter's Hill;
   Sunset the time, the place the same declivity
Which looks along that vale of good and ill
   Where London streets ferment in full activity;
While everything around was calm and still,
   Except the creak of wheels, which on their pivots he
Heard,—and that bee-like, bubbling, busy hum
Of cities, that boil over with their scum:—

I say, Don Juan, wrapt in contemplation,
   Walk'd on behind his carriage, o'er the summit,

And lost in wonder of so great a nation,
  Gave way to't, since he could not overcome it.
"And here," he cried, "is Freedom's chosen station;
  Here peals the people's voice, nor can entomb it
Racks, prisons, inquisitions; resurrection
Awaits it, each new meeting or election.

"Here are chaste wives, pure lives; here people pay
  But what they please; and if that things be dear,
'Tis only that they love to throw away
  Their cash, to show how much they have a year.
Here laws are all inviolate; none lay
  Traps for the traveller; every highway's clear;
Here"—he was interrupted by a knife,
With—"Damn your eyes! your money or your life!"

Although they are talking about the same physical scene, Wordsworth's sonnet and Byron's stanzas clearly move in diametrically opposed directions. Wordsworth's transcendent vision in effect apotheosizes London. His London is before us vividly enough, but as a redeemed city, an impressionistically sketched capital, built, not of stones and bricks and mortar, but of glittering light and air that is permeable to the grace of the imagination and the creative life of the spirit. This sonnet is one of the supreme Romantic demonstrations of Coleridge's belief that

  we receive but what we give,
And in our life alone does Nature live.

Wordsworth's London is a solitary city in which the social order does not figure because he has left it behind. He is already at home in the heaven of his imagination, and he has carried London with him in his ascent. It becomes the symbol of man's purified heart. Being such, it cannot also exist as the focus of a society organized around commerce and greed.

Blake's short lyric "London" is another Romantic poem that begs comparison with the two we are considering. When

they were a very old couple, Mrs. Blake replied to the enquiry
of a young admirer of her husband's that she rarely saw him
now, Mr. Blake was so much in Paradise. Blake entered his
heaven early in life, but unlike Wordsworth he had no desire
to carry either London or any other of the earth's productions
along with him. Even more than Wordsworth Blake possessed the "transfiguring" vision, but he had a social consciousness that made the process more arduous for him, and
he did not believe that William Pitt's London could turn into
the New Jerusalem so easily:

In every cry of every Man,
In every Infant's cry of fear,
In every voice, in every ban,
The mind-forg'd manacles I hear.

How the Chimney-sweeper's cry
Every black'ning Church appalls;
And the hapless Soldier's sigh
Runs in blood down Palace walls.

But most thro' midnight streets I hear
How the youthful Harlot's curse
Blasts the new born Infant's tear,
And blights with plagues the Marriage hearse.

Among other things, *Lyrical Ballads* is a volume of social
protest, and we know that Wordsworth spent a great deal of
his time pressing for decent social legislation for the benefit
of the poor. But perhaps because he grew up in the Lake
Country and not in a shabby district of London, social evils
did not weigh his spirits down in the way they did Blake's.
For Wordsworth it was easier after all: he found little difficulty in utilizing the Romantic imagination as an antipoverty
program. Nevertheless, Blake's "London" *is* a Romantic
poem. Its protest is revolutionary in character, and if it seems
to approach something like despair, the grim sociological

survey that it makes (and which carries overtones of the eighteenth century) is a preliminary action towards effecting man's redemption through the release of imaginative energy. Blake believed that error had to be defined before it could be expelled, and his "London" is an exercise in definition for the sake of arriving at goals that are specifically revolutionary and Romantic in nature.

On the other hand, the stanzas we have looked at from *Don Juan* are eighteenth-century in character; they are not Romantic. I am referring primarily not to their stylistic development, but to their underlying attitudes. As F. R. Leavis has conclusively shown, Byron faltered whenever he tried to write in the Augustan mode, as he had done in *English Bards and Scotch Reviewers*.

It is strange that in lining up Byron's "colloquial" antecedents in "Byron and the Colloquial Tradition in English Poetry," Ronald Bottrall failed to mention Swift, a poet whose command of colloquial speech and rhythms was extraordinary, and frequently nearer to the earlier seventeenth century than to the Augustan Age, with which his life more or less coincided. Byron, we know, admired Swift's poetry, and he appears to have returned to it rather often. On his last voyage to Greece aboard the *Hercules*, Swift was his principal reading matter. One of his fellow travelers later recalled: "On the passage to Cephalonia, Byron chiefly read the writings of Dean Swift, taking occasional notes, with the view possibly of gleaning from that humourous writer something towards a future canto of *Don Juan*." In the matter of elaborate, startling, multiple-syllabled rhymes, Swift had anticipated Byron in the great satires, and Byron was well aware of this. Trelawney records Byron as having said to him: "If you are curious in these matters, look into Swift. I will send you a volume; he beats us all hollow, his rhymes are wonderful."

Without pausing at this point to discuss common elements shared by Swift's and Byron's respective colloquial styles, I should like to place beside the stanzas from *Don Juan* quoted above, and also beside Wordsworth's sonnet, a poem by Swift that is widely familiar, "A Description of the Morning," written in 1709:

> *Now hardly here and there a Hackney-Coach*
> *Appearing, shew'd the ruddy Morn's Approach.*
> *Now Betty from her Master's Bed had flown,*
> *And softly stole to discompose her own.*
> *The Slip-shod 'Prentice from his Master's Door*
> *Had par'd the Dirt, and sprinkled round the Floor.*
> *Now Moll had whirl'd her Mop with dext'rous Airs,*
> *Prepar'd to scrub the Entry and the Stairs.*
> *The Youth with broomy Stumps began to trace*
> *The Kennel-Edge, where Wheels had worn the Place.*
> *The Small-Coal Man was heard with Cadence deep;*
> *Till drown'd in shriller Notes of Chimney-sweep.*
> *Duns at his Lordship's Gate began to meet;*
> *And Brick-dust Moll had scream'd thro' half a Street.*
> *The Turnkey now his Flock returning sees,*
> *Duly let out a-Nights to steal for Fees.*
> *The watchful Bailiffs take their silent Stands;*
> *And School-boys lag with Satchels in their Hands.*

In a companion poem written a year later, "A Description of a City Shower," Swift gets his effects by describing in a parody of the heroic manner the squalid details of the city streets during a rainfall. This is a better poem than "A Description of the Morning"; at least, Swift thought so. But it is more intent on deflating the pretensions of neoclassical poetry than it is concerned to give us a picture of Queen Anne's London in a rain. "A Description of the Morning," however, is presented, more simply, in terms of Hogarthian realism. Nothing could be further removed from Words-worth's London morning than Swift's. There is no transfigur-ing vision here but an eye that is intent on seeing what is existentially in front of it. But that is putting it too simply. The poem appears to be totally uncontrived, but it cleverly presents us with Swift's prejudice that man is a very mean creature.

Wordsworth, looking at the London houses from his coach, would write later:

> *Dear God! the very houses seem asleep;*
> *And all that mighty heart is lying still.*

Swift, looking inside the same houses, had seen something else:

> *Now* Betty *from her Master's Bed had flown,*
> *And softly stole to discompose her own.*

One is surprised that Swift is able to sustain the atmosphere of morning throughout this little poem so well, for his morning ends up by looking rather like other men's night:

> *The Turnkey now his Flock returning sees,*
> *Duly let out a-Nights to steal for Fees.*
> *The watchful Bailiffs take their silent Stands;*
> *And School-boys lag with Satchels in their Hands.*

In the full context of the poem these are no Shakespearean schoolboys with "shining morning face," but rancorous little malcontents waiting under the eyes of the bailiffs to perpetuate the tainted world to which they are the heirs. It is this felt sense of man's essential meanness, of his niggling corruption, that fuses the accumulated details into an emotional unity of a kind Gay does not succeed in giving us when he deals with a similar subject matter in his *Trivia*.

Unless we believe that the mere naming of a criminal or an improper action carries a built-in moral judgment with it, it is futile to read this poem in the hope of discovering any values or norms, even suggested or implicit, by which to "place" or condemn the world that is shown us. The presence of some positive judgment within the poem would be like a door through which one could escape into the air. But the reader can find none, and the poem closes in on him so that he may feel trapped in the festering atmosphere of these unspacious streets. It is this feeling of enclosure and uneasiness which the poem engenders that constitutes, in the end, its moral comment on the world it presents for our contemplation. Wordsworth lifts *his* London to heaven, while Blake walks the streets of *his* like an angel to pass a judgment on it drawn out of eternity. But Swift encloses himself inside the city walls and locks the gates. Here we have one of the striking differences between the closed world of the earlier eighteenth century and the open universe of Romanticism. I do not mean that eighteenth-century poetry invariably, or even frequently, instills this haunting sense of entrapment in the reader, as "A Description of the Morning" does. By imparting a feeling of claustrophobia it could be plausibly argued, indeed, that Swift's poem is subversively working in the interests of Romantic dilation. But the eighteenth century's conception of human nature—how it functions, what its limitations and possibilities are—is fixed.

I have already implied that Swift was not the representative poet of his age. As an Anglo-Irishman that was denied him. There is an invigorating lack of ultimate commitment to the loyalties and patterns of the period that was essential for the development of his peculiar brand of irony (Sir Herbert Read would have called it sardonic humor). And even more than by his curiously poised distance from the English scene, his verse was saved from that anonymity the eighteenth century often mistook for universality by the presence of a personality that no decorum or canons of taste could do much towards confining. All this makes us think ahead to Byron. Nevertheless, Swift had no doubts about man, his nature, and his role. He might be capable of decent behavior, but by overwhelming odds if you studied him closely enough you would surely find a rogue at last.

In his attractive poem "Helter Skelter," Swift gives us a vivid picture of young attorneys riding circuit. The visual impression of the poem is as significantly weighted as that of any of Daumier's lawyers. But it is the unexpected musical pattern of the poem that makes the deepest impression, and through which we feel the impact of Swift's intention. The incantatory music, which becomes insistent as the poem progresses, induces a sense of unreality that makes its own ironic comment on the law. The young attorneys, blurred by the sound to a shadowy, dreamy movement, appear like monstrous children who corrupt the roles from adult life that they parody in play:

> *And, if they begin a fray,*
> *Draw their swords and—run away:*
> *All to murder equity,*
> *And to take a double fee;*
> *Till the people all are quiet,*
> *And forget to brawl and riot,*
> *Low in pocket, cow'd in courage,*
> *Safely glad to sup their porridge,*
> *And Vacation's over—then*
> *Hey, for London town again.*

This is splendid, but the corrective intention of satire is a little blunted by our sense that these creatures were predestined by the constitution of their natures and the history of man for the grim farce they play, and that they can never escape their roles, nor their sons after them. Closure is complete.

Where, in relation to these two perspectives, does Byron's poetry take its place? Returning to the stanzas given earlier from *Don Juan*, we find that, for all the differences, Byron's poetry relates to Swift's world more closely than to that of the

Romantics. There is, of course, the topographical realism of Byron's description, which strikes an eighteenth-century note. But it is the *moral* realism that is important here. One of the most amiable young men in English literature, Juan is also one of the most accurate gauges of representative human nature. He combines folly and heroism, youthful sensualism and idealistic courage, total honesty and a capacity for self-deception, in a completely convincing way, and proves to us how winning and how unsubtle man ordinarily is. As he approaches London, caught up by Britain's self-publicized tradition of liberal manners and representative rule, Juan permits his imagination an idealistic orgy. For a brief interval Juan's London, in its own awkward fashion, threatens to become a celestial city. But Juan is mercifully recalled to reality by a knife in his ribs as the *real* London reasserts itself in the person of Tom the highwayman. The recall *is* merciful, because Byron is as sure of human nature as Swift was, and he knows Juan would be ridiculous strolling on golden pavements. Among the English Romantic poets Byron is unique in having brought his hero to town, and giving him control of the situation. One of the few young men given us by the other English Romantics who ever gets to London is Luke the shepherd's son in Wordsworth's "Michael," and we are positively startled by the precipitancy with which he goes to the dogs.

If Byron's attitudes here bear some resemblance to Swift's, there is also a difference which weighs heavily in Byron's favor. There is none of that sense of close confinement in Byron's stanzas that I noted in Swift's poem. If Byron differs from the other Romantics in having a comparatively closed vision of man, it is also fundamentally a generous one. His lack of illusion concerning man's possibilities remains remarkably tolerant and free of cynicism in contrast to Swift's morbid distaste for physical humanity. But no less than Swift's, Byron's London is a real city beyond any possibility of transfiguration. Because the physical world continuously impinges on Byron's consciousness, he writes a poetry of confrontation rather than of transcendence, and this sets him apart from his contemporaries. Alone among the English Romantics, only Byron could have been a great novelist.

Masks & Mirrors

II

DEATH AND
THE JAMES FAMILY

T HE DIARY OF ALICE JAMES makes exacting
demands of those readers who are not content with
sickroom gossip or a few random anecdotes about William
and Henry, but who wish to arrive at a responsible evaluation
of the diarist, and the intellectual or spiritual style with which
she occupied her niche in the James family. The task is not
easy because for most readers Alice James will not, on first
acquaintance, seem an appealing personality. There is often
an aggressive shrillness in her voice which, coupled with an
overdeveloped frankness, is sometimes accompanied by a
slightly sour fragrance. But even on the level of the jeering
invalid, she can often rise to the amusing or the wittily just.

Reading her diary after her death, Henry James wrote to
William that "she was really an Irishwoman." He was not,
one would guess, referring to her ardent devotion to Irish
Home Rule, which is a frequent subject in her pages, but to
certain mannerisms of speech and tone one suspects most
readers today must find slightly distressing, and which might
be described as a blend of self-irony and unpalatable whimsy.

Perhaps it is this "Irishness" as much as the uneventfulness of an invalid's life that persuades her to fill space with "funny" stories. It is sometimes difficult to be amused:

> A young man took his young woman to a restaurant and asked her what she would have to drink with her dinner. "I guess I'll have a bottle of champagne." "Guess again!" quoth he.

> A woman was brought to the London hospital the other day with a very bad bite on her arm. The doctor asked her whether she had been bitten by a dog. "No, sir, 'twas another lydy did it."

Nor is this quality of "Irishness" (if that is what it is) enhanced by her humorous habit of frequently substituting the pronoun *me* for the possessive *my*.

Alice James possessed an extraordinary moral courage, but one becomes aware of this slowly, and only as one nears the end of her diary, because it is often obscured by an intrusive stoicism and denigration of pain more nearly related to vanity and self-aggrandizement than anything else. The pulling of a tooth provides an occasion for this quality to be put on view:

> The dentist seized my face in his two hands and ex-claimed, "Bravo, Miss James!" and Katherine and Nurse shaking of knee and pale of cheek went on about my "heroism" whilst I, serenely wadded in that sensa-tional paralysis which attends all the simple rudimentary sensations and experiences common to man, whether tearing of the flesh or of the affections, laughed and laughed at 'em.

This pose of the doughty little woman who comes through without a fuss where strong men break causes one to remem-ber with gratitude and pleasure those richly orchestrated epical moans of self-pity Coleridge was in the habit of posting to his friends whenever he was suffering from atonic gout, looseness of the bowels, or the pains of drug withdrawal. It is unpleasant in Alice James because it is perfectly self-conscious, and it falsifies the true courage that she really possessed. Furthermore, she seems not to have permitted her "stoicism" to get in the way of that petulance to which, as a chronic invalid, she may have felt herself entitled:

> I am in a Porcupine fit with little Nurse—she is no more bewildered than I am and we both have simply to undergo it as one of the endless forms of moral dyspepsia. There is one comfort—she doesn't suffer 100th of what I do.

Alice James is decidedly not an ingratiating woman to meet for the first time. If the character sketched in above represented the totality of her personality, one would find extenuating circumstances for her in her long illness and the restricted society to which it necessarily limited her, and forget her diary. But as one continues to read, one becomes aware of a personality or mind behind the invalid's capricious entries that only occasionally flashed through, but with a light so serene and fine that it sustains one across the prickly pages until the signal lights again. During the last months of her illness, when she knew she was dying of cancer, the signaling lights become almost a steady beam, until, on March 4, 1892, too weak to write, she laboriously dictated this final entry to her friend Katherine Loring:

> I am being ground slowly on the grim grindstone of physical pain, and on two nights I had almost asked for K's lethal dose, but one steps hesitantly along such unaccustomed ways and endures from second to second; and I feel sure that it can't be possible but what the bewildered little hammer that keeps me going will very

shortly see the decency of ending his distracted career; however this may be, physical pain however great ends in itself and falls away like dry husks from the mind, whilst moral discords and nervous horrors sear the soul. These last, Katherine has completely under the control of her rhythmic hand, so I go no longer in dread. Oh the wonderful moment when I felt myself floated for the first time into the deep sea of divine *cessation*, and saw all the dear old mysteries and miracles vanish into vapour. The first experience doesn't repeat itself, fortunately, for it might become a seduction.

Whatever earlier entries may have suggested of petulant stoicism or the vanity of invalidism has been replaced by a courage and serenity that is wholly authentic and perfectly faultless. One is reminded, reading this last entry, of the closing passage of Tolstoy's story *The Death of Ivan Ilyich*. Both Alice James and Ivan Ilyich, as they sink towards death, experience something similar. This consists of a triumph over pain which diminishes or qualifies the personality of the sufferer; there is a stripping away from the mind and heart of the irrelevancies and distorted images of worldly life, of neurotic fears, and false values; and this brings a sense of release and purification. For each there is a sense of the imminent discovery of something unknown, perhaps even unknowable, but immensely desirable.

There is no point whatever in our asking what the nature of this discovery, if it is made at all, may be. The importance here is that the sense of death, being fully accepted and assimilated to the consciousness, virtually constitutes, for a mind like Alice James's, a new and transcendent *form* in which to apprehend earthly existence and its inevitable termination. The last entry in the diary is greatly enriched and deepened in meaning if we read it in conjunction with an earlier entry, dated August 18, 1890—for it must not be supposed that the tone and attitude of the last entry developed overnight. I make no claim to philosophic competence, but it hardly requires special knowledge to find in the following passage a remarkable anticipation of the central belief of Heidegger (who was then one year old) that only in one's profound and searching acceptance of the unavoidable "possibility" of one's own death, which annihilates all other possibilities, can one achieve an authentic personal life and freedom. For Heidegger, this consistent orientation towards death has a transfiguring effect on one's vision and knowledge, and consequent control, of existence. As one reads through Alice James's diary, it appears that some such transfiguration, springing from her complete, almost loving, acceptance of her death, is in progress:

> There has come such a change in me. A congenital faith flows thro' me like a limpid stream, making the arid places green, a spontaneous irrigator of which the snags of doubt have never interrupted nor made turbid the easily flowing current. A faith which is my moral and mental respiration which needs no revelation but experience and whose only ritual is daily conduct. Thro' my childhood and youth and until within the last few years, the thought of the end as an entrance into spiritual existence, where aspirations are a fulfillment, was a perpetual and necessary inspiration, but now, although intellectually non-existence is more ungraspable and inconceivable than ever, all longing for fulfillment, all passion to achieve, has died down within me, and whether the great Mystery resolves itself into eternal Death or glorious Life, I contemplate either with equal serenity. It is that the long ceaseless strain and tension have worn out all aspiration save the one for Rest! And also that the shaping period is past and one is fitted to every limitation through the long custom of surrender.

In the light of this perfect acceptance of death, **Alice James's** life appears gradually to have assumed a proportion, a dignity, and a beauty it would not otherwise have had. Through the later pages of her diary we often find her using her suffering and her dissolution as a frame within which to experience and express those feelings and values that she seems to have felt more intensely, and in a new way, under the radiance of her sense of death. In a late entry, she transforms the malignant cancer in her breast into an almost shocking, yet strangely beautiful, metaphor for her friendship with Katherine Loring:

> As the ugliest things go to the making of the fairest, it is not wonderful that this unwholy granite substance in my breast should be the soil propitious for the perfect flowering of Katherine's unexampled genius for friendship and devotion. The story of her watchfulness, patience and untiring resource cannot be told by my feeble pen, but all the pain and discomfort seem a slender price to pay for all the happiness and peace with which she fills my days.

If, in all this, one catches existentialist overtones, it is still to her own remarkable family that one must relate her. The James family was much possessed by death, but with them it carried no mortuary sentiment or gloom. The family's attitude doubtless had its origin in the theology of the father, Henry James, Senior. As with William Blake, the theology of the elder James, developed through more than a dozen published volumes, represents an original and independent improvisation on certain central tenets of Swedenborg. As everyone knows, Blake saw the soul of his younger brother rise from his deathbed clapping his hands for the joy of his release. If something like this never happened to the elder James, one is almost tempted to believe it is only because his children outlived him. For both Blake and James,

Senior, the individual identity was not separable from God. In his expository introduction to *The Literary Remains of the Late Henry James*, William James gives as succinct a description as possible of his father's concept of the individual self:

> The theology that went with all this was the passionate conviction that the *real* creature of God—human *nature* at large, *minus* the preposterous claims of the several selves—must be wholly good. For is it not the work of the good God, or rather the very substance of the good God, there *being* nought beside?

Unfortunately, *in this world* man constructs for himself a false selfhood, which he nourishes and sustains by his lust for self-righteousness, power, social prestige, possessions, and so on, and he hides in this false selfhood from the Divinity in himself, and from that freedom and spontaneity that is the very presence and life of God in his soul. To acknowledge this Divine life in himself would be to deny his absolute separateness, which is the illusion cherished by his false selfhood. As William James pointed out, although his father was by no means a complete Monist, the system he developed was almost Monistic because "it makes of God the one and only *active* principle," while the individual self "has no positive existence, being really *naught*, a provisional phantom-soul breathed by God's love into mere logical negation." It is obvious that in such a system which undervalues individuality as that term is commonly understood, the fact of death would receive a radically new and different emotional evaluation. The termination of a merely "provisional phantom-soul" is something quite different from the death of a substantive selfhood.

Apparently none of the children accepted the theological faith of their father, but they all appear to have been immersed in an attitude towards death that was contingent on it.

In January, 1882, Mrs. James died, and Bob, the youngest son, has left a vivid picture in one of his letters of the James household in bereavement:

> We have all been educated by Father to feel that death was the only reality and that life was simply an experimental thing and for this reason it may be that it is why we have taken Mother's going as such an orderly transition. None of us would recall her for we feel that we are more near to her now than ever before, simply because she is already at the goal for which we all cheerfully bend our steps. . . . The last two weeks of my life have been the happiest I have known. . . .

Before that year was over, the elder James also died. William was in London then, and during his father's last illness he wrote him his final letter, which, tender and compassionate, yet strikes that note that always slightly astonishes the ear when one of the Jameses speaks of death:

> Darling old Father . . . We have been so long accustomed to the hypothesis of your being taken away from us, especially during the past ten months, that the thought that this may be your last illness conveys no very sudden shock. You are old enough, you've given your message to the world in many ways and will not be forgotten; you are left alone, and on the other side, let us hope and pray, dear, dear old Mother is waiting for you to join her. If you go it will not be an inharmonious thing. . . .

His father was dead by the time William's letter arrived, and Henry wrote to his brother:

> I went out yesterday (Sunday) morning to the Cambridge cemetery. . . . I stood beside his grave for a long time and read him your letter of farewell—which I

am sure he heard somewhere out of the depths of the still bright winter air. He lies extraordinarily close to Mother, and as I stood there and looked at this last expression of so many years of mortal union, it was difficult not to believe that they were not united again in some consciousness of my belief. . . .

The concluding line of Henry James's letter is an early statement of a theme he was to strike again more insistently in his strange story "The Altar of the Dead." This story is often condemned because it appears to exploit religious ritual without the sanctions of religious faith. It is in fact very easy to be puzzled about this story of a man who (without a religion at all, one gathers) endows an altar in a Catholic church so that he may keep perpetual candles burning there to commemorate each of his friends who dies. Over the years, until his own death, the shrine with its radiant candles becomes the scene of his meditation and the source of spiritual peace to him.

This is indeed a precarious theme, carrying as it does a note of religious estheticism; but in view of the attitude towards death in the James family, it is far less dangerous artistically than one might suppose. "My being," wrote the elder James, ". . . lies, in fact, *in honestly identifying myself with others*." Because God was incarnated in all men who had broken down their false selfhoods, the Divine-Natural Humanity in which he believed was, from one point of view, communal in nature. To say that in "The Altar of the Dead" James was concerned with celebrating a miracle of consciousness, a vital community with the dead in the thought of the living, is perfectly true, but it was a habit of thought, a point of view, that had been engendered in him in his youth in the house of his father, and it did not require a belief in his father's theology for him to persist in it. The best descriptive definition of James's meaning in "The Altar of

115

the Dead" I have ever come across is, rather oddly, in an expository essay not on Henry James but Sartre. The commentator is paraphrasing an argument from *L'Etre et le néant*:

> . . . dying *has no future* open to phenomenological inspection; not having a future, it is denied the possibility of having that significance that always accrues to human action. Indirectly, however, there is a future to *my* death, a future that is not for me but for *others*. On the occasion of my death, my entire life is past. But the past is not a nonbeing: it *is*, on the contrary, in the mode of the in-itself. In and by itself the in-itself is without meaning, but the in-itself that is my past may have meaning bestowed upon it by other human beings who are therefore cast in the role of the guardians of my life.

If this is the real meaning of "The Altar of the Dead," as I think it is, it is a meaning Henry James shared with Alice James, and it seems quite possible to me that the suggestion for his story may have come from her diary. At the end of May, 1894, James received a copy of his sister's diary from William James, which he then read for the first time. When he speaks in *The Notebooks* of "The Altar of the Dead" in the early autumn of that same year, his thoughts may well have started from the following entry, dated August 13, 1890:

> As they drop, how we bury ourselves, bit by bit, along the dusty highway to the end! The especial facets of our being which turned towards each one will nevermore be played upon by the rays which he gave forth. How darksome then the last stages if we have not made our own his individual and inextinguishable radiance, to warm the memory and illuminate the mind.

However that may be, in Alice James's diary the particular consciousness of death which she inherited from her father, and which was fostered in the bosom of the James family, divested in her of theological sanctions, renewed itself in a form of radical acceptance that impresses one as peculiarly contemporary. As for Ivan Ilyich, so for Alice James, the process of dying was a process of concentration, of divesting oneself of the inessential—as her father might have said, of escaping from the artificial selfhood. In one of the last entries in her diary she writes:

One sloughs off the activities one by one, and never knows that they're gone, until one suddenly finds that the months have slipped away and the sofa will never more be laid upon, the morning paper read, or the loss of the new book regretted; one revolves with equal content within the narrowing circle until the vanishing point is reached, I suppose.

Vanity, however, maintains its undisputed sway, and I take satisfaction in feeling as much myself as ever, perhaps simply a more concentrated essence in this curtailment.

The language and imagery in which she speaks of death often has a quality that makes one think of Emily Dickinson, whose 1890 volume of poems she read and admired. She speaks of "Magnificent Death," and hearing of the death of one of Henry's friends, she frames a conceit that reminds one of the poet:

I ne'er saw the youth, but I wonder if we shan't soon meet in that "twilight land," swooping past each other like Vedder's ghosts. Will he pause and ask: "What is your name?" And shall I say, "I do not know, I only died last night" . . . ?

117

In December, 1915, as Henry James collapsed from his first stroke that preceded his death in the following February, he heard a voice in his room saying: "So here it is at last, the distinguished thing!" The final effect of the diary on one's imagination is to make one believe it must have been the ghost of Alice, come back to reassure and congratulate her favorite brother on the threshold of his absolute moment.

HENRY JAMES'S
ENGLISH HOURS

In 1905 Henry James collected and published under the title *English Hours* a group of travel sketches which had received periodical publication in American magazines between the years 1872 and 1890. Many of these pieces had already been collected in 1883, in *Portraits of Places*, a volume which also contained travel essays on France, Italy, Saratoga, Newport, Quebec, and Niagara. Now, with the prospect of a set of illustrations by the distinguished expatriate American artist Joseph Pennell to accompany the text, James reissued the English essays from the earlier collection under the new title, to which he added a number of additional sketches also written during his first years in England. Therefore, despite its date of publication, *English Hours* represents the style of the younger James.

Two years after the appearance of *English Hours* James published what must certainly be his most richly textured and brilliant book of nonfiction. *The American Scene* exemplifies the "late style" at its best. In 1904 James returned to America after an absence of twenty years. It seemed to James that

America had changed in the interval almost beyond recognition. The London that had confronted the young Henry James of twenty-three when, in 1869, he made his first independent incursion into what he was pleased to call "the capital of the human race," hardly presented a greater surface of novelty or a more formidable challenge to penetration and discovery than the New York of skyscrapers and high finance to which he returned at the age of sixty-one. The contrast between the style of *English Hours* and that of *The American Scene* makes an illuminating comment on the artistic growth that had occurred between the younger and the elder James; but what we are faced with is unmistakably a phenomenon of organic development, not one of disruption or arbitrary change. The underlying continuities that, like a complex circulatory system, impart *one life* to all of James's writings are at times more clearly perceived in his nonfiction than in his stories and novels.

In any insistent meaning of the phrase, James was not a political being; yet Hartley Grattan, in his splendid study *The Three Jameses*, was correct when he said that Henry James was "a conservative son of a radical father, a man who positively idealized ancient institutions and customs hardened by usage into principles of conduct." The danger in such a formulation is that it may discourage one from seeing how supremely flexible James's application of such principles of conduct to the moral situation in any given fiction can be. But on the whole, James's values begin with the traditional and the established, however quickly thereafter they may seek their independent insights and directions. An artist whose values are so deeply immersed in traditional considerations, so mellowed by "the tone of time," must incline of temperamental necessity towards a conservative, a *conserving*, political establishment. James has nowhere expressed this deep personal bias more straightforwardly than in *English Hours*, in his sketch on Chester:

. . . conservatism has all the charm and leaves dissent and democracy and other vulgar variations nothing but their bald logic. Conservatism has the cathedrals, the colleges, the castles, the gardens, the traditions, the associations, the fine names, the better manners, the poetry.

But throughout James's fictions there is, in addition to his poignantly personal love of England, a strain more darkly carnal. There is an admiration, more rarely, more guardedly, expressed, for Britain as a power structure—in short, for Victorian imperialism. There is of course very little of Kipling in James's attitude. It is not Empire itself, but the massive surfaces of marble and manners and mellowed opulence that Empire supports that James is powerfully attracted to, albeit, as he grew older, against his better judgment. Nevertheless, Prince Amerigo's feelings at the opening of *The Golden Bowl* remain essentially his own:

Brought up on the legend of the City to which the world paid tribute, he recognized in the present London much more than in contemporary Rome the real dimensions of such a case. If it was a question of an *Imperium*, he said to himself, and if one wished, as a Roman, to recover a little the sense of that, the place to do so was on London Bridge, or even, on a fine afternoon in May, at Hyde Park Corner.

In a man of James's rare intelligence such an admiration was necessarily qualified, and the ironic ambivalence of his later attitude is apparent in his fine rendering of Aunt Maud in *The Wings of the Dove*, that redoubtable "Britannia of the Market Place," who is virtually an embodiment of Victorian England at the height of her imperial power, "an eagle, with a gilded beak as well, and with wings for great flights." "She was vulgar with freshness, almost with beauty, since there was beauty, to a degree, in the play of so large and bold a temperament." If Maud Lowder does not personify, she none-theless richly incarnates, the Victorian power structure, and in the latitude for both affectionate rendering and satiric raillery that James permits himself in his treatment of her, we have a measure of how he subtly qualified his earlier admiration for British power.

One sees that earlier admiration at its most unqualified in certain passages of *English Hours*. There is, for example, the concluding paragraph of "London at Midsummer," a sketch which James originally published in 1877. Fearing that the influence of England as a world power may be on the wane, James, through the lips of a "sympathetic stranger," inquires if preventive measures may not be found. "This greatness of England . . . was formerly much exemplified in her 'taking' something. Can't she 'take' something now?" And James sympathizes with a suggestion in the *Spectator* that Britain should occupy Egypt—a course of action that was, in fact, followed several years later.

In the following passage, also from "London in Midsum-mer," the visual elements of the Thames vista that James describes as he travels by boat from Westminster Bridge to Greenwich become little more than a vehicle for an emotion, a moral *feeling*, about British imperialism. Despite its pretense of being only a travel note, the description exists to communi-cate this feeling, this moral persuasion, to the reader:

The little puffing steamer is dingy and gritty—it belches a sable cloud that keeps you company as you go. In this carboniferous shower your companions, who belong chiefly, indeed, to the classes bereft of lustre, assume an harmonious grayness; and the whole picture, glazed over with the glutinous London mist, becomes a mas-terly composition. But it is very impressive in spite of its want of lightness and brightness, and though it is ugly it is anything but trivial. Like so many of the aspects of

English civilisation that are untouched by elegance or grace, it has the merit of expressing something very serious. Viewed in this intellectual light the polluted river, the sprawling barges, the dead-faced warehouses, the frowsy people, the atmospheric impurities become richly suggestive. It sounds rather absurd, but all this smudgy detail may remind you of nothing less than the wealth and power of the British Empire at large; so that a kind of metaphysical magnificence hovers over the scene, and supplies what may be literally wanting. I don't exactly understand the association, but I know that when I look off to the left at the East India Docks, or pass under the dark hugely piled bridges, where the railway trains and the human processions are for ever moving, I feel a kind of imaginative thrill. The tremendous piers of the bridges, in especial, seem the very pillars of the Empire aforesaid.

By comparison with James's later mastery, this descriptive prose is not yet quite adequate to its purposes; but the purposes of the younger James—as I have already suggested—anticipate those of the later. The notoriety of T. S. Eliot's statement about James, written two years after the novelist's death, has a little overshadowed its validity: "He had a mind so fine that no idea could violate it." James's prose deals in perceptions rather than in discursively presented ideas. To say this is to limit neither the range nor the depth of his fine intelligence. But it is to recognize that as a creative artist he preferred a presentation of his moral vision in a language that eschewed equally ideological exposition, special pleading, and the suasion of logic.

Behind the passage I have quoted there is the pressure of a very simple recognition: British imperial power, while no doubt a mixed bag of goods, is ultimately conducive to a state of mind—indeed to a condition of social culture—that is much to be desired. Thus paraphrased into its "idea," the passage may strike one as a little mean. But we are not invited to confront the naked idea as such. Even at so early a date, James's strategy is elaborate if not yet wholly successful. He causes the blemished qualities of the river front and the more grasping aspects of Empire to cancel each other out, so leaving us in a mood of mild acceptance. The squalid pictorial elements of the river are presented unsqueamishly with disarming candor and blunt relentlessness. But then the sordid details almost imperceptibly "compose" themselves into a scene that, with its narrow range of darks and grays, reminds one of a Whistler Nocturne. In disclaiming elegance or grace for the picture, James invests it with those very qualities, having, in the meantime, pinned down for our appreciation its unmistakably British, even Dickensian, character.

Unfortunately, at this point the passage falters. James undertakes too broad a leap from the picture so carefully lighted and drawn to the "metaphysical magnificence" of the British Empire. He betrays his uncertainty by such phrases as "It sounds rather absurd," or "I don't exactly understand the association." His failure exists in the fact that British imperial "metaphysical magnificence" obtrudes itself here as an "idea" rather than as a perception, and so the fusion between the subtly transfigured river front and Victoria's greatness never *really* takes place. Nevertheless, despite its final deficiencies, the strategy is brilliant in conception, and looks forward to James's late, most mature, style.

As an example of the later mastery of which *English Hours* is a charming but modest forecast, one may consider the following passage from *The American Scene* in which James confronts the new skyscrapers on the Battery which had been built during his absence of twenty years:

You see the pin-cushion in profile, so to speak, on passing between Jersey City and Twenty-Third Street, but you get it broadside on, this loose nosegay of architectural flowers, if you skirt the Battery, well out, and embrace the whole plantation. Then the "American beauty," the rose of interminable stem, becomes the token of the cluster at large—to that degree that, positively, this is all that is wanted for emphasis of your final impression. Such growths, you feel, have confessedly arisen but to be "picked," in time, with a shears; nipped short off, by waiting fate, as soon as "science," applied to gain, has put upon the table, from far up its sleeve, some more winning card. Crowned not only with no history, but with no credible possibility of time for history, and consecrated by no uses save the commercial at any cost, they are simply the most piercing notes in that concert of the expensively provisional into which your supreme sense of New York resolves itself. They never begin to speak to you, in the manner of the builded majesties of the world as we have heretofore known such—towers or temples or fortresses or palaces—with the authority of things of permanence or even of things of long duration. One story is good only till another is told, and sky-scrapers are the last word of economic ingenuity only till another word is written. This shall be possibly a word of still uglier meaning, but the vocabulary of thrift at any price shows boundless resources, and the consciousness of that truth, the consciousness of the finite, the menaced, the essentially *invented* state, twinkles ever, to my perception, in the thousand glassy eyes of these giants of the mere market.

This prose is far more rich, more complex, than what we have seen in *English Hours*. Yet, paradoxically, it is also more spare, less contrived. The skyscrapers—the new temples of finance—are, with fine irony, "American beauty" roses "of interminable stem," and James's condemnation of the perverted values that prevail in the transformed city comes through the horticultural imagery all the more devastatingly because couched in a language so natural and simple. "Such growths, you feel, have confessedly arisen but to be 'picked,' in time, with a shears; nipped off, by waiting fate, as soon as 'science,' applied to gain, has put upon the table, from far up its sleeve, some more winning card." A reader might well consider behind how many of the innocent words in that sentence a sinister implication is lurking to spring.

We saw, in considering the Thames passage from *English Hours*, that an imperfect fusion—or perhaps no fusion at all—occurred between James's rendering of the river front and the idea of British imperial power. The latter remained only an idea, and the connection between the two terms was no more than an arbitrary nexus. But in *this* passage meaning and metaphor are one as flesh and blood are one, and the prose is as functional as the structure of a living body. James has achieved a style in which meaning and metaphor exist in indissoluble unity. The whole passage vibrates with intelligence of a rare order; yet this "intelligence" is not recognized through its "ideas" as such, but by the perfection and easy authority with which it orders language towards the most subtle discoveries and delicate assessments of value. James's final achievement of style was a victory for which he had labored long; but he had set his goals from the beginning, and if we read *English Hours* with attentive care we can see the later style already implicit in these earlier sketches.

II

IN FEW OF James's works does one more often encounter references to the impoverished and excluded, and for this reason *English Hours* must have an added interest for the student of his writings. Social conscience and consciousness are by no means identical. The question of James's social conscience will probably remain a subject for discussion, but of the range of his social *consciousness* there can be little reasonable doubt. On the evidence of his stories and novels it would be unjust to assert that his consciousness, as it occasionally probed into the deprived and wretched corners of existence, was unattended by sympathy and human understanding. Yet it must be confessed that there is nearly always a note of detachment, of nonparticipation, that may leave the reader, regardless of how searching James's observations or analysis may have been, with a slight sensation of hollowness. To put the matter in the worst light possible, one is sometimes reminded of Hawthorne's description of Ethan Brand —that tragic hero who cultivated his intellect and powers (Hawthorne intends Brand as a type of the creative artist) at the expense of his human sympathy:

> He was no longer a brother-man, opening the chambers or the dungeons of our common nature by the key of holy sympathy, which gave him a right to share in all its secrets; he was now a cold observer, looking on mankind as the subject of his experiment, and, at length, converting man and woman to be his puppets, and pulling the wires that moved them to such degrees of crime as were demanded for his study.

Two episodes recorded in *English Hours* are particularly suggestive of James's manner of observing and treating experiences not ordinarily falling within the scope of his art. In his sketch "An English Easter," he describes having accidentally come upon the funeral of Mr. George Odger while walking through Piccadilly. "Mr. George Odger, it will perhaps be remembered, was an English Radical agitator of humble origin, who had distinguished himself by a perverse desired to get into Parliament. He exercised, I believe, the useful profession of shoemaker, and he knocked in vain at the door that opens but to the refined." Apparently the funeral was also in the nature of a workingman's demonstration, for James goes on to say:

> The crowd was enormous, but I managed to squeeze through it and get into a hansom cab that was drawn up beside the pavement, and here I looked on as from a box at the play. Though it was a funeral that was going on I will not call it a tragedy; but it was a very serious comedy.

In the scene that James presently describes, filled with "the London rabble, the metropolitan mob," we may well be in at the genesis of a train of thought that would issue in *Princess Casamassima* nearly ten years later. In that novel James treats the revolutionary movement among the working poor with unusual understanding. But here, as we watch him staring intently across the apron of his hansom at the drama unfolding in the street, the image of Brand rises almost irresistibly.

Whatever gains there may be, there is likely to be an attendant loss for the artist in such detachment, and what those losses can on occasion amount to is suggested by a second episode recorded in "An English New Year," first published in 1879. The incident occurred while James was a guest in "a populous manufacturing region, full of tall chimneys and of an air that is gray and gritty":

> A lady had made a present of a Christmas-tree to the children of a workhouse, and she invited me to go with her and assist at the distribution of the toys. There was a drive through the early dusk of a very cold Christmas eve, followed by the drawing up of a lamp-lit brougham in the snowy quadrangle of a grim-looking charitable institution. I had never been in an English workhouse

before, and this one transported me, with the air of memory, to the early pages of *Oliver Twist*. We passed through cold, bleak passages, to which an odour of suet-pudding, the aroma of Christmas cheer, failed to impart an air of hospitality; and then, after waiting a while in a little parlour appertaining to the superintendent . . . we were ushered into a large frigid refectory, chiefly illuminated by the twinkling tapers of the Christmas-tree. Here entered to us some hundred and fifty little children of charity, who had been making a copious dinner and who brought with them an atmosphere of hunger memorably satisfied—together with other traces of the occasion upon their pinafores and their small red faces. I have said that the place reminded me of *Oliver Twist*, and I glanced through this little herd for an infant figure that should look as if it were cut out for romantic adventures. But they were all very prosaic little mortals. They were made of very common clay indeed, and some of them were idiotic. They filed up and received their little offerings, and then they compressed themselves into a tight infantine bunch and, lifting up their small hoarse voices, directed a melancholy hymn toward their benefactress. The scene was a picture I shall not forget, with its curious mixture of poetry and sordid prose—the dying wintry light in the big bare, stale room; the beautiful Lady Bountiful standing in the twinkling glory of the Christmas-tree; the little multitude of staring and wondering, yet perfectly expressionless faces.

It would, I think, be difficult to find a more disappointing passage in all of James. The hundred and fifty charity children, except as literary echoes from Dickens, do not exist at all. And even as "echoes" they are oddly negative in effect because not one of them rises to James's cherished image of

Oliver. Few novelists have been more successful in creating children, and one bears in mind that he has still to write that deeply moving account of little Hyacinth Robinson's visit to his mother dying in prison—a scene in some of its components not so far removed from the workhouse visit described here. But the latter fails because James's remoteness and deliberately "literary" perspective are such, on this occasion, as to preclude a full recognition of the human reality before him—a recognition such as William Blake made in fullest measure when he wrote of the charity children in his two "Holy Thursday" poems.

This is not, however, to imply that, for the service of his art, James's power of detached observation was not a highly useful commodity. If, at certain levels of experience, it sometimes seemed to delimit his active sympathy, it gave him the faculty of rendering detail of surface with an acuity that can make his descriptions of the London poor memorably perceptive:

> They are ill-dressed as their betters are well-dressed, and their garments have that sooty surface which has nothing in common with the continental costume of labor and privation. It is the hard prose of misery—an ugly and hopeless imitation of respectable attire. This is especially noticeable in the battered and bedraggled bonnets of the women, which look as if their husbands had stamped on them, in hob-nailed boots, as a hint of what may be in store for their wearers.

III

OSTENSIBLY *English Hours* is a book of travel sketches, and as an account of English scenes and manners the reader may well ask how informative, how illuminating, it really is. In this regard it is instructive to compare it with a book on England by Hippolyte Taine. In 1872, the year from which the earliest sketches reprinted in *English Hours* date, Taine published his *Notes sur l'Angleterre*, which James promptly reviewed for *The Nation* with appreciation and generosity. In the scenes they treat, the places they go, the activities that attract their attention, the American and the Frenchman run startlingly parallel courses, and I suspect that a reader innocent of the identity of the two authors would guess Taine to be the novelist. But such a reader would be thinking of novels like Zola's, not like James's. Writing of his own theories of critical and historical interpretation, Taine had said: "It is not my intention to comment or moralize . . . only to investigate, to *expose*, to lay all before you." In *Notes sur l'Angleterre* the reader has the sensation of having literally *everything* in England of that day laid before him. Landscape, architecture, customs, and people are delineated with an incisive sharpness of outline by a pen that utterly abjures the chiaroscuro. And surprisingly enough, despite an inevitable strain of Gallic irritability in the presence of things English, especially in the opening pages, Taine's final judgments are, in their own manner, quite as sympathetic as James's, though considerably less partial. But this is no doubt irrelevant, because one would scarcely guess that the two men were speaking of the same country.

Their most fundamental difference is on the subject of English weather, and this makes *all* the difference. Taine abominates it, is cast into the depths of misery by it. James adores it and glories in it, which is the sign of the true Anglophile. As James has written in another place, the English climate, "if not the most cheerful, is surely the most picturesque and, so to speak, the most pictorial in Europe. For a single 'effect' in landscape and interior scenery produced in France or Italy at a given moment by the play of

131

light and shade, there are a hundred in England."

Writing of London weather in his opening pages, Taine descends so nearly to despair that one is astonished that he was finally able to accept England as generously as he did:

A wet Sunday in London: shops closed, streets almost empty; the aspect of a vast and well-kept graveyard. The few people in this desert of squares and streets, hurrying beneath their umbrellas, look like unquiet ghosts; it is horrible. . . . On the façades of the British Museum the fluting of the columns is full of greasy filth, as if sticky mud had been flowing down them. . . . That hideous Nelson, planted upon his column, like a rat impaled on the end of a stick! Here any classical form or idea is against the grain. Such a bog as this is, for the antique arts, a place of exile.

Then, by way of happy contrast, comes the American Henry James a few years later, visiting the same scenes on an afternoon equally "dreary":

There are winter effects, not intrinsically sweet, it would appear, which somehow, in absence, touch the chords of memory and even the fount of tears; as for instance the front of the British Museum on a black afternoon, or the portico, when the weather is vile, of one of the big square clubs in Pall Mall. I can give no adequate account of the subtle poetry of such reminiscences; it depends upon associations of which we have often lost the thread. The wide colonnade of the Museum, its symmetrical wings, the high iron fence in its granite setting, the sense of the misty halls within where the treasure lies—these things loom patiently through atmospheric layers which instead of making them dreary impart to them something of a cheer of red lights in a storm.

Whatever else it may be about, *English Hours* is a book about English weather, English light and shadow and atmosphere, and it is for the sake of the "weather" one goes back to it as often as one does. It is largely because of the "weather" that James's England, and especially his London, are so convincingly realized in his prose, and not merely "exhibits" in a museum case stared at under an artificial glare, which, despite the intense interest and appreciation they excite in the reader, is what Taine's England and London come to in the end.

Since "weather" and "atmosphere" are so important in *English Hours*, it is only fair to give the reader a few specimens of the climate he will be exposing himself to when he begins to read. The following passages have been selected almost, but not quite, at random:

. . . the atmosphere, with its magnificent mystifications, which flatters and superfuses, makes everything brown, rich, dim, vague, magnifies distances and minimizes details, confirms the inference of vastness by suggesting that, as the great city makes everything, it makes its own system of weather and its own optical laws.

London is pictorial in spite of details—from its dark green, misty parks, the way the light comes leaking and filtering from its cloud ceiling, and the softness and richness of tone which objects put on in such an atmosphere as soon as they begin to recede. Nowhere is there such a play of light and shade, such a struggle of sun and smoke, such aerial gradations and confusions.

Then the great city [London] becomes bright and kind, the pall of smoke turns into a veil of haze carelessly worn, the air is coloured and almost scented by the presence of the biggest society in the world, and most of

133

the things that meet the eye—or perhaps I should say more of them, for the most in London is, no doubt, ever the realm of the dingy—present themselves as "well-appointed." Everything shines more or less, from the window-panes to the dog-collars.

Such passages might be multiplied indefinitely if space permitted. Their value is that they allow, indeed require, the "weather" to become an imaginative solvent in which official buildings, warehouses, cathedrals, ruins, parks, and Englishmen themselves become, in the country of one's own mind, an organic and homogeneous world of which the final effect is composition, harmony, unity. Focus, not dispersal, is the end of James's art, and it would doubtless repay investigation to examine how, in so many of his stories, an impression of form and cohesion is won precisely through his control of atmosphere and light. It is surprising that James never became more than half-heartedly reconciled to the French Impressionists, but, after all, the light that filters through his prose is mostly the light of Constable and Turner, though he had the white glare of America at his finger tips as well.

In one of the "weather" passages I quoted above James remarked, in his tribute to English atmosphere, that it "minimizes details." In his writing generally James is a master of elimination, and it is an art that he no doubt partly learned from the dappled light of England. James's "elimination" of detail is not that, say, of Reynolds, in whose less successful canvases one is sometimes confronted by forlorn and staring blanknesses. Rather, James gives us a glittering haze crowded with incident—voices from a luminous cloud, fragrances from a hidden bank. Even when details appear to congest the page, the principles of selection will usually prove to have been austere.

Of all the classic occasions of English life it is possibly Derby Day at Epsom which, for its impression of life and color when treated in art, most exorbitantly demands an accumulation of the circumstantial and the secondary. Whether in Frith's huge and visually bristling canvas *Derby Day* in the Tate Gallery, or in George Moore's "Derby Day" chapter in *Esther Waters*, form, insofar as it is achieved, evolves through a tesselated pattern of anecdote, incident, and pictorial persiflage. Such being the indiscriminate demands of the subject, one might well hesitate to commit it to the hands of an artist so dedicated to singleness of effect and to the claims of the essential. Yet James's description of Derby Day in the sketch called "Two Excursions," written in 1877, is among the best things in *English Hours*. It is not, on this occasion, the habit of "eliminating," but rather a temptation to "include," which may strike the reader, erroneously, as the compelling impulse behind the treatment. James's rendering of the scene is as bright and gay and relentlessly busy as Frith's; yet this sense of teeming activity and general noise is, in fact, the effect of a happy concentration on one beguiling incident. James brushes in, impressionistically, the idling clouds, the blue-green distances of the Epsom Downs, the jockeys seen over the heads of the crowd in pink, green, orange, scarlet, white, and the "beggars and mountebanks and spangled persons on stilts"; and then he brings the irresponsible gaiety to focus in the little drama enacted on the adjacent carriage:

On a coach drawn up beside the one on which I had a place, a party of opulent young men were passing from stage to stage of the higher beatitude with a zeal which excited my admiration. They were accompanied by two or three young ladies of the kind that usually shares the choicest pleasure of youthful British opulence—young ladies in whom nothing has been neglected that can make a complexion superlative. The whole party had been drinking deep, and one of the young men, a pretty

lad of twenty, had in an indiscreet moment staggered
down as best he could to the ground. Here his cups
proved too many for him, and he collapsed and rolled
over. In plain English he was beastly drunk. It was the
scene that followed that arrested my observation. His
companions on the top of the coach called down to the
people herding under the wheels to pick him up and put
him away inside. These people were the grimiest of the
rabble, and a couple of men who looked like coal-heav-
ers out of work undertook to handle this hapless youth.
But their task was difficult; it was impossible to imagine
a young man more drunk. He was a mere bag of liquor
—at once too ponderous and too flaccid to be lifted. He
lay in a helpless heap under the feet of the crowd—the
best intoxicated young man in England.

For a sense of how much, in the full treatment, James has
left out to achieve this air of brightness and slightly wicked
fun, one should turn to Taine's description of Derby Day in
the closing pages of the first chapter of *Notes sur
l'Angleterre*. His handling, in its own manner, is splendid,
but it is the documentary method, and it leaves ample room
for the squalid and the sordid, which James either ignores or
—as here—transmutes. Taine's Derby Day, one is sure, has
the shocking truth of fact, but James's has the truth of art,
arrived at by discriminations that are not the concern of the
historian, the documentarist, or even, perhaps, the writer of
travel books in the usual sense.

James often seems to write more suggestively, more *exactly*, of architecture than of painting. He has a genuine
feeling for three dimensional form, for space and mass and
situation, that enables him to plant the great old buildings of
England as solidly on his pages as they stand on their historic
sites; and he invests them with all the softly gleaming ambience of ancient association and cherished tradition. There are

moments, perhaps, when for some tastes the call to the picturesque may become a shade insistent, as in this charming
description of the façade of Exeter:

The front, however, which has a gloomy impressiveness, is redeemed by . . . a long sculptured screen—a
sort of stony band of images—which traverses the façade
from side to side. The little broken-visaged effigies of
saints and kings and bishops, niched in tiers along this
hoary wall, are prodigiously black and quaint and primitive in expression; and as you look at them with whatever contemplative tenderness your trade of hard-work-
ing tourist may have left at your disposal, you fancy that
they are broodingly conscious of their names, histories,
and misfortunes; that, sensitive victims of time, they
feel the loss of their noses, and toes, and their crowns;
and that, when the long June twilight turns at last to a
deeper gray and the quiet of the close to a deeper
stillness, they begin to peer sidewise out of their narrow
recesses and to converse in some strange form of early
English, as rigid, yet as candid, as their features and
postures, moaning, like a company of ancient paupers
round a hospital fire, over their aches and infirmities and
losses, and the sadness of being so terribly old. The vast
square transeptal towers of the church seem to me to
have the same sort of personal melancholy. Nothing in
all architecture expresses better, to my imagination, the
sadness of survival, the resignation of dogged material
continuance, than a broad expanse of Norman stone-
work, roughly adorned with its low relief of short columns and round arches and almost barbarous hatchet-
work, and lifted high into that mild English light which
accords so well with its dull gray surface.

The poetic quality of such passages doubtless owes something to the influence of Hawthorne. James gave particular

care to his treatment of the great cathedrals which, like so many venerable Churchmen, file through his book in a dignified and commodious procession. They emerge from his descriptive characterizations, each with its unique, its distinctive, essence laid bare as if it were a human personality rather than an ecclesiastical monument. In the description of Exeter it is not so much James's handling of architectural feature that strikes one, though he is always competent at that, but rather the way he proceeds, by the intimations and persuasions of his style, to grasp and reveal the inner life of the building.

But when all is said, it is London itself that is the chief protagonist of *English Hours*. The quality that most attracted James to it was what he called its "multitudinous life," and his book is filled with a hundred eloquent attempts to convey to the reader his ever-abiding sense of the tremendous energies, the unceasing flow of passions and impressions, the immeasurable variety of its streets and squares and crowds.

TWO AMERICAN PAINTERS:
COPLEY AND ALLSTON

THE PICTURES of John Singleton Copley and Washington Allston offer an interesting comment on the dilemma that has always faced the American artist. It is a dilemma we are accustomed to bringing to focus in the novels of Henry James, but the lines were not always as clearly marked as he draws them there. For Copley, the problem of the American artist had not yet been formulated in its most blighting terms, and this helped to make possible his considerable achievement in painting. His answer to the problem involved no more than an original modification of the European stem by an essentially American but delicately flexible and receptive sensibility. The tradition to which his work conformed necessarily remained European, but there was as yet no emotional urgency to superimpose a self-conscious national pattern on top of it, nor yet any nervous rebellion against doing so. Copley's paintings exhibit a free and natural air, and they are almost the last American paintings that do until comparatively recent times. But Copley was born in 1738, and the kind of problem that confronted the Colonial artist was perhaps less invidious than the problem posed by the inhibiting nationalism that grew up after the American Revolution. Their paintings reveal a superficial similarity between Copley's and Allston's problems, but the similarity exists only in the poverty of cultural background which drove them both, perhaps too vehemently, to the study of ancient masterpieces when they finally became accessible to them in Europe. The psychological barrier between Europe and America, insofar as it exists for Copley at all, is an obstruction easily got over.

Copley went to England shortly before the Revolution began, and he stayed there. Although his English pictures represent a change from the direct, rather cold, vision of his American work, they usually (but not always) exhibit a quality that distinguishes them from the work of his European contemporaries. But this "difference" is not due to a New England local coloring of feeling, or a national narrowness of perception—which might easily have been the case had Copley been born fifty years later; it is a "difference" that embodies a large part of his distinction, and it may be glimpsed, for example, in his *Portrait of Midshipman Augustus Brine*, which hangs in the Metropolitan Museum. In this portrait, despite its large indebtedness to the English school, Copley reveals, through the pinched, supercilious face of the little midshipman, a quick apprehension of personality, a shrewd lightning grasp of the elusive, individual identity rather than of the impressive aristocratic type resemblances that predominate in Reynolds and Lawrence. The portrait is an extremely interesting anticipation of Eakins, and it is, one is convinced, something that only an American would be likely to have done. It represents the kind of crafty insight, the shrewd, calculating intuition, the sense of the hidden weakness which, vested not in an artist's eye, but in a nation at large, would guarantee that nation's commercial prosperity. On the surface it is a thoroughly English portrait, and yet it is thoroughly un-English at last. For Copley there was not enough distance between England and America either to exclude or embarrass him as an artist—there was just enough to give him a detachment which he knew how to make the most of.

There is no doubt that *Brook Watson and the Shark* is Copley's masterpiece. Some years ago when the Museum of Modern Art showed it in an exhibition called "Romantic Painting in America," the tyranny it exercised over the imagination was so complete that one returned to it again and again at the expense of everything else in the show. It is therefore a little surprising to find Flexner writing, "Even that fierce rendition of terror, *Brook Watson and the Shark*, is fundamentally literal-minded. Far from frightening us with imaginative symbols, Copley makes us feel that we are actual spectators of the tragedy as it occurred." [1] At one level this remark is true, but it too easily assumes that an image cannot be simultaneously literal and symbolic. Actually, the impact of this picture is owing to its inexhaustible capacity to take interpretation. There is more than mere literalness (however brilliantly executed) in the mysterious suggestiveness of the open jaws of the shark, in the ghostly nakedness of the man floating through the green water, in the highly conventionalized, almost ritualistic, gestures of the men in the boat, and in the enigmatic repose of the Negro, whose extended arm, raised in a kind of benediction, carries into the foreground of the action the weight and solidity of the great vessels riding at anchor in the harbor. Not until Melville would an American produce anything with quite this kind of imaginative power. The important thing to remark here is that, although the directness of vision is insistently American, it is realized with a maturity possible only as long as an American could function without nervousness in the presence of the European

1. *John Singleton Copley*, by James Thomas Flexner.

tradition. The figures at first seem wooden and awkward (this was Copley's first important London picture), but his understanding of what could be accomplished in terms of that very limitation makes the picture a wonderful success. And it is an understanding that Allston's contemporaries would scarcely have been capable of.

Washington Allston was born forty-one years after Copley, while the American Revolution was still in progress. Consequently, he grew up in an environment from which the absence of paintings to study was the least of the difficulties confronting the American artist. The problem was no longer the simple one of going to Europe to study or live: it had become the complex problem of "escaping" to Europe—and one had to deal also with the uneasy conscience that followed on the heels of that alternative. The ease with which Copley's art had managed to be both American and European—or rather, English—without embarrassment, and to achieve real stature in terms of a culture not yet hopelessly fragmentary, gave place to the nervous high spirits of Washington Allston viewing the galleries of Europe for the first time, filching romantic fragments from hundreds of ancient paintings with the voracious appetite of a starved American. Allston's paintings are charming, and they are also admirably executed; and one cannot view them without participating in the exhilaration with which he delightedly utilized parts of Raphael, Titian, Poussin, Prud'hon, Crome, Gainsborough, Bonnington, Michelangelo, Claude, Lorenzo Lotto, Hogarth, Rubens, and probably dozens of others. But the pleasure at last becomes a little boring and one prefers to remember how Copley had complained from France on first viewing the works of Raphael, Correggio, Titian, and Guido that he hoped the Paris pictures did not represent the best works of those artists from whom he had anticipated so much in America. If one compares the feeling and knowledge with which Copley assimilated the influence of Raphael in his painting *The Ascen-*

sion in the Boston Museum of Fine Arts with the exuberant
virtuousity with which Allston could paint *anybody's* manner, the difference between, not so much two men as two
societies, becomes apparent.

It is difficult not to think of Allston in terms of *Roderick
Hudson*. James's novel is the most valid and revealing comment we have on the dilemma that confronted the contemporaries of Allston. The following dialogue between Roderick
and his patron, Rowland Mallett, as they talk beneath "the
long-stemmed pines of the Villa Ludovisi" mentions most of
the significant elements in Allston's own charm and failure as
a painter: the eagerness of response, the quickness of assimilation with its superficial sophistication, the engaging innocence, and finally that sense of guilt, that moral nervousness
which was to prove a nearly incurable disease with American
artists:

"It came over me just now that it's exactly three
months since I left Northampton. I can't believe anything so ridiculous."

"It certainly seems more."

"It seems ten years. What an exquisite ass I was so
short a time ago!"

"Do you feel," Rowland asked all amusedly, "so
tremendously wise now?"

"Wise with the wisdom of the ages and the taste of a
thousand fountains. Don't I look so? Surely I haven't the
same face. Haven't I different eyes, a different skin,
different legs and arms?"

". . . you're in the literal sense of the word, more
civilized. I dare say," added Rowland, "that Miss Gar-
land would think so."

"That's not what she would call it; she would say I'm
spoiled; I'm not sure she wouldn't say that I'm already
hideously corrupted."

After Allston's return to America he produced a few pictures in which there is a small but personally felt vein of poetry that is new in his work. And yet Richardson's attempt [2] to argue that Allston's homecoming was not an artistic calamity for him is not only unconvincing, but absurd, when he argues that Allston finally failed, not because New England presented an unfavorable environment, but because the exact opposite was the case. "The world was too interested and friendly, too eager to encourage him. . . ." This represents a misunderstanding of the whole problem, which centers in the relationship of the American artist with the European tradition, and one has to go back to the concluding pages of *Roderick Hudson* to understand what really happened, why Allston back in New England again turned more and more to esthetics and literature, and neglected painting, which was his true art. It was not merely for the sake of ending his novel that James brought Roderick Hudson to disaster at the cliff's edge:

> Roderick's stricken state had driven him, in the mere motion of flight, higher and further than he knew; he had outstayed supposably the first menace of the storm and perhaps even found a dark distraction in watching it. Perhaps he had simply lost himself. The tempest had overtaken him, and when he tried to return it had been too late. He had attempted to descend the cliff in the treacherous gloom, he had made the inevitable slip, and whether he had fallen fifty or three hundred feet little mattered now. Even if it had not been far, it had been far enough.

2. *Washington Allston: A Study of the Romantic Artist in America,* by Edgar Preston Richardson.

MRS. WHARTON'S MASK

EDITH WHARTON'S very reticent autobiography, *A Backward Glance*, first published in 1934, three years before her death, was reissued with other of her books in 1962 to mark the centenary of her birth. Certainly her autobiography is indispensable for understanding the New York social structure of her girlhood, which forms the essential subject of some of her best work. But, delightful as it is in all respects, it tells us surprisingly little about Mrs. Wharton herself. It is somewhat disconcerting to reflect that if we wish to know something about her more essential than that she was a very *grande dame*, the only place we can go for a hint is to the brief biographical essay by Wayne Andrews introducing a collection of Edith Wharton's short stories, published by Scribner's in 1958.

Percy Lubbock's *Portrait of Edith Wharton* (1947) is primly tight-lipped concerning everything that one seriously interested in her work might want, or need, to know. Reviewing the book when it first appeared, Edmund Wilson made a list of things it did not tell us about its subject. The questions Wilson asks provide a frame for a portrait that is still missing, and they seem to me more illuminating than the

145

"official" likenesses we have been given. For this reason he is well worth quoting:

> Mrs. Wharton was always quite rich. Where did her money come from? Was it her own or was it her husband's? And why did she marry Edward Wharton, with whom she obviously had little in common and was not very much in love? What, precisely, was the matter with him when he became deranged and Mrs. Wharton finally divorced him? Mr. Lubbock tries to put their relationship in as attractive a light as possible, but then he later speaks of Walter Berry, the American lawyer in Paris with whom Edith Wharton's name has always been associated, as "the man she had loved for a lifetime, in youth and age." To what kind of situation had this given rise? There is a legend that Edith Jones's first love was broken up by her mother, who disapproved of it and sent her abroad; and that her first book of poems, which she had secretly had printed, was discovered and destroyed by her family. Is it true? And is it true that she began writing fiction some years after her marriage, as a result of a nervous breakdown, at the suggestion of S. Weir Mitchell, the novelist and neurologist? It has been asserted by persons who should be in a position to know that Edith Wharton had some reason for believing herself an illegitimate child and that her family rather let her down from the point of view of social backing. . . .

The dearth of information that exists concerning Mrs. Wharton's real personality has not been fortunate for her critical reputation. Art is not quite so autonomous as twentieth-century criticism often likes to think, and as one grows increasingly familiar with her fiction one recognizes that she belongs among those artists whose work, however obliquely, is an extension of their personal tensions and their intimate personalities, a knowledge of which may do more to illuminate their creative motives and the particular effects their art achieves than anything else can. The quality that so many of her heroines and heroes have of being hopelessly trapped by the demands or the refusal of their society, or by the vacuity of their social aspirations, or by the various deprivations imposed on them by life, seems projected from some deep center in herself, from some concealed hopelessness, frustration, or private rage that we are never allowed to see except at several removes in the disguising medium of her art.

Mrs. Wharton is rarely seen except as a public figure. With her twenty-two servants, her splendid houses, her beautifully landscaped gardens in which nothing so common as a geranium was permitted, her retinue in attendance of ambassadors, French academicians, international hostesses, duchesses, and distinguished men of letters, her beloved Pekineses, and her luxurious motor cars in which Henry James so often found courage to face the long hot summers, she seems less a woman novelist than a princess royal; and there is little in the façade, so exquisite and perfect in taste, so carefully prepared and jealously preserved, that gives much inkling of the private personality that was responsible for the art. Even her photographs are "official." *A Backward Glance* reproduces one taken about the time she wrote *The House of Mirth*, in 1905, in which she might easily be mistaken for Ellen Terry as Lady Macbeth reading the letter from her husband. It is this redoubtable "public" personality that, one fancies, has sometimes intruded itself between her work and even the most sympathetic of critics.

Somewhat surprisingly, the subtle relation that exists between her art and her life is nowhere better exemplified than in *Ethan Frome*. Not to admit the relation is to be impelled towards an adverse judgment on a work that deserves to rank with such brilliant achievements as *The House of Mirth*, *The Custom of the Country*, and *The Reef*.

147

A few years ago, in an essay on *Ethan Frome*, Lionel Trilling said, a little severely, of Mrs. Wharton: "she was a woman in whom we cannot fail to see a limitation of heart, and this limitation makes itself manifest as a literary and moral deficiency of her work, and of *Ethan Frome* especially." He bases his judgment on what he takes to be her cruelty, even (one gathers) her sadism, in her attitude toward her characters, whom she submits to needless and gratuitous suffering—gratuitous because in the given situation they are incapable of acquiring moral knowledge from their pain. Speaking of that last horrifying scene in which we see the three principals trapped, as it were forever, in that impoverished New England kitchen, Trilling writes: "all that Edith Wharton has in mind is to achieve that grim tableau . . . of pain and imprisonment, of life-in-death. About the events that lead up to this tableau, there is nothing she finds to say, nothing whatever." He calls his essay "The Morality of Inertia"; in his reading of the novel Ethan Frome falls short of the specifications of the Aristotelian tragic hero because he is one of those people "who do not make moral decisions, whose fate cannot have moral reverberations."

Against this reading of *Ethan Frome* it is possible to oppose a quite different reading in which the movement and meaning of the whole narrative depend on two crucial moral decisions made by Ethan, the second of which cancels the first and entails tragic consequences because it is the *wrong* decision. The two moral decisions are painstakingly prepared for in the text, and given as sharp a focus as possible. The first decision is made when Ethan, tormented by his love for his wife's young cousin Mattie, plans to run away with her, and for that purpose considers the possibility of securing money from the Hales on false pretenses:

He started down the road toward their house, but at the end of a few yards he pulled up sharply, the blood in his face. For the first time . . . he saw what he was about to do. He was planning to take advantage of the Hales' sympathy to obtain money from them on false pretenses. That was a plain statement of the cloudy purpose which had driven him in headlong to Starkfield.

With the sudden perception of the point to which his madness had carried him, the madness fell and he saw his life before him as it was. He was a poor man, the husband of a sickly woman, whom his desertion would leave alone and destitute; and even if he had had the heart to desert her he could have done so only by deceiving two kindly people who had pitied him.

He turned and walked slowly back to the farm.

Ethan's second choice, which reverses the one that has been quoted, is to die with Mattie rather than to face the intolerable pain of parting from her forever. It is not a rational choice in the sense that the first decision was. As Mrs. Wharton finely presents it in the last chapter but one, it is the result of an all but irresistible compulsion of love and despair—almost irresistible, but not quite, for in that first decision of Ethan's that Mrs. Wharton rendered for us with such clarity, she showed us a will and a moral intelligence capable of overcoming even this last temptation.

In the sled crash that brings the main story of the action to a close, Ethan and Mattie are not killed but hopelessly crippled. As Ethan painfully regains consciousness under the great elm towards which he has steered, Mrs. Wharton gives us a remarkable paragraph:

The sky was still thick, but looking straight up he saw a single star, and tried vaguely to reckon whether it was Sirius, or—or— The effort tired him too much, and he closed his heavy lids and thought that he would sleep. . . . The stillness was so profound that he heard a little animal twittering somewhere nearby under the snow. It made a small frightened *cheep* like a field mouse, and he wondered languidly if it were hurt. Then he understood that it must be in pain: pain so excruciating that he seemed, mysteriously, to feel it shooting through his own body. He tried in vain to roll over in the direction of the sound, and stretched his left arm out across the snow. And now it was as though he felt rather than heard the twittering; it seemed to be under his palm, which rested on something soft and springy. The thought of the animal's suffering was intolerable to him and he struggled to raise himself, and could not because a rock, or some huge mass, seemed to be lying on him. But he continued to finger about cautiously with his left hand, thinking he might get hold of the little creature and help it; and all at once he knew that the soft thing his hand had touched was Mattie's hair and that his hand was on her face.

Ethan's half-delirious desire to help the little animal he imagines he hears is not the reaction of a morally lethargic character; but apart from its immediate effectiveness in deepening still more our sense of his humanity, the passage rises to a bleak revelation when he becomes aware that the agonized *cheep* is not from an animal in pain but from the crushed body of the only person who has ever satisfied his instinct to love. The presence of the little field mouse does not act as a reductive agent on the dignity, the suffering, or the moral natures of Ethan and Mattie, nor does it suggest that they exist on a *sub*-tragic level; rather, it precipitates them into a nonhuman void beyond tragedy where the sufferings of mice and men are one, where moral decisions and love and decency appear to be obliterated in the face of a blank indifference.

But this was a resolution which, however much she may have felt impelled towards it, Mrs. Wharton would not ac-

cept any more than she accepted Ethan's *second* moral decision to find an escape in self-imposed death with Mattie. The
horrifying closing scene in the kitchen in which Ethan, Mattie, and Zeena seem to confront each other forever is not
suffering wantonly imposed on her characters by an embit-
tered female writer, but a punishment that grows ineluctably
out of a moral act deliberately performed, and the punishment is meant to exist as an evaluation of that act. In the
prologue to *Ethan Frome* the narrator of the story exclaims
when he first sees Ethan's face: "He looks as if he was dead
and in hell now." One might argue with some plausibility
that *Ethan Frome* is a moral parable, and the sequel played
out in the farmhouse kitchen is really an epilogue in hell.

Since the purpose of these comments is not to offer a
critique of the novel but to suggest a relation between Mrs.
Wharton's biography and her art, it will be necessary to
glance quickly at her situation during the several years that
preceded the publication of *Ethan Frome* in 1913.

In 1908, according to Wayne Andrews, Mrs. Wharton's
husband, "who had already developed symptoms of neuras-
thenia, suffered a severe nervous breakdown." Two years
later he was placed under the care of a psychiatrist. Something of the blackness of the period comes through in a letter
Henry James wrote to her at the time, and from which
Andrews quotes: "Only sit tight yourself *and go through the
movements of life*. That keeps up your connection with life—I
mean of the immediate and apparent life, behind which, all
the while, the deeper and darker and unapparent, in which
things really happen to us, learns under that hygiene, to stay
in its place."

Andrews gives us for these same years quotations from
Mrs. Wharton's unpublished diaries that reveal the passionate intensity of her love for Walter Berry, not more than
hinted at in *A Backward Glance* or in Percy Lubbock's
Portrait. His excerpts are immensely more moving than pas-

sages of this kind commonly are, and they reveal a woman who has little apparent relation with the "official" Edith Wharton. They also reveal a human being with a hopeless sense of entrapment. Returning from Paris to her husband, mentally ill in their home in Lenox, Massachusetts, she entered in her journal, which seems to be addressed to Berry, the following passage:

> I heard the key turn in the prison lock. That is the answer to everything worth-while!
>
> Oh, Gods of derision! And you've given me twenty years of it!
>
> *Je n'en peux plus.*
>
> And yet I must be just. I have stood it all these years, and hardly felt it, because I had created a world of my own, in which I had lived without heeding what went on outside. But since I have known what it was to have someone enter into that world and live there with me, the mortal solitude I come back to has become terrible. . . .

It requires no very strenuous effort of the imagination to conceive the possibility that *Ethan Frome* may well have grown out of the double ordeal that Mrs. Wharton went through between 1908 and 1913, when the novel was published. All the constricting circumstances in which Ethan finds himself entrapped, Mrs. Wharton may have carried over, suitably disguised, from her own situation, to scrutinize and question in the pages of her book. But the ultimate resemblance between her situation and the one depicted in *Ethan Frome* is a moral one. From neither situation does there appear to be a possible issue in terms of happiness. Even though Mrs. Wharton was divorced in 1913, she remained apart from Berry, and the moral decision she made in her own life would appear to correspond more or less to the *first* moral decision made by Ethan—the one she was to punish him so severely for forsaking in his second decision.

There is no question of suggesting here that Mrs. Wharton was vulgarly capitalizing on her private experiences in *Ethan Frome*. Despite what may be a personal origin, her art is ultimately a highly impersonal one. But her own moral crisis appears to be reflected with remarkable fidelity in *Ethan Frome*, and one might even venture to suggest that it may have become for her, as she worked with it through the year of her divorce, a moral laboratory in which she tested creatively the alternatives that confronted her in her impossible situation. If she was cruel, the cruelty was in the severity with which she judged herself. So far from indicating a limitation of heart, *Ethan Frome* would seem to be, if the relation between Mrs. Wharton's art and life that has been conjectured here is true, the expression of a remarkably sensitive moral nature.

SCOTT FITZGERALD:
THE APPRENTICE FICTION

ALTHOUGH nearly all critics recognize today the quality of Scott Fitzgerald's best fiction, from time to time one still hears a violent dissenting opinion. The case against Fitzgerald was succinctly stated in a 1951 essay by Leslie Fiedler: "And so a fictionist with a 'second-rate sensitive mind' . . . and a weak gift for construction is pushed into the very first rank of American novelists, where it becomes hard to tell his failures from his successes. Who cares as long as the confetti flies and the bands keep playing!" It is a little difficult to know in the context what Fiedler means by a "second-rate mind." But a novelist who discovers and is possessed by an important subject, one which is centrally significant in the experience of his country and time, and who gives that subject vivid and effective embodiment in his work, hardly deserves such an epithet, however intended. Fiedler knows perfectly well that Fitzgerald has a subject, but he doesn't like it. As he tells us in his book on the American novel published in 1960: "There is only one story that Fitzgerald knows how to tell. . . . The penniless knight . . .

goes out to seek his fortune and unhappily finds it. . . . He finds in his bed not the white bride but the Dark Destroyer." Apart from the fact that one is sick to death of categories like these, the interpretation is likely to seem prejudiced and less than honest to anyone who disagrees with Fiedler's bright but falsifying decription of Fitzgerald as the "laureate" of "the American institution of *coitus interruptus*."

Fitzgerald's discovery of his subject was a progressive one, and he moves into a fuller consciousness and control of it until the end. Although Mr. Fiedler's intention is not complimentary, he comes close to an exact formulation when he describes Gatsby, Fitzgerald's most representative hero, as "the naif out of the West destined . . . to die of a love for which there is no worthy object." In writers who are, in a sense, born with an innate subject to write about, their early work can be peculiarly revealing, both as to subject matter and tone, and this is true of Fitzgerald.

In *The Apprentice Fiction of F. Scott Fitzgerald*, John Kuehl has collected the early stories written between 1909 and 1917—the earliest written while he was at St. Paul's Academy, three while he was at Newman School in Hackensack, and the remainder while he was an undergraduate at Princeton. While these stories are clearly "apprentice fiction," several of them are remarkably good, and collectively they indicate that Fitzgerald had already found his subject, although there are few intimations that he was yet aware of the moral dimensions of it which he would exploit so wonderfully in *The Great Gatsby*.

Kuehl has provided a series of excellent critical commentaries on the stories, which relate them to Fitzgerald's later development. Recognizing that nearly all of them deal with frustration or moral defeat, however disguised, he writes in his introduction: "Inevitably, Scott Fitzgerald's juvenile protagonist, through personal weakness or some external force or both, would become the *homme manqué*, a term Fitzgerald himself would use to describe Dick Diver." And in a later comment on one of the Princeton stories he says: "All the plots he thought of 'had a touch of disaster in them.' He anticipated that lovely girls would go to ruin, that wealth would disintegrate, that millionaires would be 'beautiful and damned.' "

A glance at his subjects will indicate how early the characteristic temper of his sensibility asserted itself. In "Shadow Laurels," which is written in dialogue, an eminently successful man returns to his native city, seeking information about his father, whom he had never known. He discovers not only that his father was a drunkard and wastrel, but there are intimations to the eyes of the other characters that the successful man is very much the son of his father. In "The Spire and the Gargoyle," part of which he incorporated in *This Side of Paradise*, an undergraduate flunks out of Princeton and is haunted by a sense of defeat and nostalgia ever afterward. In "The Ordeal," a Jesuit novice about to take his vows is sorely tempted to refuse them. He overcomes the temptation, but in a way that disturbingly suggests the victory has been mechanical and external only. In what is perhaps the best of the stories, "The Pierian Springs and the Last Straw," a writer who somewhat resembles the novelist Fitzgerald was to become, after many years marries the girl he had loved in his youth, and finds that it destroys his talent. In these stories it is not only subject matter and a propensity towards disaster that anticipate the mature writer: their romantic alignment is particularly insistent.

All during Fitzgerald's life, Keats was his favorite poet. "For awhile after you quit Keats all other poetry seems to be only whistling or humming," he wrote to his daughter; and he has several times remarked on the frequency with which he read Keats when he was very young. In the year of his death he wrote that he still could not read "Ode to a Nightingale" "without tears in my eyes." Keats's strong verbal influence in the more poetic passages of Fitzgerald's prose is obvious—perhaps in *The Great Gatsby* most of all. But one guesses that essentially it was Keats's attitude to experience that seized and dominated his imagination, and may have exerted some influence on Fitzgerald's choice of themes and subject matter.

Throughout Keats's poetry there is a sense of transience and loss, at times an almost unbearably poignant sense of passage and dissolution. The origin of this is understandable in terms of Keats's biography; but there is a somewhat similar sense of transience in Fitzgerald's writing. In the latter case it is a little difficult to guess its cause, but it is pervasive. His second novel, *The Beautiful and Damned*, has a good many passages like these:

> Beautiful things grow to a certain height and then they fail and fade off, breathing out memories as they decay. And just as any period decays in our minds, the things of that period should decay too, and in that way they're preserved for a while in the few hearts like mine that react to them.

> There's no beauty without poignancy, and there's no poignancy without the feeling that it's going, men, names, books, houses—bound for dust—mortal—

This sense of loss soon grew sharper and more bitter. It is of the essence of Gatsby's ordeal that he believed the past could be repeated, almost as Keats had written to Benjamin Bailey, "We shall enjoy ourselves here after by having what we called happiness on earth repeated in a finer tone. . . ." But Fitzgerald is not to be identified with Gatsby. He understands, as his heroes do not, the element of irrevocable, tragic loss in which his vision is grounded. "Winter Dreams," one of his better short stories, concludes with a statement which makes its own comment on Gatsby's private dream:

"Long ago," he said, "long ago, there was something in me, but now that thing is gone. Now that thing is gone. I cannot cry. I cannot care. That thing will come back no more."

Fitzgerald never learned to triumph over this theme of loss and defeat in his fiction as Keats does in his poetry. In Fitzgerald's case it moves from the elegiac to the tragic but never to victory, as it does, for example, in the great speech from "Hyperion" in which Oceanus, the vanquished Titan, accepts the infinite loss entailed in a fall from divinity:

As Heaven and Earth are fairer, fairer far
Than Chaos and blank Darkness, though once chiefs;
And as we show beyond that Heaven and Earth
In form and shape compact and beautiful,
In will, in action free, companionship,
And thousand other signs of purer life;
So on our heels a fresh perfection treads,
A power more strong in beauty, born of us
And fated to excel us, as we pass
In glory that old Darkness.

In this superb vision of an endless evolution into beauty and perfection, forever canceling out the stages past, the redemptive factor for Keats is of course the power of his genius and splendor of his poetry. But although Fitzgerald's sense of loss is in many ways strangely Keatsian, a resolution similar to Keats's is beyond him—and not merely because he has not Keats's astounding genius. Fitzgerald's ultimate subject is the character of the American Dream in which, in their respective ways, his principal heroes are all trapped. If the American Dream seems delusively to carry a suggestion of infinite possibilities, it tolerates no fresh perfections beyond its own material boundaries. If it engenders heroic desires in the hearts of its advocates, it can only offer unheroic fulfillments. For this reason Fitzgerald's novels, and *Gatsby* above all, are tragedies. The heart of the tragedy is that these heroes must die of a love for which there is no worthy object. Fiedler was quite right about that, but hopelessly wrong in seeing this theme as trivial. An abiding faith in the paradox that infinite satisfactions can be had in the devout pursuit of success, money, and romantic love has always been the corrupting element in American society. To have invented a series of fables dramatizing this central truth and its consequences for America is not indicative of a "second-rate mind."

In Kuehl's well-edited collection of Fitzgerald's apprentice fiction we encounter this kind of hero in whom the seeds of defeat and tragedy are suggested, even in the flush of success, in perhaps a majority of the stories. Not until *The Great Gatsby* would Fitzgerald gain full control of the subject, and transform it into an effective instrument for probing the nature of the American experience, but partly for this very reason these early attempts are illuminating. The Romantic tone, the tragic bias, the critical irony, have all already been established.

PROBLEMS OF AMERICAN
LITERARY BIOGRAPHY

I

LONGFELLOW
by Newton Arvin

I T IS UNFORTUNATE that the late Newton Arvin
should have chosen Longfellow as the subject of his last
book. Arvin's three critical studies of Hawthorne, Melville,
and Whitman were valuable additions to literary biography.
The *Hawthorne* in particular, which appeared in 1929, was
as judicious in its assessment of its subject as one could find
before Matthiessen's *The American Renaissance*. The critical
judgments in *Melville* (1950) are sometimes more debatable, but it is one of the most stimulating and useful brief
studies of him that we have. Arvin was lucky three times in
his subject and his timing, the first biography antedating the
Hawthorne revival by a few years, the *Melville* riding the full
wave of its subject's "rediscovery."

Arvin's new book is proof that Longfellow is a subject in

whom it is very difficult to become interested. This is in fact a downhearted book. Mr. Arvin exhibits a certain embarrassment by seeming to undermine, in a running series of remarks, the sufficiently modest claims he makes for Longfellow's talent. The text is studded with discouraging statements like these:

> Even in his own day he had done nothing to extend the boundaries of poetic speech or to revivify the diction of American poetry.

> *The Spanish Student* is much too fragile and weightless a piece of work to deserve the injustices of labored treatment.

> . . . we are inclined to feel that, on the whole, in spite of its lapses, there are a good many things worse than *The Song of Hiawatha*.

> . . . the slack commonplace of these inferior poems ["Excelsior," "A Psalm of Life," "The Village Blacksmith"] insured their universal currency for many decades.

> . . . if we are looking for either a heroic largeness or a novelistic roundness of characterization [in *Evangeline*], we shall be badly let down.

> In spite of his ambitions for it, *Hyperion* is at best a slight and imponderous book, and in some stretches the thinness of the air makes one breathe in gasps.

> It goes without saying, now, that there is much that is facile and flaccid in these five volumes.

> Longfellow's moralizing poems fail, either wholly or relatively, because he was not a moralist.

> One regrets that, with all this ardor behind it, *Outre-Mer* is no more impressive than it is.

161

Such remarks can be found on most pages, and the cumulative effect is very depressing. On the positive side, Arvin's extended discussions of the poems he considers best do little to dispel the grayness. The book ends with a curious epilogue that is, in fact, an apology for writing on Longfellow. It is labored in tone, and if some of its observations are just, they are also obvious. One of the points that Arvin makes here is that Longfellow's critical reputation has suffered in our time because of "the revolution in taste, associated with the names of Eliot, and later, Tate, Ransom, and others. . . . The valuation, in poetry, of such qualities as ambiguity, tension, and irony was bound to result in the repudiation of much romantic poetry. . . ."

I doubt if one need go so far afield to explain the decline in his reputation. Longfellow is not unpleasant to read, but there is no important nineteenth-century American poet who has written so little of what is unmistakably poetry as opposed to the mere competence of middling verse. Longfellow has written no poem that proclaims a poet as clearly as a single line of Emerson's is able to:

In May, when sea winds pierced our solitudes . . .

Although he was notoriously "literary" in half a dozen languages, a translator, and something of a literary antiquarian, Longfellow never established an interesting relation in any of his poems with an earlier tradition. The conscious and effective use that Emerson was able to make of the seventeenth century in his beautiful "Threnody" for his little boy who had died would have been entirely beyond Longfellow's competence—perhaps even beyond his comprehension:

For flattering planets seemed to say
This child should ills of ages stay,
By wondrous tongue, and guided pen,
Bring the flown Muses back to men.

162

Perchance not he but Nature ailed,
The world and not the infant failed.
It was not ripe yet to sustain
A genius of so fine a strain,
Who gazed upon the sun and moon
As if he came into his own,
And pregnant with his grander thought,
Brought the old order into doubt.
His beauty once their beauty tried;
They could not feed him, and he died,
And wandered backward as in scorn,
To wait an aeon to be born.

To write a book on Longfellow should be, first of all, a matter of carefully devised critical strategy, in which the subject as humanist, man of letters, and benevolent representative of American culture, living in estate at Craigie House, should hold the center of the picture. There is no doubt that Longfellow played this role well, and that American letters remains in his debt because he did so. His real function was not unlike that of his contemporary Charles Eliot Norton. A few years ago Kermit Vanderbilt published a biography, *Charles Eliot Norton: Apostle of Culture in a Democracy*, which, it seems to me, might provide the ideal model for a book on Longfellow. The limitations of the two men were a little similar, Longfellow perhaps having a margin of advantage in that he was less a puritan and hence more generous in his response to literature. There is no special pleading, no condescension, no apology in Vanderbilt's book, but lucid analysis of Norton's teaching, scholarship, literary criticism, and very considerable public services. I can think of no biography offhand that gives as rewarding an insight into the intellectual life of this particular milieu in America, and it is difficult to see why the Master of Craigie House could not have been presented as significantly in this respect as the

Master of Shady Hill.

Vanderbilt did not assume that Norton's scholarship and writing were still of much intrinsic interest in themselves, whatever the figure of the man himself might be. Arvin makes the mistake of assuming that Longfellow's poems either are, or ought to be—hence the tone of embarrassment which I have already remarked on. From the moment he is committed to an extended critical examination of the poetry, Arvin, Longfellow, and the reader are in for trouble. It is difficult to see why this kind of detailed attention should have been given the poems at all; they are incapable of supporting it. For example, Arvin devotes two more pages to a discussion of *Hiawatha* and *The Courtship of Miles Standish* than he gave to *The Scarlet Letter* in his *Hawthorne; Evangeline* receives fourteen pages of commentary to only seven for *Billy Budd* in his *Melville;* he analyzes *Hyperion* at as great length as he treated *The Confidence Man;* "Bartleby the Scrivener" receives two pages of discussion in the earlier biography, *The Spanish Student* four in *Longfellow*. One's first response to this disproportion in a biography written on the same scale is an insistent "Why?" But there is nothing in Arvin's book that will provide an answer.

As a critic of poetry Arvin is far from being as satisfactory as he usually was with the novel. There is too much old-fashioned impressionism in his method:

If *Der arme Heinrich* suggests a small window of stained glass, in pure and primary colors, *The Golden Legend* suggests a softly hued but loosely composed mural, perhaps in a library, in the manner of some nineteenth century Pre-Raphaelite.

The Courtship of Miles Standish has

. . . the tonality of the Massachusetts seacoast when the wind is from the east, the rather bleak landscape washed with a grey mist.

. . . the minor key in which many of these poems are written suggests the plaintive nocturne of some lesser romantic composer.

. . . he is an accomplished, sometimes an exquisite, craftsman, like a master in some minor art, a potter or a silversmith.

Much space is devoted to critical comments that persist in seeming pointless—that, at best, do nothing to take one into the poem, and which consist largely of prose paraphrase. In a representative passage, he says of *Hiawatha:*

It is an Indian Summer poem, and it is also a late-afternoon or sunset poem. The sunsets abound in the feeling of romantic landscape painting. The setting sun is sometimes seen as a beautiful bird, a flamingo, dropping into her nest at night fall, and sometimes as a more purely mythical bird.

He writes of *The Courtship of Miles Standish:*

There is only one sunset in *The Courtship*—for this is a poem about beginnings—but there are two fine sunrises, and the more splendid of these is the sunrise on the morning of the wedding when the sun appears out of the sea like Aaron out of his tent.

Perhaps there is no particular harm in this kind of criticism, but also is there any point? If the last quotation leads into an observation of some interest on the Old Testament Oriental opulence of one aspect of the Puritan imagination, the point is muffled by the way in which Arvin has chosen to present it.

As a subject, Longfellow undoubtedly tempts his critics towards a certain obviousness, but one cannot help wishing Arvin had resisted more. *Tales of a Wayside Inn* is probably Longfellow's most successful single book, and Arvin rightly points to his skill in writing sustained narrative verse of a popular kind. The stories Longfellow gives us in this volume are, as everyone knows, put in the mouths of seven Americans who have met at the Red Horse Inn in Sudbury, Massachusetts. The idea of the framework comes of course out of Boccaccio and Chaucer, but one cannot help wondering what conceivable audience Arvin was writing for that he thought it in need of the following information: "There is no portrait here remotely comparable in vigor with that of the Wife of Bath, the Prioress, or the Pardoner; Longfellow's portraits, though they were drawn from actual individuals, are dim and sketchy side by side with these." Arvin expands the remark for more than a page.

The criticism of the shorter poems is no more satisfactory. Arvin offers a number of critical and descriptive commentaries on a few dozen poems by Longfellow. Some of his comments are detailed. But the cold fact remains that no amount of good will or artificial respiration can put the breath of life back into poems that are no longer viable. There are of course certain poems that we still derive some pleasure from—for which we can still feel some admiration: "The Fire of Drift Wood," "The Tide Rises, The Tide Falls," "My Lost Youth," "The Jewish Cemetery at Newport," and a few others. But the critical emphasis they should have received is lost in the undiscriminating welter of poems brought forward for analysis.

Nor is it always possible to agree with Arvin's particular judgments, even within the context of the Longfellow canon. During his lifetime Longfellow was the most popular poet in America, and his mass audience had an admirable instinct for picking out as its favorite pieces poems with a crudely sentimental or didactic life. However one may wish to qualify it, life *was* there. I am very far indeed from sharing Arvin's contempt for "Excelsior," "The Village Blacksmith," and "A Psalm of Life." He prefers, as specifically opposed to

166

them, "The Light of Stars," which seems to me an offensive poem. He finds in it a nice balance "between the confession of suffering and the voice of the resisting will." But this is surely to contribute a complexity that is by no means present in the poem. Here are the last three verses:

> *The star of the unconquered will,*
> *He rises in my breast,*
> *Serene, and resolute, and still,*
> *And calm, and self-possessed.*

> *And thou, too, whosoe'er thou art,*
> *That readest this brief psalm,*
> *As one by one thy hopes depart,*
> *Be resolute and calm.*

> *O fear not in a world like this,*
> *And thou shalt know ere long,*
> *Know how sublime a thing it is*
> *To suffer and be strong.*

Longfellow had his own griefs and one respects them: but one can only reply to this: Preach this to the concentration camps, or the martyrs of Vietnam, or (in our great democratic phrase) the victims of your choice. It is impossible to know whether one's teeth are put more on edge by the woolly syntax or the bogus moral superiority that is nothing less than insulting.

On the other hand, the three poems that Arvin condemns in the comparison are among the few through which a decided charm still shines. I have always admired the gallant youth bearing "A banner with the strange device, Excelsior!" It is easy to understand why Thurber once drew a set of illustrations of him. Unlike "The Light of Stars," it has nothing invidious in its moral tone. Indeed, the attitude expressed there probably has a certain validity for the imagination of brave boys of a certain age. The verse is much more effective than usual with Longfellow, and the mounting action is as sharp and straight as a sky-pointing icicle. I fail to see why anyone should object to the over-purity and simplification of motive. One is not concerned with human beings here, but with charming dolls. Like some of Dryden's heroic tragedies, it ought to be enacted on the stage of an elegant puppet theater. It is easy to visualize the final apotheosis (which really has a good deal of style) against the background of an Alp two feet high:

> *There in the twilight cold and gray,*
> *Lifeless, but beautiful he lay,*
> *And from the sky, serene and far,*
> *A voice fell, like a falling star,*
>   *Excelsior!*

While "A Psalm of Life" may be an inferior poem, it is difficult to join wholeheartedly in Arvin's total condemnation. In certain of the verses there is an intensification of the cliché that approaches originality, and a resounding authority in dealing with the obvious that commands assent. I particularly like the fourth verse:

> *Art is long, and Time is fleeting,*
>   *And our hearts though stout and brave,*
> *Still, like muffled drums, are beating*
>   *Funeral marches to the grave.*

The echo from Henry King's "Exequy" is probably unconscious, but it touches one. The surprising thing is the stanch way in which Longfellow's lines, coarsened, even vulgarized as they are, refuse to be utterly extinguished by the comparison.

As for "The Village Blacksmith," there is less "slack commonplace" in it than in many of the poems Arvin prefers. There is a direct simple authority in the description of the

Blacksmith that even approaches style, just possibly by way of "The Ancient Mariner":

> *His hair is crisp, and black, and long,*
> *His face is like the tan;*
> *His brow is wet with honest sweat,*
> *He earns whate'er he can,*
> *And looks the whole world in the face,*
> *For he owes not any man.*

Arvin praises "The Goblet of Life" because he finds in it "an almost Hardyesque harshness." On the other hand, he disdains "The Children's Hour." But "The Children's Hour" resembles Walter de la Mare's most characteristic poems so closely it might have been written by the later poet, and it seems to me almost as much a matter of praise to resemble Walter de la Mare as to resemble Hardy.

If one is going to write a book on Longfellow, it is precisely his popular successes—what Arvin calls his "inferior" poems—that have to be faced. They are not important poems —not always even good poems—but they can still move when prodded. "The Building of the Ship," one of Arvin's favorite pieces, seems to me totally inert. It is difficult not to think that, faced with the problem of finding anything relevant or exciting to say about the poems, the chance to speak of literary influences (in this case Schiller) and symbols (the ship, rather as an afterthought, stands for the Union) may have proved seductive. At any rate, it was unlucky that Arvin brought up Whitman:

It is what Whitman would call a Song for Occupations —for one Occupation of course—and it abounds in the materials of construction. . . . Almost as Whitman, one hears the sound of axes and mallets plied "with vigorous arms."

169

"A Song for Occupations" is by no means one of Whitman's great poems, but it grows out of an overpowering central impulse or perception, just as "Song of Myself" does. Life is pervasive in it. The genre painting of Longfellow's poem is all brown varnish beside it.

A few years ago Arvin published an essay on Emerson that seemed to me one of the most perceptive discussions of him I had ever read. This is the kind of distinction one rightly associates with Arvin, and one regrets he did not choose Emerson rather than Longfellow as the subject of his last book. American criticism is in Arvin's debt. Probably the best way to pay it is simply to acknowledge that *Longfellow* is much inferior to the earlier biographies, which deserve, and will have for a long time to come, distinguished status in their field.

II

SINCLAIR LEWIS: AN AMERICAN LIFE

by Mark Schorer

M ARK SCHORER'S *Sinclair Lewis: An American Life*, belongs to that peculiarly American genre of writing known as the "definitive" biography. Other books that belong in this category are Ralph L. Rusk's biography of Emerson, W. A. Swanberg's book on Dreiser, and more recently, Carlos Baker's life of Hemingway. But the list is long and formidable. In the case of Schorer's biography of Lewis, his publishers announced at once that the book "will stand for years to come in the select company of definitive American biographies." The nature of the definitive biography, as conceived by blurb writers and some reviewers, will be commented on later, but one characteristic of these books may be mentioned here. The biographer-critic, or artist, who should be in control, gives way to the chronicler of the quotidian; an extended analysis of the subject's artistic production is likely to give place to the address of his tailor or the school of his analyst. In short, we learn everything except what it is important for us to know.

But I mention this important shortcoming of the "definitive" American biography as we have come to know it in order to say at once that in several important respects Schorer's book is a fortunate exception. He has included too much trivia—a few hundred pages too much. But he has also given us a very good critical analysis and evaluation of Lewis as an artist. When we have broken and cleaved our way through the unpruned biographical irrelevancies, we find ourselves in the presence of a comprehensive critical statement, fine enough, judicious enough, to revive the spent spirit.

As an artist Lewis does not present a difficult case. "Perhaps it is futile," Schorer says at one point, "to approach any Lewis novel as a work of art." This is the cornerstone of his critical edifice, and while the observation is perhaps easily made, it is right. Most of all, it must have required critical courage to state so simply such a truth about a novelist to whom one had just dedicated nine years of one's life. Nothing is easier to concede than that Lewis never rose to be an artist, but the case is, after all, more complicated than that. The four or five major novels retain, even today, a gaily gruesome attraction, and while *Elmer Gantry* is by no means Lewis's best work, there are many better American novels one would more willingly relinquish. In odd and oblique ways, American art would be much poorer without these rather artless books. It is his sense of this paradox that gives strength to Schorer's evaluation.

Part of Lewis's appeal arises from the fact that he seems to write from a much earlier American world than that of his contemporaries, and his satiric bitterness is qualified by a nostalgic glow. Schorer analyzes this quality well when, commenting on certain tensions in Lewis's sensibility, he writes:

It is precisely this complex of qualities in the novels of Sinclair Lewis that marks him as having been formed before 1914 and sets him off sharply from only slightly younger writers who matured during the First World War and were publishing their exciting early books— *The Great Gatsby*, *The Sun Also Rises*, *Manhattan Transfer*, *Soldier's Pay*—simultaneously with Lewis's big ones. The same complex of qualities revealed in the early novels remains in the big books and all through his decline to his last book in 1951, and beside the work of these younger men, even in the 1920s, even the big books already seemed in some ways curiously old-fashioned. It was an older America than theirs that Lewis loved and praised and chided, and an older vision that supported his effort.

In fact, what one assumes to have been Lewis's satiric formula in creating characters like Babbitt and Dodsworth had been more than anticipated as early as James Fenimore Cooper's satiric novels. Steadfast Dodge from *Homeward Bound* (1838) might have come straight from Gopher Prairie or Zenith.[1] Cooper's prose is hardly distinguished; his intelligence is. The similarities between Dodge and Lewis's boosters are marked, but there are even more marked differences between the two authors' attitudes. For Cooper, Dodge is only contemptible, and the laughter dies away thinly in the recognition of the threat this kind of creature poses to American civilization. Dodge is completely framed by Cooper's hatred. But as Schorer recognizes, there is a curious affinity between Lewis and Babbitt that gradually moves towards identification. In *Main Street* and *Babbitt* satiric purpose wanes. Perhaps it was never really there at all. Small town values and Rotary triumph benignly in the end. It is this ambivalence of attitude that helped to guarantee Lewis's great public success. It also guaranteed his ultimate failure as an artist, and worst of all, his tragic failure as a human being.

Schorer's account of Lewis's preparations and research for the major novels is valuable. The pages devoted to his research for *Elmer Gantry* among the ministers of Kansas City are not only as entertaining as the novel, they lift anecdotage to the level of illuminating critical comment. It is when Schorer turns his attention from the work to the man that one has some serious doubts, and here it will be necessary to return briefly to the American bias for "definitive" biogra-

1. Cooper's description of Steadfast Dodge is quoted in "James Fenimore Cooper: America's Mirror of Conscience." See pages 160–61.

phy, which might better be termed "catchall." The merits of these biographies vary greatly, but several generalizations may be made. Length (perhaps better still, poundage) is regarded as a virtue in itself. The researching or collecting rather than the evaluating intelligence is esteemed, and its invidious presence is exhibited everywhere by the undiscriminating accumulation of *facts*, collected with the obsessive compulsion of a passionately dedicated jackdaw. So much attention is paid to background that the foreground often becomes a blur. Relevance is lost, focus distorted, perspective ignored, proportion denied. My favorite passage from one of these "definitive" books comes from Ralph Rusk's *The Life of Ralph Waldo Emerson*. Here is a picture of Waldo's father, William, walking along the Boston waterfront:

If William Emerson could have found time during the overcrowded hours of May 25 to make the rounds of the waterfront and the chief business streets, he would unquestionably have been impressed by the rich stores of goods for sale. . . . Shops and warehouses were crowded with a bewildering variety of desirable things: silk ribbons, men's silk hats, Italian artificial flowers, Roman violin strings, marble chimney pieces with hearths to match, thousands of excellent Havana segars, fine flour, first and second quality ship bread, haddock, pollock, herring, mackerel, hundreds of quintals of codfish and barrels of alewives and hogsheads of molasses, boxes of white and brown Havana sugar, Canton sugar, Calcutta sugar, Welsh's fresh chocolate, numerous chests of fresh hyson and hyson skin and bohea and Souchong tea, tons of the best green coffee, bottled cider, pipes of country gin and Rotterdam gin, St. Vincent's rum, cherry rum, New England rum, St. Kitt's and Granada rum, London porter, cognac, sherry, Madeira, Lisbon and Vidonia and Málaga wines, Bordeaux claret, table beer and strong beer by the barrel, kegs of tobacco, boxes of Turkish figs, prunes, muscatel raisins, fresh oranges, lemons, apricots, Baltimore flour, Richmond flour, pork, casks of rice, nuts, seeds, tons of whale oil, Georgia upland cotton and cotton from the Carolinas, hemp, bales of Madras handkerchiefs, umbrellas, fans, gloves, hose, ear jewels, ear hoops and knots, English and Genevan watches, finger rings, knee buckles, swords and hangers, gold and silver and tinsel epaulettes, satins, laces, broadcloths, calicoes, ginghams, cassimeres, chintz, Marseille quiltings, sprigged and tamboured muslin, long lawns, Irish linens, sheeting, diapers, shawls, black and coloured hats for men, razors, straw hats and bonnets as high as $15 each, fancy rosettes, veils, cloaks, mantels, silk gloves, superfine fancy colored kid gloves and shoes of the same material, sewing silks of all kinds, nankeens, dimities, elegant morocco and cabinet work, shaving and dressing cases, satteen wood tea caddies with cut glass sugar basins, elegant family medicine chests, paints and water colors in scores of varieties.

One is impressed by the extensive research among old lading bills and the advertisements of ancient Boston newspapers that must have gone towards compiling this list, meant to add verisimilitude to a walk there is no reason for supposing William Emerson to have taken. One is no less surprised at the materiality of the thoughts that were engaging William's mind the morning he took this hypothetical walk. But surely it would be better to sacrifice the "definitive" in such a passage to the interests of the relevant. Schorer is not guilty of this kind of excess, but neither is he altogether innocent. I find the footnote with which he ends his book interesting in this respect. It is concerned with weather conditions in Rome the day Sinclair Lewis died, and it says in part:

It may still have been raining on January 10, 1951. Roman weather reports, even on outlying districts like Monte Mario, are no doubt available to anyone who wishes to continue these researches. *Per me ho finito.*

The sigh of relief with which Schorer must have ended his nine years of labor seems clearly registered in that concluding sentence: *Per me ho finito.* And his specific suggestion for continued research into the "climate" of Lewis's background I am inclined to think of as ironical. But then again, in view of much of the evidence provided by the biographical portions of the book, one wonders.

In dealing with the novels, Schorer discovered the right attitude: the stance of the good critic who is dedicated to his task, and who knows what he wants to say. The problem of finding the proper attitude towards Lewis himself is much more difficult, and here the role of literary critic is not entirely helpful. It is not until the closing pages, when Schorer approaches Lewis with something of the imaginative insight of the novelist, that a satisfactory relation is established between them. During much of the book Schorer seems to be hiding his embarrassment with Lewis's personality by concentrating on "definitive" spadework until the uncovered data towers so high we almost lose sight of Lewis himself. Schorer, in a rather dry analysis of Lewis's character, puts his finger on the difficulty:

One might list his conflicting qualities in opposite columns and suggest that there were two selves in Sinclair Lewis; but all these qualities existed together and simultaneously in him, and in their infinite, interacting combinations there must have been not two but six or eight or ten or two hundred selves and, because they could never be one, a large hole in the center. When he peered into that, what could we expect him to see?

176

A much more interesting question for us is what we could expect Schorer to see. Confusion is not complexity, a mere multiplicity of "selves" is not richness of organization, and one understands that a personality dominated by "a large hole in the center" will not easily become the beautiful form of any book of which it is the subject. But it is more difficult to understand why Schorer decided to throw vast—*really vast!*—quantities of literary refuse in the form of anecdotes, gossip, and circumstantial detail down that hole in the hope of filling it up. The hole remains as empty as ever because, as Schorer knows so well, Lewis had no real artistic or creative identity at all.

It is interesting to inquire why, in the last pages, Schorer is able to deal so much more satisfactorily with Lewis than in the earlier parts. I believe it is because he finds it possible to place the human wreck that Lewis became in a literary context at last, to see him as part of a pattern larger than himself. Perhaps it is too much to ask anyone to relate Sinclair Lewis, the best-selling novelist, the bumptious Rotarian, the American boob, to any significant literary meaning. The imagination balks. Paradoxically, the dying alcoholic, wracked with delirium tremens and suffering from a painful skin disease, distrusting and rejecting his friends, is a more impressive man than Schorer has had to deal with before. At the end, Lewis may not assume the dignity of a tragic character, but the horror of that death seems laden with meaning. At one point Schorer quotes Hemingway's well-known remark: "We do not have great writers. Something happens to our writers at a certain age. . . . You see we make our writers into something very strange. . . . We destroy them in many ways." It comes as something of a shock that it is Sinclair Lewis of all writers who proves this most in our century—more even than Hart Crane and Scott Fitzgerald. That Schorer makes this clear in the last part of his book is one of his achievements, but that the earlier parts of the book are not directed towards this discovery more consciously and deliberately is unfortunate. But this, of course, is one of the penalties of being "definitive."

However, it is graceless to complain, because when Schorer does make his point he makes it with a macabre magnificence I have not encountered since the funeral of Gloria Swanson's chimpanzee in *Sunset Boulevard*. The remarkable description of Lewis's first heart-attack in Florence has become my favorite piece of American Gothic writing:

> Parties . . . did not interest him very much any more, as, alone in his house, he slumped into a long bout of reckless, solitary drinking. Then finally, on one wild stormy December night, a telephone call came from Lady Una Troubridge to Dr. Vincenzo Lapiccirella, a distinguished and cultivated Florentine diagnostician and cardiologist. He must come at once to Villa La Costa! The wind roared in the cypresses, rain tumbled from the black skies in torrents, the doctor lost his way and found it again, came finally to the great door and pounded on it only to have it opened and slammed in his face by a servant who did not know that he had been called. A dog came bounding round the corner of the house and added its barking to the tumult. The doctor pounded again, this time to be admitted and to meet Alexander Manson, who took him to the upper floor. Past the two bathrooms out of Hollywood (one apple-green, one orchid, the two separated by a wall consisting chiefly of an illuminated aquarium in which huge goldfish swam lazily back and forth) he entered the master bedroom, a large chamber that, with all its new green-and-gold furniture in heavy Renaissance imitation, seemed crowded. Here there was no respite from the gilt: on the doors, on the ceiling, on the fireplace, on the wide headboard of the bed where lay this incredibly

178

ugly man, red-faced and drunk. He had suffered his first heart-attack. . . .

Dr. Lapiccirella, who had seen some lepers, feared that it was leprosy that afflicted Lewis, and he took him to Dr. Marcello Comel, one of the finest dermatologists in Europe, who was then in the medical school at Pisa.

I suspect that this passage will fix the image of Sinclair Lewis in our imagination, just as few of us ever think of Bertrans de Born except as Dante saw him in Hell with his severed head swinging like a lantern from his hand. We are amazed to find that Lewis had such potentialities in him after all. The exaggerated theatricality of this passage—the roaring cypresses, the black torrents, the barking dog, the fantastic baths—are right. No other inverted commas could possibly enclose this literary career, at the end, in its proper, final frame. And Dr. Lapiccirella's ghastly suspicion has, in context at least, the effect of a symbolic judgment reaching all the way back to Sauk Centre, Minnesota.

Schorer's publishers have referred to this biography as "a monumental study." It is. But I hope that sometime Schorer will add a couple of months to the nine years he has already devoted to it, and chip out the perfect book on Sinclair Lewis that is at present walled up in its "definitive" crypt, and screaming to be freed.

III

MR. CLEMENS AND MARK TWAIN

by Justin Kaplan

O NE EVENING, so the story goes, when Mark Twain was in London he dined out in society with Whistler and Henry James, and the latter, broaching a subject that seemed innocently appropriate for the occasion, inquired: "Do you know Bret Harte?" "Yes," Twain replied, "I know the son of a bitch." Justin Kaplan in his new biography of Mark Twain regretfully acknowledges the story may be apocryphal; but even if it is, Twain and James achieve in the exchange that unity in dissimilarity that is often said to characterize the best images of metaphysical poetry.

It is well known that neither Twain nor James had any admiration for the other's work. Nevertheless, there has been a persistent tendency on the part of critics to pause from time to time from more strenuous reflections and imagine the two in some kind of relation. One of the first to do so was Edmund Wilson, who, in "The Ambiguity of Henry James," wrote: "It is curious to compare *A Sense of the Past* with *A Connecticut Yankee in King Arthur's Court*, with which it really has a good deal in common." Wilson's remark is more than a passing insight: It marks an important conjunction in the orbits of two major American writers who are moving in opposite directions. But even before Wilson, Constance Rourke in *American Humor* wrote of Christopher Newman in James's *The American:* "He might have been in San Francisco or Virginia City with Mark Twain; he had the habits of the time and place."

Such examples could be multiplied very easily. Later we

shall glance at one of the reasons why critics are disposed to associate two writers so unlike: but here one may simply observe that, in a curious way, Twain's attitudes sometimes appear to be a kind of distorting mirror held up to James's. "It was wonderful to find America, but it would have been more wonderful to miss it," Twain caused Pudd'nhead Wilson, who is a persona of himself, to write in his calendar. James never held a sentiment even remotely like that, but old-time critics sometimes thought he did, and Twain's attitudes often conform with remarkable fidelity to the erroneous image of James that once circulated in this country among American literary patriots.

The so-called definitive edition of Twain's work is in thirty-seven volumes. Probably the collected edition of no other major American writer contains so uneven a body of work, or work whose attitudes and point-of-view are so uncertain and wavering. Twain criticism has, for the most part, showed remarkable efficiency in recognizing the several masterpieces, and in sifting, among the remainder, the good from the indifferent and the inept. In what is probably the best critical book on the work itself, *Mark Twain: The Development of a Writer*, Henry Nash Smith writes: "The main line of his development lies in the long preoccupation with the Matter of Hannibal and the Matter of the River that is recorded in 'Old Times' and *The Adventures of Tom Sawyer* and reaches a climax in his book about 'Tom Sawyer's Comrade. Scene: The Mississippi Valley. Time: Forty to Fifty Years Ago.' "

"Old Times on the Mississippi" is the seven installments published in *The Atlantic Monthly* in 1875, to which Twain subsequently made the disappointing additions that rounded them out to book size under the title *Life on the Mississippi*. The collected edition contains a good many titles of interest and importance beyond the three named above; but the point is that in the work of no other great American writer is the discrepancy between the best, the average, and the worst so great. It is rather as if Emily Brontë, having written *Wuthering Heights*, had gone on to write *East Lynne*, *Lady Audley's Secret*, and *Three Weeks*. Perhaps one's bewilderment arises not because the worst is so bad (which it isn't, except in a few unimportant instances) but because the best is so superb that one is oppressed by a sense of grotesque incongruity.

This kind of discrepancy does not exist, for example, in the collected novels of Fenimore Cooper, about whom Twain was so unfairly insulting. A good deal of Cooper may be virtually unreadable today, but the thirty and some volumes that make up the collected edition are informed by political, social, and moral attitudes that are consistent and constant, and by a play of intelligence that is only dimmed because Cooper comes through as a genuine artist in only a handful of his novels. And certainly this discrepancy does not exist in The New York Edition of James, where themes, attitudes, and technique are all the product of a creative sensibility intellectually and emotionally at ease with itself. This results from a seriousness of creative purpose that Twain seems only occasionally, and never consciously, to possess. Both Cooper and James are always in dead earnest when they write. Neither could be deflected from his purpose, whatever the cost to his personal popularity or prosperity. Refusing to compromise with the failures of their society as each understood them, they incorporated their insights and their dissatisfactions in their fiction in such a way that there is an organic connection between their art and their social values. The fiction of each is continuous with, not disjunct from, the social and political world in which he lives. For them writing was a form of practical action by which they tried to make their critical vision effectively operative, and so through their writing they achieved an integration of themselves as men and artists.

Twain was a greater artist, if a less critically intelligent man, than Cooper; his native endowment of genius may even have approached James's, though this is a highly risky speculation. But he lacked—and lacked ruinously—the kind of integration, that continuity between the outer and the inner worlds, that characterized the other two novelists. Something like this interpretation of Twain as man and artist was first advanced in 1920 in Van Wyck Brooks's *The Ordeal of Mark Twain*, Brooks's best book, and one of the best interpretations of an American writer we have, despite the disagreement and controversy it has provoked for more than forty years. Commenting on the sense of guilt, the pessimism, and the self-accusations that steadily increased as Twain grew older. Brooks wrote:

> It is an established fact, if I am not mistaken, that these morbid feelings of sin, which have no evident cause, are the results of having transgressed some inalienable life-demand peculiar to one's nature. It is as old as Milton that there are talents which are "death to hide," and I suggest that Mark Twain's "talent" was just so hidden. That bitterness of his was the effect of a certain miscarriage in his creative life, a balked personality, an arrested development of which he was himself almost wholly unaware, but which for him destroyed the meaning of life.

In such a view any critical evaluation of Twain's achievement in art must necessarily look for corroboration to the facts of biography. Brooks's volume relied heavily on biographical background in making its case, but *The Ordeal of Mark Twain* remains essentially an interpretative criticism— an attempt to understand the limitations of Twain's genius through the frustrating social and cultural conditions in which he passed his life. An interpretation of this kind is not a biography in any strict sense, and such biographies as we have possessed, beginning with Albert B. Paine's authorized life, have in various ways been unsatisfactory. Justin Kap-

lan's *Mr. Clemens and Mark Twain* is now not only the best
life of Twain that we possess, but it is also one of the best
among those long, detailed, and "definitive" biographies of
American literary figures that have appeared with somewhat
monotonous regularity from our presses over the past fifteen
years or more.

Kaplan's book is long—388 pages of actual text; but it is
not as long as these "definitive" American biographies,
which sometimes seem to have replaced the late Victorian
vogue for the three-volume novel, usually are, and Kaplan's
discretion here has given him a strong advantage. His Twain
is not buried under a plethora of information. Details are
plentiful, but handled with a discriminating sense of relevance and proportion. The result is that we have a finely
rendered portrait of a man and a personality, not an anatomy
chart. And it *is* a portrait, in the true sense of the word, that
we are given. Mr. Kaplan appears to urge no particular
interpretation of Twain on the reader, but to allow the days
and the years of his life to speak for themselves. Nevertheless, behind this seemingly artless presentation there is a firm
and controlling conception of what Twain was, and what
made him so.

Although Kaplan mentions Van Wyck Brooks at no point,
in important respects his Twain is very much the same divided and frustrated figure that we encounter in *The Ordeal*
—in this strictly biographical context all the more convincing
because Kaplan's intentions appear to be so little polemical.
There are differences in interpretative details, of course. In
Kaplan's account, Twain's wife, Livy, is much more attractive—not at all the restraining and defeating influence on his
art she appeared to be to Brooks. And as Kaplan really begins
his narrative only at the end of 1866, when Twain sailed
from California for New York, where he was to be the
correspondent for the San Francisco *Alta California* during
the next year, we are given no detailed account of his boyhood

and youth. Hence, the disastrous influence of his mother, Jane Clemens, in laying the deadly hand of convention and conformity on her son, of which Brooks makes so much, is not treated at all.

We begin, in effect, with the young writer who, back from his trip to the Holy Land on the *Quaker City*, and having already written *The Innocents Abroad*, is about to marry the daughter of the coal and iron monopolist Jervis Langdon. Although Twain was already a nationally known writer of humorous sketches with substantial expectations, the contrast between the young Westerner of modest origins and the coal tycoon of Elmira, New York, who embodied on a moderate scale (the Langdon household expenses ran to $40,000 a year) the opulent positives of what Twain would soon christen the Gilded Age, was dazzling to him. But it was even more frightening. Few of his contemporaries reacted more strongly against the business and financial corruption of the age than Twain did, and there is plenty of evidence that when he permitted himself he saw through his father-in-law (who wanted Twain to write a life of Christ) clearly enough. But if he deplored the age, it was quite a different thing when it came to deploring his father-in-law, who was one of its representatives. So Twain had to arrive at a workable *modus vivendi* with a great deal that he hated most, while ostensibly keeping his hands and his conscience clean.

"Mark Twain," writes Kaplan, "all his life had plutocratic ambitions but at the same time believed that money was evil and created evil." During most of his career he squandered many thousands of dollars promoting get-rich-quick schemes, usually in the form of some mechanical gadget— or sometimes a protein food supplement, or a self-pasting scrapbook of his own invention. When the fortune he had sunk in the Paige typesetting machine drew him into bankruptcy, his good angel turned out to be a man whom he hardly knew, Henry Huttleston Rogers (otherwise known as

"Hell Hound" Rogers), one of the major figures in the Standard Oil trust and a symbol of all that was least attractive in American financial and business philosophy of the period. "We are not in business for our health, but are out for the dollars," Kaplan quotes him as telling a governmental commission. Twain had every reason to be grateful to Rogers, whose kindness and help were his financial salvation, but the friendship serves to illuminate the conflict of motives that ravaged Twain to the end of his life, the ease with which sentiment blotted out critical intelligence. "He is not only the best friend I ever had," Twain wrote of Rogers in 1902, "but is the best man I have ever known." When Charles Dudley Warner suggested to Twain that he might profitably and appropriately become the publisher of Henry Demarest Lloyd's *Wealth Against Commonwealth*, a book attacking the "Standard Oil fiends," the co-author of *The Gilded Age*, according to Kaplan, "swallowed his rage and the temptation to tell Warner that it was one of those fiends who . . . was keeping him and his family out of the poorhouse."

This ambivalent attitude towards American wealth and the kind of society promoted by its pursuit amounts to a genuine confusion in Twain's thinking and writing. And it is matched by a corresponding ambiguity of attitude towards Europe and England. The engaging old man who liked to entertain wearing the scarlet academic gown he had acquired when Oxford gave him an honorary degree felt an emotional affection for England that was extremely remote from the crass American cynicism mouthed by the narrator of *The Innocents Abroad* towards the past and everything European. When Twain went to England in 1872 to collect material for a satire on the English, he fell in love with the island and the people. "I would rather live in England than America—which is treason," he wrote his wife; and he said that he felt like "a Prodigal Son getting back home again." Kaplan gives an excellent analysis of Twain's feelings for the English at this point in his life:

He . . . adored the English because their way of life offered him for the first time a baseline by which he could measure his discontent with his own country, and instead of a satire on the English he wrote *The Gilded Age*, an angry and reactionary book about Americans. . . . He saw about him stability, government by a responsible elite, the acceptance of a gentleman's code. These were painful contrasts with the chicanery and cynicism, the demoralized public service, the abuse of universal suffrage and legislative power, and all the excesses and failures of American society in the 1870's going through the most dynamic but least governable phase of its growth.

Twain fell away from this earlier enthusiasm, but if *A Connecticut Yankee in King Arthur's Court*, published in 1886, is badly marred by Anglophobia, it is also a novel, as Henry Nash Smith has shown in his detailed discussion of it in *The Development of a Writer*, which is built upon unresolved ambiguities and confusions of attitude of which Twain is not even conscious. Hank Morgan, the Connecticut mechanic who undertakes to industrialize and republicanize sixth-century Britain, ends up with a desecrated country and twenty-five thousand rotting corpses he has electrocuted. The stench from which threatens his own life. "So much for the ideals and achievements of nineteenth-century American civilization!" Twain might be saying. Of course he meant to say, and thought he *was* saying, something quite different, and so did the enthusiastic American audience for whom he wrote the book. But the unresolved ambiguity is there, a literary memorial to a lifelong personality split.

In his reactions to great wealth Twain never managed to achieve that purity of vision with which Henry James wrote *The Ivory Tower*—or that part of it which he finished. But the extraordinary thing is that so far as his hands and conscience went, Twain did manage to keep them reasonably clean. It was his art that ended up by being harmed because it was rarely able to bridge the gap between his sense of what was wrong with the times and his personal commitments to his family, friends, and society. Kaplan, like Van Wyck Brooks before him, recognizes Twain's moral and emotional schizophrenia as the radical flaw in his creative temperament. Like Brooks, Kaplan finds in Twain's story "Those Extraordinary Twins," which deals with the temperamental conflict of Siamese twins who share only one pair of legs between them, a symbol of the destructive tension in Twain's own personality. On the subject of Twain's split identity Kaplan writes:

> Twinship was one of Mark Twain's favorite subjects, often one of his fatal temptations. He could manipulate it into melodrama and farce by exploiting its possibilities and surprises and discoveries. *Pudd'nhead Wilson* became viable only after the *débridement* of a "comedy" called *Those Extraordinary Twins*. But twinship, along with the cognate subject of claimants of all sorts, also offered Clemens an enormously suggestive if misleadingly simple way of objectifying the steadily deepening sense of internal conflict and doubleness which is suggested by two sets of near homonyms: Twain/twins and Clemens/claimants. And soon he would begin to explore the doubleness of Samuel L. Clemens and Mark Twain through concepts of "dual personality," "conscience," and, toward the end of his life, a "dream self" that seemed to lead a separate life.

One begins to perceive at least one reason why, against all the evidence, critics have so often tended to associate the names of Twain and Henry James in the manner described earlier. The cultural polarity represented by Europe and America, which is at the center of James's fiction, has its fragmentary counterpart in the double commitment of Twain to the integrity of his own creative conscience, and to the values represented by the age in which he lived. On the level at which James approached the problem of two ostensibly opposed sets of values, an imaginative synthesis could be realized in art, but for Twain each commitment was irrevocably opposed to the other, and so his double allegiance was destined to remain a pair of monstrous twins. It was only when he rejected the claims of the present altogether, and the responsibilities imposed by his society and family, and retreated to the past—to the Matter of Hannibal and the Matter of the River—that he was free at last to realize the full potential of his genius.

Towards the end of his life when he felt freer to speak out, to write as he would against the false values of his age, a synthesis between the two commitments was still impossible in his art; for he found that he was no longer committed to anything at all except, to use a phrase of his own, the Great Dark. Out of this Darkness came the most interesting of his second-rank novels, *The Mysterious Stranger*, and several fragments of nihilistic stories, interesting indeed but easily overestimated in an age like ours. The kind of mordant despair that Twain embraced in his last years was as little likely to produce the creative tensions essential to great work as that deflection of his satiric genius into "safe" channels of indignation that, through his prime, left his prosperity and popularity unchallenged.

The Twain whom Kaplan gives us shares a great deal with the Twain that Van Wyck Brooks gave us nearly half a century ago. In saying this, one has no intention of suggesting that Kaplan has necessarily been influenced by Brooks. Kaplan's Twain is before us as the solid and convincing result of many years of discriminating labor. Brooks's Twain has often been under critical attack, and so it is good to have, in support of the only credible Twain, this authoritative and strongly corroborative study.

Biographers working on the scale of Kaplan are often inclined to scant their critical chores, and trace the genesis and reception of an author's books, or their autobiographical content, rather than attempt an evaluation of them as art. But one cannot have a "literary" biography without the literature, and in his treatment of Twain's work Kaplan shows himself to be a thoroughly reliable and astute critic. This indeed is one of the strong points of the biography. In a work of this nature a series of detailed critiques of the individual books and stories would be out of place; but it is clear that Kaplan has made them in the abbreviated critical comments he permits himself. It is his critical understanding of Twain's books, his trained ability to measure either literary success or failure, that leads him by a direct and economical route to so firm and convincing a portrayal of so difficult and ambiguous a subject.

PROBLEMS OF AMERICAN
CULTURAL HISTORY

I

O STRANGE NEW WORLD

by Howard Mumford Jones

Howard Mumford Jones could probably best be described as a cultural historian. That is how he is described on the dust jacket of his recent book, *O Strange New World*. The chief interest of this book may well lie in certain questions it raises implicitly, and leaves unresolved, about the nature of cultural history itself. I know of no attempt to make a neat and succinct formulation of its problems and goals comparable to the late A. O. Lovejoy's essay "The Historiography of Ideas." No doubt the reason is that the general term *cultural history* is too broad, and admits of too many approaches, to tolerate a definition or even a description that would be adequately or usefully delimiting. Nevertheless, cultural history demands, even more than political, military, or economic history, a rigorously defined perspective, a firmly held criterion of relevance, and a keenly developed sensibility that has been trained in literature and the arts. Cultural history more than any other kind exercises the creative faculty and makes the heaviest demands on critical discrimination. Scholarship and breadth of erudition are not secondary, but they are pointless without these other qualities that can put them effectively to work.

O Strange New World appears to be almost disastrously deficient in all these qualities. In the concluding paragraph of his book, Jones asks: "Who was this new man, this American? We do not yet know. But finding an answer to Crèvecoeur's famous query dominates our cultural history for decades." This, I suppose, is the question on which the ten chapters composing the body of the book converge, and the chapters are to be taken as separate but related essays, each treating a distinct component or factor in the tradition that, beginning with the sixteenth century, has gone to make up this still unknown quantity—an American.

When Crèvecoeur first asked this question in the 1780's it had a good deal of point; but although it has been asked so often in this century that it is in some danger of becoming a chestnut, one wonders if there is much sense in asking it at all. If we still do not know what an American is, as Jones says, it may be because the question is not absolute in itself, and carries as many possible answers as there are persons to address themselves to it. *O Strange New World* adopts the paradoxical strategy of exploring and illuminating the character and reality of this *still unknown* American by sifting a mass of historical evidence from the sixteenth century to the mid-nineteenth—thereby using the *unrevealed* as the criterion of relevance by which to select and discriminate among the limitless clutter of facts. As a result, the figure of this American sometimes seems more in danger of being buried under information than excavated from it. In the end, neither a sharper definition of the American essence, nor a new illumination of our historical past, is achieved. Instead we are given facts whose interrelationships are examined under somewhat arbitrary chapter headings that may, indeed, shackle them together, but nowhere succeed in revealing an organic or living unity among them.

Jones undertakes to show us the slowly evolving American against the largest possible geographical and temporal background. In theory this is admirable, for every moment of time is, in one sense, rooted in all the ages. In practice, however, this plan soon encounters difficulties. There is a distinct limit to the amount of material on which a scholar who is not also a greatly gifted creative mind can impose form and imaginative order. Jones is, of course, a scholar of large erudition in his field, but it is an erudition that sometimes behaves on wanton associationist principles in this book.

Space does not permit a detailed analysis of the material in any one chapter, but one might consider the opening ten-page section of Chapter VIII, "Roman Virtue," in which the impact of the classical tradition on the new nation is considered. After being told that we were never part of the Roman Empire, and that "no battered statues are dug up in America as they are dug up in Greece or Israel or Italy," we are given a description of the classical motifs on the great seal of the United States, and something is said of classical iconography on early American coins and medals. We are told in considerable detail about the Latin mottoes on the great seals of twenty states, and this somehow moves into a discussion of James Russell Lowell's "Commemoration Ode" of 1865. Several pages are then devoted to the recovery of classical antiquity during the Renaissance, with selected anecdotes, and after a paragraph on Ivan III, who, by marrying in 1472 the niece of Constantine Paleologus, last Emperor of Byzantium, projected the idea of Moscow as the third Rome, we are shown George Washington, "the Cincinnatus of the West," who "took his oath of office on the balcony of the 'classical'

United States building in New York City and became president of a new republic eight times as large as the Republic of
Rome when Rome included all Italy." The next two pages
concern themselves with the vitality of the classical tradition
from the fifteenth century. We are in at the excavation of the
Laocoön, see the Apollo Belvedere set up in the Vatican, hear
words of praise for Elizabethan translations of the classics,
are reminded that Spenser "portrays English rustics conversing as he thought Roman or Greek shepherds might have
talked," and that "Ralegh's *History of the World* comes
down to the period when Macedonia became a Roman province." On the next page we are shown Jefferson in Paris
designing the Virginia capitol in the classical manner, are
told of the popularity of Piranesi etchings of Roman ruins
with wealthy Americans, are referred to Healy's "charming
if sentimental picture of Longfellow and his daughter Edith
under the arch of Titus," and after additional references to
Byron, Hawthorne, and Mark Twain, are informed that "the
long, continuous emotional thrust of antiquity into the United
States [is] not quite validated by Elizabeth Taylor in *Cleopatra*." This is cultural history as Leonard Lyons might write
it up, and it not surprising that the index runs to thirty
columns of very small type.

Although the last three sections of Chapter VIII are a little
more concentrated, the general impression is of facts as thick
as crab grass across the lawn of history. But more serious
than their proliferation is the more than passing doubt one
feels about Jones's dealings with them. He is, for example,
much concerned with the idea of a Machiavellian tradition in
the New World. One agrees with him of course in rejecting
those older writers who tried to suggest that the nastier
aspects of human nature were washed away by the sea spray
when the white man first invaded this continent; but an
elaborate theory about Machiavelli and America, which the
facts hardly seem to support, is not necessary to explain why

194

human behavior remained constant. Jones has erred in requiring what is at best a pseudo-idea to bear a weight in his argument that is beyond its strength. As part of his strategy for integrating America with the European past, his development of the Machiavellian tradition in the American wilderness invites a closer glance.

Machiavelli is carefully prepared for in the text by several pages on the horrifying crimes of the Italian tyrants that might have been torn out of J. A. Symonds' *The Age of the Despots*, and Machiavelli is given in his own person as much space as John Adams, twice as much as Alexander Hamilton, a third more than George Washington, and only slightly less than Jefferson. Jones is of course arguing that the condition of the New World, remote from royal authority and control, called for qualities of force, ruthlessness, and duplicity of leadership that had been recommended in *Il Principe*. It is well known that Ralegh was a serious student of Machiavelli, but apart from him there is virtually no evidence that any of the conquistadors, buccaneers, explorers, and frontiersmen whom Jones puts in the tradition had ever read him. Certainly none of the Indians, who are also placed in the tradition, had done so: and although Jones, in somewhat muffled tones, asserts that "some knowledge, however slight, of such Renaissance authors as Machiavelli, Cervantes, and Shakespeare" persisted through the Colonial period, it is difficult to suppose that Henry Morgan or Captain Kidd was much influenced by the dubious Florentine. Yet repeatedly Jones *implies*, without affirming, the existence of a very palpable tradition of Machiavellianism in America. He sees it (p. 145) as somehow involved "in California during the gold rush to the Klondike."

The existence of this tradition is never established by anything approaching a demonstration, but by a curious performance of scholarly legerdemain it is insistently present. One cannot even be sure of the kind of claims Jones is really making for it because his prose, when he speaks of it, is kept at a level of baffling ambiguity:

> The lack of any definitive study of the vogue of Machiavelli in North America seems to indicate that *Il Principe* has no such influence as the cult of the gentleman. But the central issue is, as I have said, not one of influence but of conduct, and it seems unlikely that the powerful traditions we have been discussing died out and left no aftermath. What happened was that the Machiavellian theory of power, so far as the mainland colonies were concerned, seemed to split into two parts. One has to do with terror as an instrument of policy, and the other with cunning.

I do not know what any of this means. If American conduct on the frontier and in the wilderness grew directly out of the environment and its dangers, then the question of Machiavelli's "influence" is irrelevant, and probably nonexistent, and need not be raised. For a moment this seems to be what Jones is saying. But then he speaks at once of the "Machiavellian theory of power" splitting into two parts, and we are back on the level of "influence" again rather than of conduct, and the rather sly reference to the nineteenth-century cult of the gentleman, which certainly *did* exist, seems to be introduced chiefly for the sake of conferring by association some of its reality on the cult of the "Machiavels," whose existence Jones has certainly not proved.

The existence of this tradition becomes even more questionable as we advance towards the present. Jones admits he does not know whether Frank Norris ever read Machiavelli, but it would be "a nice exercise in logical discrimination" to distinguish between Machiavelli's concept of power and Norris's concept of force in *The Octopus*. Mentioning the novelist Winston Churchill, whose fictional character Jethro Bass manipulates the New Hampshire legislature in a way that reminds him of Cesare Borgia, Jones remarks: "Machiavellianism, whether as finesse, fraud, or force, has long been a standard component of American political life."

I said earlier that Machiavellianism in America seems in this book to be less an idea than a pseudo-idea; but even worse, it becomes at last little more than the abuse of a word. Jones is sorely beset in this book by a specific problem and a specific temptation. The problem that plagues him—as it does many cultural historians, especially American ones—is the problem of relevance and proportion in dealing with factual data. He riddles the target with the introduction of names like Constantine Paleologus and Ivan III, but leaves the bull's eye ("Who is this new man, this American?") intact. The temptation he is unable to resist is that of conferring an importance and status on a phantom idea (Machiavellianism in America) which is not inherent in the situation or the data he is examining, but is wheeled forward under special lighting for the given occasion.

II

PATRIOTIC GORE
by Edmund Wilson

IT IS AN unusual American who hasn't an abolitionist or a planter hiding in him somewhere. This kind of partisanship is not complicated, and neither for the most part are the books on the Civil War that it produces. Edmund Wilson's *Patriotic Gore: Studies in the Literature of the Civil War* is a good deal more complex than that. I believe some critics have found it simply pro-Confederate in sympathy, but his attitudes towards the issues involved are sufficiently elusive to exonerate him from conventional allegiance to either side, and they call for close examination. Rewarding as the book is in most respects, certain questions never seem to be satisfactorily resolved. Wilson judges the Civil War from his appalled sense of what he believes to be its consequences in the present. What he abhors in the modern world he abhors with good reason, but the historical genealogy of these abominations is neither convincingly nor forthrightly presented here. This is a slighter qualification of the book's merits than one might suppose, but it should be appreciated from the first. Wilson is profoundly opposed to certain forces or tendencies in the modern state that he regards as far more sinister than anything to be found in Confederate ideology. These tendencies were given a tremendous impetus by the Civil War and by the philosophy of government developed in the North both during and after the conflict. Hence the war as a whole, but particularly the North's role in it, is open to grave censure.

It may be possible to understand Wilson's position more

198

clearly by comparing his attitude to the Confederacy with his attitude to the American Indians. Several years ago, in *Apologies to the Iroquois*, Wilson wrote an admirable exposé of those processes of coercion and bureaucratic bullying by which the state in our time is able to impose its will on a minority—or even on an apathetic majority—at the expense of individual rights and decency. Wilson was dealing with the shameful attempt of the Power Authority of New York under the chairmanship of that Apostle of Leveling, Robert Moses, to dispossess arbitrarily a handful of Indians of a part of their reservation guaranteed to them by the existence of eighteenth century treaties. Happily in this case Moses' idea of the good life—or of life-in-death—did not prevail. In detailing the story Wilson brilliantly presented the image of the twentieth-century public servant in his most distasteful and dangerous guise: an irresponsible wielder of official authority whose idea of progress and public development is at odds with basic concepts of individual human dignity. Emotionally Mr. Wilson seems to see the war of the North against the South in somewhat the same way that he saw the war of the Power Authority of New York against the Tuscarora nation. Wilson hates the modern state with its arbitrary exercise of power and its denial of the individual's limited responsibility for the direction of events. He hates bureaucracy, governmental anonymity, the absorbent power of the Federal authority. He hates these things because they produce Power Authorities and arrogant public servants that think God created man for them. It is difficult not to hate with him. But despite the brilliance of *Patriotic Gore*, it seems doubtful if the Civil War can really be judged in a frame this narrow.

As I have already said, this book is not conventionally pro-South in the way some have suggested. In dividing the honors between the two sides Wilson is remarkably bipartisan, and those chapters are best in which he deals with persons, whether of the North or of the South, whose understanding of issues is comprehensive enough to confer a dialectical centrality on their thought. The essay on Alexander H. Stephens, the Vice President of the Confederacy, is especially suggestive of the nature of Wilson's partisanship—such as it is. After a vivid sketch of Stephens' character the essay concerns itself principally with his political philosophy as presented in his monumental work, *A Constitutional View of the Late War Between the States*. Perhaps this work may have suggested the form in which *Patriotic Gore* itself is written. It consists of colloquies which, as Wilson describes the work, "take place between Stephens himself and a set of three imaginary Unionists who have come to see him at Liberty Hall. . . . The Professor, the Judge and the Major are allowed to express themselves, to counter the statements of Stephens with their Unionist version of recent events. . . ." The contending voices of the two sides, present in Wilson's book by copious quotation, must have a somewhat similar effect. Stephens' constitutional philosophy, which Wilson describes at some length, is based on the legality of secession. This is of course a self-contained point that is not directly related to the question of slavery, and if there is an implicit assumption running through *Patriotic Gore*, it seems to be that Stephens had the better of the argument with his Unionist friends. It is easy to understand Wilson's partiality for Stephens. He goes to the heart of the matter when he says: "The 'Monster,' as he calls it, that Stephens fears is 'the Demon of Centralism, Absolutism, Despotism'; and the warning against the danger of this is the burden of all his post-war writing." In many respects Stephens was one of the most admirable figures of the Confederacy. He nearly broke with Jefferson Davis when the latter found it necessary to restrict civil rights in the South in the prosecution of the war. Wilson quotes Stephens as saying that he opposed "the impressment of provisions at arbitrary prices—the suspension of the Writ of *Habeas Corpus*, and the raising of the necessary military forces by conscription. These last I considered not only radically wrong in principle, but as violative of the Constitution, and as exceedingly injurious to our Cause in their effects on the people." By way of chilling contrast, Wilson has quoted a few pages earlier the remark of Lincoln's Secretary of State, Seward: "I can touch a bell on my right hand and order the arrest of a citizen of Ohio. I can touch the bell again and order the arrest of a citizen of New York. Can Queen Victoria do as much?" And then Wilson rather mischievously adds the flea circus version of this shocking utterance by quoting Robert Moses in a footnote: "I can take your house away from you and arrest you for trespassing if you try to get back into it." Clearly Stephens seems to come off well in the comparison. He is more concerned with civil rights than Lincoln was; he seems a better sort than Seward; he stands for individual dignity and is no violator of private property. Wilson and Stephens are like one man in their fear of "the Demon of Centralism," and Wilson quotes Stephens on his conception of the radically limited powers of the Presidency with pleasure.

But there is a darker side to Stephens' political theory that does not come off as well. Speaking of the role of slavery, he said that the Confederacy rested "upon the great truth that the Negro is not equal to the white man, that slavery—subordination to the superior race—is his natural and normal condition. This our new government is the first in the history of the world based upon this great physical, philosophical, and moral truth." Although Wilson does not quote this specific remark, he quotes similar ones, too long to include here, and with a complacency I find difficult to reconcile with the defender of the Iroquois. "From the moment this man of principles," he says, "has established a principle that makes slavery obligatory, every step of the course of the South follows logically from his previous postulates." Perhaps: but who can any longer put faith in Stephens' interpretation of civil rights or of the meaning of despotism? At this point the Confederacy begins to resemble the Power Authority of New York more than it does the Tuscaroras.

The "Centralism" and "Despotism" of the Federal government that were given such an impetus by the Civil War have been incredibly accelerated, Wilson would say, by the historic developments of the twentieth century, and it is from our present darkness that he views the ancient events. On the nature of this present darkness he comments in his introduction with great persuasiveness:

After [the last World War] the troops and agents of the U.S.A. moved in all over Europe and Asia, from West Germany to South Korea, and we found ourselves confronted by the Soviet Union, which was also moving in. Neither the Soviet Russians nor we were very much beloved by the peoples in upon whom they had moved. The rivalry of power units had now reached an even more gigantic scale than that of the British and German Empires. The Russians and we produced nuclear weapons to flourish at one another and played the game of calling bad names when there had been nothing at issue between us that need have prevented our living in the same world and when we were actually, for better and worse, becoming more and more alike—the Russians emulating America in their frantic industrializing and we imitating them in our persecution of non-conformist political opinion, while both, to achieve their ends, were building up huge government bureaucracies in the hands of which the people have seemed helpless. We Americans, whose public officials kept telling us we were living in "the Free World," discovered that we were expected to pay staggering taxes of which it has been estimated that 70 per cent has been going not only for nuclear weapons capable of depopulating whole countries but also for bacteriological and biological ones which made it possible for us to poison the enemy with every abominable disease from pneumonia and encephalitis to anthrax, cholrea, diptheria and typhoid, as well as with such new devices as the chemical agent called "GB," which imitates the natural weapons of the Australian stone fish and the black widow spider in paralyzing the nerves of its victims so that a drop of it no larger than a dot can kill a man in fifteen minutes. We discovered that if we should refuse to contribute to these researches, we could be fined and clapped into jail—that we could even be clapped into jail if we protested against any of this by taking part in public demonstrations. We are, furthermore, like the Russians, being spied upon by an extensive secret police whose salaries we are required to pay, as we are required to pay, also, the salaries of another corps of secret agents who are infiltrating foreign countries. And while all this expenditure is going for the purpose of sustaining the United States as a more and more unpopular world power, as few funds as possible are being supplied to educate and civilize the Americans themselves, and generations of young people are growing up who at worst live a life of gang warfare, the highest objectives of which are brawling and killing and robbing, in the buried crowded slum streets of cities outside of which they can imagine no other world, and at best find little spur to ambition when they emerge from four years in college to face two years in the armed services in preparation for further large-scale wars at the prospect of taking part in which they rarely feel the slightest enthusiasm.

This is very well said—indeed, beautifully said. The description could scarcely be bettered in itself; but the relation between this picture of horror with which Wilson introduces his essays and the Civil War itself remains, to me at least, ultimately evasive and confusing. Wilson makes it a matter of implication and suggestion rather than of clear definition and reasoned argument, but it is fairly obvious what the implications are as far as the Civil War and the guilt of the North are concerned. "The truth is that the South since the Civil War," he says, "in relation to the Washington government, has been in a state of mind that has fluctuated between that of Hungary and that of the Ukraine in relation to the government of Moscow." One is impelled to ask: If the legality of secession had been granted by the North, would it really have checked the kind of "Centralism" Wilson deplores? Could that Kafka-esque night of the modern soul he has described so well have been avoided? Had the Confederacy really been able to found a nation on Alexander Stephens' philosophy of racial inequality and subordination, would there have been any less likelihood of our persecuting nonconformist political opinion today? Despite its rather flamboyant acknowledgment of civil rights, would that political philosophy, based as it was on the cornerstone of slavery, have discouraged the Nazis? And if America now has gang warfare of the worst kind, what reasons are there for supposing that the Ku Klux Klan and the White Camellia represented higher moral types than our own juvenile criminals? Have the senators from the South represented, on the whole, an ideal of human dignity one could wish to see strengthened? Is it not possible that an independent Dixie might have become merely another political asylum for discredited European fascists?

But it would be unfair to emphasize this aspect of *Patriotic Gore* unduly. Taking the book as a whole, Wilson is not *for* the South as much as he is *against* the whole disastrous fact of the Civil War. In dealing with the men and women who were the leaders of thought and action, he measures out honors and demerits with a superbly bipartisan hand, while he sees both the North and the South falsifying equally the image of itself under which each fought the war. Any warring nation is compelled to justify itself by devising a conventional image of its aims and behavior, designed primarily to delude itself rather than the enemy. Both the North and the South created false masks through which they peered, admiring their own disguised reflections in the literature and oratory of the time. Wilson is particularly good in suggesting the existence and progress of that deliberately cultivated mystical bent that persuaded so many Northerners that the Lord had handed them His sword of vengeance. No doubt the decline of Calvinism in New England had left a residue of mystical aspirations that the more unemotional worship supplanting it could not utilize, but which the war could. Certainly there is something pathological about many of its manifestations. Wilson's discussion of Harriet Beecher Stowe's husband, Calvin Stowe, is very revealing. All his life he had had weird visions of little animated creatures, usually in human form, of "a darkly bluish color spotted with brown," who lived in constant terror of black funnel-shaped clouds that floated overhead. If one of the little creatures were touched by a cloud, "the body was drawn into the cloud and became a part of its substance. It was indeed a fearful sight," Stowe says, "to see the contortions, the agonizing efforts, of the poor creatures who had been touched by one of these awful clouds, and were dissolving and melting into it by inches without the possibility of escape or resistance." On one occasion he awakened to find a large blue skeleton in bed beside him, and Harriet herself seems to have had a *Doppelgänger* that on at least one occasion embarrassed her husband. Stowe had been born in Massachusetts and later taught at Bowdoin College. Wilson's portrait of him is suggestive of that peculiar ambience of frustrated Calvinism and mystical yearning that would help to stimulate the North's sense of divine mission.

The image the North formed of itself is better defined in the work of the almost forgotten Francis Grierson, to whom

Wilson devotes some of his most interesting pages. After Calvin Stowe, who resembled a rabbi according to George Eliot, Grierson presents an unexpected version of the Northern saint. A young man who had met him wrote: "I had never seen a man with lips and cheeks rouged and eyes darkened. His hair was arranged in careful disorder over his brow, his hands elaborately manicured and with many rings on his fingers; he wore a softly tinted flowing cravat." One can mention Grierson here only in relation to the Lincoln cult. Wilson quotes this from one of his books: "Abraham Lincoln, the greatest practical mystic the world has known for nineteen hundred years, is the one man whose life and example ought to be clearly set before the English-speaking people. . . . His genius was superhuman. And since this world is not governed by chance, a power was at work which foreordained him for his unique mission. . . . That Lincoln possessed intuition and illumination without resorting to human aid is clear. His words were simple and his actions were simple, like those of the Hebrew seers. . . ." It is perhaps appropriate that Grierson's last book, written as an old man, should have been published in Los Angeles—a series of "psycho-phone" communications from, among others, Lincoln and Grant. The Northern sense of divine mission that is found in "The Battle Hymn of the Republic," that is powerfully present to the imagination in the figure of Lincoln, and that, indeed, was a kind of holy atmosphere that the North breathed in those days, was certainly not hypocritical. Even today it has a note of irresistible beauty about it. But it was a false and dangerous image: how false, Wilson makes cruelly clear by his sharply drawn contrast between the Northern picture of the martyred God-commissioned John Brown and the barbarous reality of his murders for the Lord.

The false image of itself that the Confederacy created is less attractive and even more untrue: an artificial Walter Scott world, sentimental, intellectually deadening, devoid of

authentic values. "The Northerner as well as the South-
erner," Wilson writes, "is likely to be taken in by an historical optical illusion which makes it appear that the life of the
South in the period just before the war was still something
majestic and lovely; but we must not forget Olmstead's discovery that the 'gentry' of the 'colony days' now consisted of
a very few families 'in a region much larger than the old
German Empire.'" The reference is of course to Frederick
Olmstead, whose sociological study of the South, *The Cotton
Kingdom*, appeared in 1861. Even though the gulf between
Southern aristocratic pretensions and the reality is familiar to
modern readers through more recent books like W. J. Cash's
The Mind of the South, Wilson's full summary of the depressing conditions described in *The Cotton Kingdom* provides a richly ironic background to his scattered discussions
of the Southern code of honor, chivalry, and dueling. The
South's fatuous faith in dueling in particular arouses Wilson's contempt, and he sees in it one of the explanations for
the South's readiness to fire on Fort Sumter. Just as the
North was sincere in its belief it was divinely commissioned,
the South was no less convinced it was playing a role of
knightly heroism. But as compared with the Northern saints,
there is something a little too self-consciously histrionic about
these Southern knights. "I was better dressed that evening
than I ever was during the war," writes the Confederate
guerrilla fighter John Mosby. "Just before starting to Richmond I got through the blockade across the Potomac a complete suit from head to foot. I had a drab hat with an ostrich
plume, with gold cord and star; a heavy, black beaver-cloth
overcoat and cape lined with English scarlet cloth, and as it
was a stormy evening, over this I wore a gray cloak, also
lined with scarlet." The values of these Southerners may be
noble enough, but one thinks of artificial rather than of living
flowers. I know of nothing better on the Georgia poet Sidney
Lanier than the critical discussion of him in this book. Lanier

accomplished some interesting work, but most of the time his sensibility seems as false and contrived as that sham code of chivalry with which so many Southern writers had become infatuated. "Perhaps you know that with us of the younger generation in the South since the War, pretty much the whole of life has been merely not-dying," he wrote to a friend. The horrors of the Reconstruction would be enough to explain such exhaustion, but one suspects that a better explanation could be found in a sensibility nurtured on artificial literary conventions and values incapable of supporting authentic life. Both the Northern saint and the Southern knight are for Wilson false images by means of which the Unionists and the Confederates duped each other, but most of all themselves. They represent "fraudulent traditions." In the wake of the saint and the knight has come the juvenile delinquent. Instead of "this absurd centennial," says Wilson, "a day of mourning would have been more appropriate."

I have remarked already on the admirable Plutarchan contrasts through which the biographical portions of the book are balanced between North and South. Rather unexpectedly, the hero of *Patriotic Gore* seems to be General Grant, who is approached by way of the *Personal Memoirs*. The simple decency of Grant, whether dealing with his soldiers, the army horses, or even the fowls in his barnyard, enables Wilson to write one of his most affecting portraits. But Grant's nobility Northern-style is conscientiously balanced by its Southern equivalent in Lee. Similarly, the fascist taint that discolors General Sherman's image is carefully matched with the repulsive Cromwellianism of Stonewall Jackson. And so it goes through a roster of some thirty names.

A considerable portion of *Patriotic Gore* deals with the literature of the Civil War. Wilson is handicapped here by the fact that this literature is for the most part inferior. Although there are good discussions of Harriet Beecher Stowe, George W. Cable, Albion Tourgée, George Washington Harris, and Sidney Lanier, Wilson's critical treatment of more important writers such as Whitman and Melville is curiously pedestrian. Without being positively unfair to Whittier, Wilson, like everybody else in our time, underestimates him. Whittier was the Archibald MacLeish of his day, but his poetry is better. The closing pages of *Snow-Bound* are great enough as poetry to redeem a corpus of verse much inferior to Whittier's. Discussing Melville's poetry, Wilson concentrates on *The Scout Toward Aldie*. "What Melville has revealed in the fanciful tale . . . is a mutual fascination of each of the two camps with the other, the intimate essence of a conflict which, though fratricidal, was also incestuous." And following this up with a glance in the direction of Julien Green's much later Civil War drama, *Sud*, he says: "The novelty of *Sud*, however, is that the central North-South relationship is a homosexual one." These are observations one wishes Wilson had left to Leslie Fiedler, but there aren't many of them, and one easily forgives them for the sake of his distinguished attack on Southern humorists like George Washington Harris and A. B. Longstreet in the essay on Sut Lovingood, the name of Harris's degraded and sadistic Southern "cracker." For some years there has been a conspiracy among certain scholars and critics of American literature to present characters like Sut Lovingood and the subhuman creatures that fill the pages of Longstreet's *Georgia Scenes* and a whole library of similar books as somehow admirable, examples of good clean fun and earthy vitality instead of the ugly monsters of degenerate sensibility that in reality they are. Wilson does a mopping-up job that ought to put an end to this farce for all time, but probably won't because too many scholars of American literature have invested entirely too much in these hideous caricatures of the human image. Once they are seen for what they are, perhaps they hold an interest of a nonliterary kind, as phenomena that are related to the Southern scene as a whole. The quality of Wilson's criticism is apparent in such insights as this: "The dreamy nobility of a man like Lanier and the murderous clowning of Harris are products of the same society, and the two men have something in common."

When the pro-Southern bias of which *Patriotic Gore* gives ample evidence is carefully analyzed, it is seen to be of an unconventional kind that resolves itself into a fear of "Centralism" in the state rather than into any love for the Myth of the Old South. The one disappointing aspect of the book lies in Wilson's failure to correlate convincingly this "Monster" of modern "Centralism" with what he considers to be its seeds germinated in the Civil War. His attempts to do so, centered in the introduction but scattered throughout the book, are not forthright—indeed, are downright devious at times. And in any case, Wilson's dislike and fear of "Centralism" are not reassuring parts of his argument. But such is the nature of the book that this objection can scarcely be called a major one. The picture of the Civil War world it gives is so vivid, its rendering of personality so dramatic, that it is easily his most entertaining work.

Masks & Mirrors

III

THE HEROIC AND THE
ROMANTIC WEST

As FIGURES, both Lewis and Clark have a simplicity, even a plainness, that seems at first to contrast strangely with the romantic aura that hovers vaguely around their expedition in the minds of most readers. Most writers on Lewis and Clark fail to resolve this tension satisfactorily. The Lewis-and-Clark expedition was a high imaginative achievement quite as much as it was a practical one; but there are many imaginative modes in which to create, to act, and to have visions, and their mode was not the romantic one that with the help of Cooper, Irving, and Parkman settled down across the American West in the generation or so that followed. To read the copious writings of the two explorers themselves is to discover the marks not of a romantic but of an heroic age. So far as I know, they alone among the early American explorers communicate this note in their writings. But if for a moment they did create something like an heroic age beyond the Mississippi, it was an age that passed very quickly.

When we open the pages of the *Journals* and the *Letters* of

Lewis and Clark, at once we are in a world of practical activities and concrete *things:* of boatbuilding, the requisitioning of horses and arms, and we are given long lists of Lewis's requirements for the expedition that succeed in being richly evocative of some early world: axes, trumpets, iron spoons, copper kettles, coils of rope, bolts of scarlet cloth, adzes, tinsel tassels, mirrors, vermilion, scalping knives, and so through many pages.

The community that existed between Lewis and Clark and the forty-three men of the first American expedition to the upper Mississippi and across to the Pacific was very much of that character we find described in heroic poetry. It was a group whose large freedom of behavior was restrained and shaped by the dominant personalities of Lewis and Clark rather than by the rigorous imposition of military discipline. We are told repeatedly how the young men of the expedition entertained visiting Indians and their chiefs by dancing for them—a charming inversion of the usual roles; and York, Clark's Negro slave, mimed for the savages. "He . . . made himself more turribal than we wished him to do," Clark writes. Curiously enough, Clark's sensitively inventive spelling ends up by enhancing rather than diminishing the natural elevation of the style. In representative notes like the following, Clark's peculiar orthography not only underlines his warm human tolerance, but conjures up a native village and its customs more vividly than he could have done with orthodox spelling:

Those people are Durtey, Kind, pore, & extravigent, pursessing national pride, not beggarley recive what is given with great pleasure. Live in warm houses, large and built in oxygon form forming a cone at top . . . a curious custom with the Souixas well as the rickeres is to give hansom squars to those whome they wish to Show some acknowledgements to . . . 2 hansom young

Squars were sent by a man to follow us, they came up this evening, and pursisted in their civilities.

Despite the exuberant spirits that buoyed the expedition up under so many difficulties, Clark was ready at a moment's notice to confront a moral crisis with archaic simplicity and resolution:

I was allarmed about 10 oClock by the Sentinal, who informed that an Indian was about to kill his wife in the interpeter's [interpreter's] fire about 60 yards below the works, I went down and Spoke to the fellow about the rash act which he was like to commit and forbid any act of the kind near the fort.

The prevailing spirit of the expedition was not romantic and reckless bravery, but a combination of courage, intelligence, and dignity that filtered down from the peculiar qualities of the two leaders, and herein particularly lies the explanation of that "heroic" quality that has been noted. This becomes especially evident in the skill, diplomacy, and fearlessness with which the party outfaced the Teton Sioux, whose terrorism and exacted tributes had virtually destroyed Spanish and French fur-trading on the Missouri. The admirable account in the *Journals* of the tact and resolution with which the expedition called the bluff of the extortionists might be used as a model of foreign policy, even today, in dealing with small, unpleasantly truculent nations.

It is necessary to remember that the Lewis-and-Clark expedition was not merely the physical conquest of a new world by brave but unlettered men. Jefferson intended it to be a conquest in knowledge also, and towards this end he had seen to it that Lewis, during his two years as the President's secretary, should be specially trained and instructed by America's leading scientists. Jefferson's letter of instructions to Lewis, June 20, 1803, reprinted in Donald Jackson's

Letters of the Lewis and Clark Expedition, with Related Documents, gives a remarkable insight into the amplitude of Jefferson's vision. It also makes clear, as little else can, the intellectual and moral, as well as physical, qualities that would be required of the men who should lead and complete the mission. Lewis turned out to be a veritable Odysseus in the wilderness, and although he lacked Lewis's education and scientific training, Clark's intelligence made him a worthy partner in the enterprise.

The capacity of both men for coping with the most difficult problems of the exploration is illustrated in their triumphant solution of the puzzle that confronted them when, in the course of the upper Missouri, they came to the embouchure of a north fork (the Milk River) of such size and current that it was impossible to determine (as they must do to complete their mission) which of the two streams was the true Missouri. No historian has shown a more sensitive appreciation of the achievement of Lewis and Clark than the late Bernard DeVoto. In *The Course of Empire* he makes this rather startling evaluation of the intelligence and ingenuity that the two men brought to the solution of their problem:

> The commanders of a momentous exploration thus answered the question that must be answered right if the expedition was not to fail. At this critical turning point, with immediate failure hanging in the balance, the answer is co-operative and joint. It is Lewis who writes down the reasoning in the *Journals*, but this analysis is as clearly Clark's as his, for it was Clark who had formulated the winter's data, had checked and re-checked and tabulated it, and must now check it again for unperceived possibilities of error in calculation or in reasoning. And this joint effort is a remarkable act of mind. Considering all that went into it and all that depended on it, it must be conceded a distinguished place in the history of thought.

It would be absurd to pretend that the achievement of Lewis and Clark has been scanted, but apart from a very few writers like Bernard DeVoto, its essentially creative and imaginative character has been missed, its essentially "heroic" quality sacrificed in the interests of Western romanticism. It was no doubt his sense of this "heroic" quality, possibly unique in American annals, that led Robert Penn Warren, at the close of that odd, often exasperating poem, *Brother to Dragons*, to bring the ghost of Lewis back to confront Jefferson with the charge of betrayal. The great vision that is implicit in Jefferson's letter of instructions to Lewis could scarcely, in the nature of things, be realized. But for a moment it seemed to be incarnated in heroic action. Nevertheless, it was bound to end (and this I take it is Warren's point) in petty commerce, avarice, cruelty, ambition, and all the usual falsifications that man is heir to.

The falsifications so far as the American West is concerned began early. The men of serious purpose and dedication, of whom there were very few to match Lewis and Clark, were soon joined by a group of sophisticated Easterners and Europeans, and the heroic West that may have existed only for the duration of the Lewis-and-Clark expedition gave way to the romantic West. The newcomers were often young, and it is easy to believe they were often charming. Certainly they had a dramatic flair in the quality of their imagination, their behavior, and their dress. Washington Irving was already forty-nine when he made his excursion described in *A Tour of the Prairies*, but he delighted in the graces of his young traveling companion, the Count, who represented the type more perfectly than Irving could ever have hoped to, even in youth. Irving's admiration glows through this description:

> His dress was a gay Indian hunting-frock of dressed deer-skin, setting well to the shape, dyed of a beautiful purple, and fancifully embroidered with silks of various colors; as if it had been the work of some Indian beauty,

to decorate a favorite chief. With this he wore leathern pantaloons and moccasins, a foraging-cap, and a double-barrelled gun slung by a bandoleer athwart his back: so that he was quite a picturesque figure as he managed gracefully his spirited steed.

To many of these young men their brief season on the frontier was a Mardi Gras with no Lent to follow. A good many of them had literary interests, and they tended to see the landscape, the Indians, the flora and fauna, as if they were out of Spenser or mythology. Colorful, indeed theatrical as their books occasionally are, there can be something a little disturbing about them at times. Most books in the literature of the West tend to be sticky with the blood of slaughtered buffalo and bucks, but in the *Journals* of Lewis and Clark the hunting accounts are usually direct and simple, and even though one may abominate hunting as a practice, it is only rarely one finds the *Journals* even slightly offensive in this regard. But the complicated pirouettes of sentiment in which Irving indulges have something noxious about them:

> There was something in this picture of the last moments of a wounded deer to touch the sympathies of one not hardened to the gentle disports of the chase; such sympathies, however, are but transient. Man is naturally an animal of prey; and, however changed by civilization, will readily relapse into his instinct for destruction. I found my ravenous and sanguinary propensities daily growing stronger upon the prairies.

By the time the two Bostonians, Francis Parkman, then twenty-three, and his friend Quincy Adams Shaw, made their Western trip to Fort Laramie in 1846, the "sanguinary propensities" of visiting Easterners had acquired a rather nasty look, and the sadistic urge was not invariably released on animals. Out of his journals kept on this expedition Parkman drew his colorfully dramatic account, *The Oregon Trail*. Parkman was a complicated (if not complex) personality. Bernard DeVoto, among others, has commented on the avidity with which he treats scenes of torture in his histories of France and England in North America. Possibly in Parkman's case this was partly motivated by his neurotic fear of weakness in himself, but its effect is often no more pleasant than outright sadism. There are doubtless much more offensive passages in reputable American literature than the following from Chapter IX of *The Oregon Trail*, but none comes to mind at the moment. Having arrived at Laramie, Parkman and Shaw developed an intimacy with the Indians living near the fort, and in their visits to a neighboring village young Shaw undertook medical ministrations to the savages:

He had brought him a homeopathic medicine-chest, and was, I presume, the first who introduced that harmless system of treatment among the Ogillallah. . . . A hideous, emaciated old woman sat in the darkest corner of the lodge, rocking to and fro with pain, and hiding her eyes from the light by pressing the palms of both hands against her face. . . . She came forward very unwillingly, and exhibited a pair of eyes that had nearly disappeared from inflammation. No sooner had the doctor fastened his grip upon her, than she set up a dismal moaning, and writhed so in his grasp that he lost all patience; but being resolved to carry his point, he succeeded at last in applying his favorite remedies.

"It is strange," he said, when the operation was finished, "that I forgot to bring my Spanish flies with me; we must have something here to answer for a counter-irritant."

So, in the absence of better, he seized upon a red-hot brand from the fire, and clapped it against the temple of the old squaw, who set up an unearthly howl, at which the rest of the family broke into a laugh.

It is surprising that Charles Eliot Norton, who undertook to expurgate references to sex and liquor from the manuscript before publication, saw nothing offensive here to delete, but his blindness carries a certain eloquence. From all these later products of the romantic West, one returns with relief to the pages of Lewis and Clark. To compare their *Journals* with most of the later accounts of the West is to appreciate and measure their stature with a new recognition, and to see clearly the differences that separate the two great explorers of America's "heroic" moment from their romantic, and sometimes slightly unsavory, heirs.

WAH-TO-YAH AND THE TAOS TRAIL:
A MINOR CLASSIC OF THE WEST

O NE OF THE BEST books to have come out of the
American West during the nineteenth century was a
small travel book which, though it has some reputation
among fanciers of the frontier, is virtually unknown to a
wider or more serious literary audience, even by name. Yet it
is a minor classic of great charm, and it has qualities of
language and observation that should give it a currency it has
never been near to enjoying. To respond to its freshness, it is
no more necessary to be an addict of the West than one must
be a committed cultural primitivist to enjoy Melville's *Typee*.
Wah-to-yah and the Taos Trail is above all else a book by a
very young man. Lewis Garrard was seventeen when he lived
through the experiences it recounts; he was twenty-one when
it was finally published in 1850. A stepson of a Justice of the
United States Supreme Court, he set out in 1846, with paren-
tal permission, for an extended trip into the West. In what is
now Kansas City, he joined a caravan headed for Bent's Fort

in southeastern Colorado, near the Spanish Peaks (the Indian name for which was Wah-to-yah). From there he traveled south to Taos in New Mexico, and returned East the following year.

While *Wah-to-yah* could not formally be described as an initiation book recounting the young hero's exposure to experience in the sense that Melville's *Redburn* may be, it has many qualities of that genre, and Lewis in many respects recalls the image of the very youthful Wellingborough. Like Redburn, he has an attractive tolerance for the peculiarities of others, and an appealing sympathy with their difficulties. And like Melville's young hero, he is sometimes inclined to think a little sentimentally of the comforts and kindnesses of home. Even along the Santa Fe Trail he is able to speak in the accents of the well-brought-up boy of proper, decent sentiment. Coming across a lonely grave, he writes:

> On the top of the rock, near the edge, was a deposit of earth, where the remains of some poor fellow had been placed. To die anywhere seems hard, but to heave the last breath among strangers, on the burning, desolate prairie, with no kind mother or sister to pay those soothing attentions which divest the bed of sickness of many of its pangs, is hard indeed.

He was in Taos not long after the murder of Charles Bent, the United States governor by appointment of the newly conquered territory. He attended the trial and the mass execution of the six Mexicans who had been convicted for Bent's death. His description of the hangings, which comprises the whole of Chapter XVII, is an extraordinarily vivid and moving piece of reportage which comes to a climax in the following brief passage:

> Bidding each other "adios," with a hope of meeting in Heaven, at a word from the sheriff the mules were started, and the wagon drawn from under the tree. No

fall was given, and their feet remained on the board till the ropes grew taut. The bodies swang back and forth, and, coming in contact with each other, convulsive shudders shook their frames; the muscles, contracting, would relax, and again contract, and the bodies writhed most horribly. While thus swinging, the hands of two came together, which they held with a firm grasp till the muscles loosened in death.

But this in itself gives little indication of the sense of dramatic contrast and descriptive skill with which young Garrard succeeds in evoking the events of that wretched morning. The soldiers softening the stiff ropes with soap, the black-gowned padres giving Holy Communion under the stares of the sentinels, the trembling prisoners marched to the gallows with halters round their necks, the obscene jocularity in the bar before and after the hangings—all this is beautifully rendered with the inherent instinct of a natural artist.

While Lewis Garrard is a modest, self-effacing boy, the freshness of his personality and writing makes his presence felt everywhere in the book. Several times we get a striking picture of the boy himself. When his buckskin pantaloons finally wore out at Fort Bent, it was necessary for him to get a new pair sewn:

> While the pantaloons were being cut out by the enterprising John Smith and sewed by his squaw with awl and sinew, I wore a breechcloth *à la mode Cheyenne*, manufactured of a leg of my old pants. They were rather the worse for wear than when I sat with them in a daguerreotype room before leaving home, trying to look my sweetest for a fond relative. With breechcloth, blanket, painted face, and moccasins, I made a very respectable looking savage.

For a period Lewis lived in a Cheyenne village, making friends with the Indians. Once when a party of braves returned with a fresh collection of Pawnee scalps, the village went into several days of celebration, marked by a ceremonial scalp dance. The immediacy and verve with which Garrard re-creates the color and rhythms of a barbaric ritual dance can be gauged by comparing his description with the much-praised account of the corn dance in D. H. Lawrence's *Mornings in Mexico*. Lawrence, it seems to me, loses in the comparison, perhaps partly because he remains essentially a spectator. Lewis, on the other hand, painting his face in Cheyenne style, joined in: "I had made the acquaintance of many young men and girls, and often I chasséd up to the scalps and joined in the chorus. . . ."

Although a properly brought-up youth, Lewis knew that the "right" sentiments for a boy in Cincinnati on Sunday morning would not get him far among the Indians. When the time came to leave the village, he parted sadly from his friends—especially from his host's beautiful daughter, Red Dress. Taking her hand, he thought of

> the gay dances around the scalps in her company, with other graceful Houris, enveloped in the same blanket, and our commingled "hay-he-a-hay" (scalp chorus) rising above the other voices. . . . I half wanted to stay. The poor shivering Indians, standing in the deep snow, saw us off.

Garrard has been much praised for the accuracy with which he has recorded dialect and speech rhythms of the Mountain Men. In his brief introduction to an edition of *Wah-to-yah* that appeared a few years ago, A. B. Guthrie, Jr., credits Garrard and another writer, the English explorer George Frederick Ruxton, with giving us what knowledge we possess of these speech patterns.

> But for the two, both of whom had ears and appetites for the lingo, we should have lost, or thought altogether

224

preposterous, such habits of tongue as: "Well, hos, I'll dock off buffler, and then if thar's any meat that 'runs' that can take the shine outen 'dog,' you can slide." Or: "Hatch, old hos! Hyar's the coon as would like to hear tell of the time you seed the old gentleman. You's the one as savvy's all 'bout them diggin's."

The quotations can be translated: "Well, friend, I'll except buffalo, and then if there's any meat afoot that surpasses dog, you're crazy." "Hatch, old boy, I'd like to hear of the time you saw the devil. You understand all about his place."

Although it appears that Garrard's accuracy would have justified an explanatory note on dialect similar to the one with which Twain prefaces *Huckleberry Finn*, the real strength of the book lies in the effortless simplicity of the prose. The best-known chapter in the book is the one in which the Mountain Man Hatcher relates his visit to hell. It is, in fact, an account of a seizure of delirium tremens, and Garrard has managed to reproduce through Hatcher's voice a combination of qualities native to the frontier—its sadism, its love of the macabre, its grisly humor and jovial brutality, its verbal recklessness, its narrowly constricted but violent imaginative capacity, especially where the supernatural is concerned. There is invariably something sinister about frontier humor, and rarely has this quality been understood better than by Garrard.

Although his framing vision of the West is doubtless best described as romantic, he is free of those stereotypes and conventions that we associate with much of the literature of Western romanticism. Garrard's West is a highly credible reality. The directness, freshness, and honesty of his vision and language convince us he was there.

JAMES FENIMORE COOPER:
AMERICA'S MIRROR
OF CONSCIENCE

I T I S A commonplace of literary history that the 1850's represent the most brilliant period of achievement in American literature. *The Scarlet Letter*, *Moby-Dick*, *Walden*, and *Leaves of Grass*, to mention only the most obvious books, were produced during the first five years of the decade. The nineteenth century had seen nothing like it before, nor would it again as the nation moved through the Civil War to the genteel vulgarity of the Gilded Age. As we look back on the 1850's from the present time, the very magnitude of those achievements, which have given a characteristic stamp to the American sensibility, acts as a kind of watershed—dividing us from a remoter American past which one may be more inclined to visit from motives of curiosity or historical interest than from any compelling sense of kinship. But in the case of James Fenimore Cooper, a kinship does exist.

Cooper died at the beginning of the 1850's, but there are aspects of his mind and writings that place him in a more direct relationship with the great writers who came after him than with his strict contemporaries. Today he is commonly regarded as a writer of boys' books. As a recent American critic has pointed out, most of the great American classics may be regarded as boys' books. But this is only one way, and a very narrow way, of looking at them: and there is more than one way of looking at Cooper. Quantitatively, a good deal has been written about him in the past, but contemporary criticism, which has had so much to say about Hawthorne, Melville, and James, has tended to shy away from him.[1] This is unfortunate, for there is a great deal in Cooper to repay scrutiny. With the exception of Hugh Henry Brackenridge, whose satirical novel on early American politics, *Modern Chivalry*, also goes unread, Cooper was the first American writer to use the novel form seriously as a vehicle of social and political criticism. He wished to argue and to communicate his ideas about society and American manners, politics, and economics. This new note of seriousness that he brought to his role as a novelist (even when he tried to disclaim it) was in itself a new recognition of the possibilities of fiction. His satiric examination of American life, and his exploration of the contrast between American and European attitudes, in novels like *Homeward Bound* (1838) and *Home as Found* (1838), look forward to Henry James, while such characters as Steadfast Dodge and Aristabulus Bragg anticipate the Babbits and Dodsworths of a later literary generation.

One of the functions and responsibilities of literature is to define nationality in the act of describing it or dramatizing it. Without Shakespeare, Milton, Jane Austen, and Dickens, it is difficult to think that the English would know how to think and act like Englishmen. The novels of Cooper are an exercise in national definition. He sets out to tell his countrymen

1. This essay was written in 1961 and first published in 1962. Since then Cooper has received a great deal of attention at the hands of critics and scholars.

what it should be to think and act like an American, and if he is too often self-conscious in his mission, he nevertheless extends the range of our self-knowledge. In the great figure of Natty Bumppo he has given us a symbolic character who seems in ways almost mysterious to embody the very genius of America itself: at any rate, of that America stretching backward in time towards that early moment when, as Scott Fitzgerald said, "a fresh, green breast of the new world" presented man "for the last time in history with something commensurate to his capacity for wonder." It is essential that in an age of concrete and steel the lines of imaginative communication with that earlier world should not be destroyed.

The American writer during the first half of the nineteenth century was in a vulnerable position. He was exposed to two dangers. He might be tempted to consider the whole idea of an American literature invalid and content himself with servile imitation of English models. An anonymous author was not a solitary voice when he wrote in 1807:

> We know that in this land, where the spirit of democracy is everywhere diffused, we are exposed as it were to a poisonous atmosphere, which blasts everything beautiful in nature, and corrodes everything elegant in art; we know that with us "the rose leaves fall ungathered," and we believe that there is little to praise and nothing to admire in most of the objects which would first present themselves to the view of a stranger.

On the other hand, he might react in the opposite direction and think the United States culturally independent of the Old World, and so abandon himself to a suffocating literary provincialism. As the Connecticut poet John Trumbull put it much earlier in *An Essay on the Use and Advantages of the Fine Arts* (1770):

> *This land her Steele and Addison shall view,*
> *The former glories equalled by the new;*

Some future Shakespeare charm the rising age,
And hold in magic charm the listening page.

In either case there would have been little truth involved in
the literature that resulted, and America would not have
discovered her true image in such distorting mirrors.

It is a tribute to Cooper's intelligence that he successfully
avoided these two pitfalls. His novels usually show a deep
sympathy with his country, and a strong faith in its possibilities: but this is always accompanied by an insight into the
limitations surrounding the conditions of life in America that
prevents him from falling into the kind of inflationary writing
that marred the work of many of his contemporaries. One of
the characters in the late novel *The Redskins* makes a measured cultural assessment of the American cultural scene that
clarifies Cooper's lifelong attitude:

> "Will New York ever be a capital? Yes—out of all
> question, yes. But the day will not come until after the
> sudden changes of condition which immediately and so
> naturally succeeded the revolution, have ceased to influ-
> ence ordinary society, and those above again impart to
> those below more than they receive. This restoration to
> the natural state of things must take place as soon as
> society gets settled; and there will be nothing to prevent
> a town living under its own institutions—spirit, *tenden-
> cies*, and all—from obtaining the highest tone that ever
> yet prevailed in a capital. The folly is in anticipating the
> natural course of events. Nothing will more hasten these
> events, however, than a literature that is controlled, not
> by the lower, but by the higher opinion of the country;
> which literature is yet, in a great degree, to be created."

This was written in 1846, shortly before the 1850's that
were to go far towards creating such a literature as Cooper
envisages here. The literature of that decade was no accident.
More than a half-century of national history leads up to it,

during which the foundations of a literary tradition were established. Without the substantial beginnings of such a tradition the later accomplishments would have been impossible, and it was Cooper who did more than any other writer to give it scope and dignity. He enlarged the function and range of the novel by making it an organ of serious intellectual criticism; he gave it a peculiarly national flavor by his celebration of American scenery and by his treatment of distinctively American problems. In some ways what Henry James was to say of Hawthorne might even more truthfully be said of Cooper: that he showed "to what a use American matter could be put by an American hand: a consummation involving, it appeared, the happiest moral. For the moral was that an American could be an artist, one of the finest, without going 'outside' about it. . . ." Above all, the international reputation Cooper achieved as an artist lent a sense of security to a new literature that was both brash and unsure of itself.

In our own time we have witnessed several notable literary revivals. When Melville died in 1891 he had already been long forgotten. "Probably, if the truth were known," said a newspaper obituary, "even his own generation has long thought him dead. . . ." But today no other writer of the American nineteenth century speaks as profoundly and intimately to us as Melville. Similarly, Henry James is no longer considered an esoteric craftsman, writing only for a small audience. It is not fashion that dictates these shifts in taste, but fundamental changes in our problems and needs. Shortly after Cooper died in 1851, Melville wrote that "a grateful posterity will take the best care of Fenimore Cooper." Cooper has never been forgotten to the extent that Melville was until the 1920's; nevertheless, Melville's words have not proved prophetic. If Cooper is conventionally honored, he is seldom read; and today much of his enormous production remains out of print. What likelihood is there of a Cooper revival, even on a moderate scale? There is this to recommend it: under his old-fashioned prose, the questions that engage his attention are similar to many that trouble us. They are not the same torturing problems of metaphysical anxiety and doubt that we share with Melville. Rather, they are political in character.

The central preoccupation, seen under a variety of aspects, that troubles Cooper in his most representative novels is the threat to democracy in action as it exists in a country where traditional values are in the process of being supplanted by economic motives; where manners and cultural standards are in the process of being reduced to the lowest common denominator, and where the intolerant tyranny of the majority threatens the liberalism of the few. In an age vitiated by concepts of conformity, Cooper's better novels demonstrate the healthfulness of a patriotic subversiveness that does not regard flank-rubbing with the herd the most satisfactory form of social contact. F. R. Leavis once described our age as one of mass civilization and minority culture. In *The American Democrat* (1838) Cooper had explained why democracies are especially prone to this cultural affliction:

The tendency of democracies is, in all things, to mediocrity, since the tastes, knowledge, and principles of the majority form the tribunal of appeal. This circumstance, while it certainly serves to elevate the average qualities of a nation, renders the introduction of a high standard difficult. Thus do we find in literature, the arts, architecture and all acquired knowledge, a tendency in America to gravitate towards the common centre in this, as in other things; lending a value and estimation to mediocrity that are not elsewhere given. It is fair to expect, however, that a foundation so broad, may in time sustain a superstructure of commensurate proportions, and that the influence of masses will in this, as in other interests, have a generally beneficial effect. Still

. . . the mass of no community is qualified to decide the most correctly on anything, which, in its nature, is above its reach.

This recognition is pervasive throughout Cooper's books. It is an attitude that is easy to misinterpret unless it is focused in the full context of his political credo, and the Americans of his day did misinterpret it. "The most intense lover of his country," wrote Thomas R. Lounsbury, his first biographer, "he became the most unpopular man of letters to whom it has ever given birth." Cooper believed in the ascendancy of the uncommon man, and it would be unwise for us to forget our first major novelist who was centrally concerned in his work with a truth that has become even more urgent with the passage of time.

But it must be confessed that certain qualities in Cooper's prose militate against a widespread revival of interest in his work. At his best, Cooper is a great writer. When he describes the wilderness or the sea, few can surpass him. As Joseph Conrad said of him:

His descriptions have the magistral ampleness of a gesture indicating the sweep of a vast horizon. They embrace the colours of sunset, the peace of starlight, the aspects of storm and calm, the great loneliness, the stillness of watchful coasts. . . .

But in local passages the prose is sometimes archaic and stilted, the dialogue wooden, the humor debatable. In the beginning, the reader must have patience and generous sympathy if he is to realize that Mark Twain's insulting essay "The Literary Offenses of Fenimore Cooper" tells more about Twain's critical incapacity than it does about Cooper's limitations as a writer. In the end, one can do nothing better than remember Conrad's words: "He wrote before the great

American language was born, and he wrote as well as any novelist of his time."

II

A YEAR before he died, Cooper is reported to have said that "it takes a first-class aristocrat to make a first-class Democrat." This might be taken as the motto of his life. It not only affected his practical political thinking to the end, but it left its mark on most of his writing, which was always a reflection of his deepest political and social convictions. It was to argue and further the cause of these convictions that it seemed worthwhile to him to write at all. There has sometimes been confusion about Cooper's politics because it has appeared to many literary historians that a man of his aristocratic predilections had no business being a Jacksonian aristocrat, especially when his father had been one of the New York State partisan leaders of the Federalists—that party out of which the Whig party grew. One well-known Cooper scholar put it this way a number of years ago:

> Cooper was a country gentleman, a Whig squire. . . .
> He wanted to be and was loyal to the United States and
> its form of government, but his social ideals were in
> conflict with the "levelling" and "majority" tendencies
> present in Jacksonian America—a most uncomfortable
> time for a traditionalist!

But Cooper was never a Whig. He was, though perhaps with qualifications towards the end of his life, an ardent supporter of Jackson's policies, seeing in the Whig party a powerful oligarchy of vested interests based on business and financial speculation. In a political pamphlet attacking the Whigs, *A Letter to His Countrymen* (1834), Cooper described in general terms the political tendencies of his time, but he meant the application to be made to the Whigs in particular:

> I had had abundant occasion to observe that the great political contest of the age was not, as is usually pretended, between the antagonist principles of monarchy and democracy, but in reality between those who, under the shallow pretence of limiting power to the *elite* of society, were contending for exclusive advantage at the expense of their fellow creatures.

In other words, Cooper in 1834 was very much in the same position as the man today who may well believe that standards must be maintained by a minority of informed and disciplined leaders, but who refuses to accept as an adequate substitute an "aristocracy" of entrenched capitalists intent on augmenting their own power and resources. Cooper, like Hawthorne, William Cullen Bryant, Hiram Powers, Horatio Greenough, George Bancroft, James K. Paulding, and most of the other intellectuals of the day, knew that one could be a Jacksonian without being a Vandal, but that it was very difficult to be a Whig without being a Philistine. The leveling tendencies and the emphasis on majority opinion were certainly present in Jacksonian America, and a reading of Cooper's political primer, *The American Democrat* (1838), will reveal how painful these were to Cooper; but they were imperfections of the political surface, not of the heart, and they might be corrected. Cooper believed that such a corrective mission could be accomplished only by men who were equally devoted to democratic principles and to standards of personal conduct and taste that were popularly described as "aristocratic" in the new equalitarian atmosphere of his America.

Perhaps it would really be more accurate to describe Cooper as a Jeffersonian Democrat, for his faith was in the land, and, like Jefferson, he envisaged America as a republic whose wealth consisted in farms and landed estates rather than in business and finance. It was natural that landed wealth should appear the best kind of wealth to him—in his boyhood he had lived with it under almost idyllic circumstances, or so it seemed when he looked back on those years from mature manhood. It seemed to him that the most precious human values attached themselves, in the course of time, to inherited property, and so were transmitted from one generation to the next. Land was the basis of social solidarity and the guarantee of social and cultural continuity. As opposed to wealth accumulated through business and financial speculation (the principal sources of Whig prosperity), landed property supported character, encouraged responsibility, and fostered tradition. Cooper knew this from the example of his father.

Judge William Cooper had been one of the most successful land agents of the Revolutionary years. By 1786 he had acquired 40,000 acres of land in western New York, near Otsego Lake, and here, in 1790, he brought his family from New Jersey. The child James (Cooper took his mother's family name, Fenimore, only later in life) was then only thirteen months old. The mansion house which Judge Cooper soon built is described in a history of Cooperstown as "a great rectangular stone house with castellated roof and gothic windows, surrounded by box hedges and wide lawns trimmed precisely by black gardeners, far surpassing any other home in the far west." Growing up between the frontier freedom of the woods and the lake—the Glimmerglass of *The Deerslayer* —and the spacious ease of Otsego Hall with its retinue of slaves and servants, it is not remarkable that Cooper found his democratic and aristocratic propensities at ease in later life.

Cooper's education was suitable for the son of a Congressman and the wealthiest man in his county. It culminated at Yale, from which he was expelled in his third year for an undistinguished undergraduate performance involving gunpowder in a keyhole and a donkey in the classroom. At home again, young Cooper had thoughts of the sea, which his father, at this point, was willing to encourage. He sailed at first before the mast of a merchant vessel, and in 1808 entered the United States Navy as a midshipman. During these years he acquired that love of the sea and detailed knowledge of ships and sailing that enabled him to become the first great sea novelist before Conrad. By the time he resigned from the Navy in 1810 his father was dead, having been struck over the head by a political opponent, and Cooper himself was about to be married. He had chosen Miss Susan Augusta De Lancey, whose ancestors had distinguished themselves in the service of the King, and whose grandfather had been royal lieutenant governor of New York. The marriage was a happy one, and almost certainly his wife's upperclass Tory background confirmed those tendencies in Cooper's character that we have already noted.

At his father's death Cooper was apparently very well off financially, but, for whatever reasons, within a few years his circumstances were considerably reduced. "Accident first made me a writer," Cooper once wrote, but the fact that it held out promise of financial reward undoubtedly encouraged him to continue on a course so casually begun. His first novel, *Precaution* (1820), was written as the result of a bet with his wife. Apparently he intended it to be an imitation of Jane Austen's *Persuasion*. It is not surprising that the future master of the American wilderness showed limited command of the English drawing room. His second novel, *The Spy* (1821), is one of the earliest of the American classics, and its success —eight thousand copies in four months—must have persuaded Cooper to continue in his new role. It is the story of a Colonial family, the Whartons, living in Westchester during the American Revolution, and the plot becomes a kind of debate in action between the American and British points of view. Cooper returned to the Revolution in later novels, and, in his use of the theme of divided loyalties, one occasionally has anticipations of the later international novel with its dialectical pattern of American and European attitudes. The most famous character in the novel is Harvey Birch, the Yankee peddler, who is Washington's favorite spy. He accomplished his missions for the Americans by posing as a spy for the British, and this device of the superimposed identity, the assumed identity, becomes a favorite one with Cooper in later books. He utilizes it in a variety of ways, but usually for the purpose of maintaining an aloofness from his material and exercising superior control over it. Though he made little of it technically, Cooper, like Henry James, was attracted to the role of the detached observer, as all writers must be whose interest is intellectual and analytic.

Cooper's third novel, *The Pioneers* (1823), sold thirty-five hundred copies on the day of publication. Natty Bumppo, who has been called the most memorable character in American fiction, was first introduced in this novel. Cooper was to pursue Natty's career in the wilderness and on the prairies through four more books, but these must be discussed as a unit later. The same year saw *The Pilot*, the first of a series of sea stories in which Cooper drew on his naval experience. By this time he had become, with the possible exception of Irving, the best-known writer in America, both at home and abroad, and his income had been greatly augmented. He was now ready to fulfill an old ambition by taking his family to Europe. The extended visit lasted over seven years, during which time Cooper, with characteristic but scarcely credible energy, published seven novels, a long book of American social criticism, *The Travelling Bachelor: or Notions of the Americans*, and collected the material for five travel books which he published shortly after his return in 1833. Cooper moved through Europe, not as an obscure American, but as a literary lion who was everywhere considered to be the peer of

Sir Walter Scott. Lafayette was his friend, and through the American minister in Paris he secured entry into the most influential governing circles and fashionable coteries. He was an indefatigable observer of foreign manners and attitudes, and always a tireless champion of America. Yet it is probable that in subtle ways these splendid years in Europe disqualified him from ever settling down happily in the United States when he came home again.

Cooper returned to America with a more detached attitude than ever, determined to instruct his countrymen in the basic rudiments of what makes a *good* American. It is not altogether surprising that the Americans objected. The period of Cooper's popularity came to an end. After the publication of *Homeward Bound*, a review of it appeared in the *North American Review* which indicates the new response:

> Professing to be a sturdy republican, he has exhausted his powers of invective upon the manners and characters of his countrymen, who are, taking his own descriptions for truth, ignorant of the first principles of social refinement, and no better than a nation of brutes and savages. If such are the friends of Republicanism, she may well pray heaven to save her from them.

Cooper's admiration for aristocratic values came to patriotic focus in his concept of the American gentleman. The American gentleman, so far as outward manners, spiritual refinement, and cultivated tastes went, was not to be distinguished from the finest flower of European nobility. Eve Effingham, the heroine of *Homeward Bound* and *Home as Found*, both published in 1838, reflected perfectly Cooper's faith in a natural aristocracy in the United States:

> Eve actually fancied that the position of an American gentleman might really become, nay, that it *ought* to be the highest of all human stations short of that of sover-

eigns. Such a man had no superior, with the exception of those who actually ruled, in her eyes, and this fact, she conceived, rendered him more than noble, as nobility is usually graduated. She had been accustomed to seeing her father and John Effingham moving in the best circles of Europe, respected for their information and independence, undistinguished by their manners, admired for their personal appearance, manly, courteous, and of noble bearing and principles, if not set apart from the rest of mankind by an arbitrary rule connected with rank. Rich, and possessing all the habits that properly mark refinement, of gentle extraction, of liberal attainments, walking abroad in the dignity of manhood, and with none between them and the Deity, Eve had learned to regard the gentlemen of her race as the equals in station of any of their European associates, and as the superiors of most, in everything that is necessary to true distinction.

This was naturally not the breed of American Cooper found most in evidence when he returned home, and the two Effingham novels are filled with satiric portraits, often scathing and penetrating, of less admirable national types who still ring as painfully true as Sinclair Lewis's gallery. Cooper was always better when he attacked than when he praised. Here is a description of Steadfast Dodge:

Mr. Dodge came from that part of the country in which men were accustomed to think, act, almost to eat and drink and sleep, in common; or, in any other words, from one of those regions in America, in which there was so much community, that few had the moral courage, even when they possessed the knowledge, and all the other necessary means, to cause their individuality to be respected. When the usual process of conventions, sub-conventions, caucuses, and public meetings did not supply the means of a "concentrated action," he and his neighbors had long been in the habit of having recourse to societies, by way of obtaining "energetic means," as it was termed; and from his tenth year up to his twenty-fifth, this gentleman had been either a president, vice-president, manager, or committee-man, of some philosophical, political, or religious expedient to fortify human wisdom, make men better, and resist error and despotism. His experience had rendered him expert in what may well enough be termed the language of association. No man of his years in the twenty-six States, could more readily apply the terms of "taking up"—"excitement"—"unqualified hostility"—"public opinion"—"spreading before the public"—or any other of those generic phrases that imply the privileges of all, and the rights of none.

But to appreciate Cooper's cruel mastery of the meannesses and hypocrisies of these Americans, it is necessary to see them in action. The social analysis in the Effingham novels, particularly of the New York scene in *Home as Found*, can occasionally be Jamesian in the quality of its comedy, and it is both accurate and ruthless with its barbs. Steadfast Dodge and Arisabulus Bragg are comic characters, but in Cooper's eyes they posed a real threat to America. Only a class of disinterested intellectuals and democrats like Edward Effingham, Eve's father, could counteract it, and today it is difficult to say that Cooper was wrong. The concentrated creative outburst of 1838 is clearly symptomatic of a crisis of mind and heart. After long years abroad, Cooper was equipped to look at his countrymen with a sharper, more critical vision than he had possessed before. The tremendous energy that he brought to the task of revaluation is amply exhibited in *Homeward Bound*, *Home as Found*, and *The American Democrat*, which, with a fourth book, *Gleanings in*

Europe: Italy, all belong to this one extraordinary year. Cooper summed the situation up admirably in this passage from *The American Democrat:*

> The democrat, recognizing the right of all to participate in power, will be more liberal in his general sentiments, a quality of superiority in itself; but, in conceding this much to his fellow man, he will proudly maintain his own independence of vulgar domination, as indispensable to his personal habits. The same principle and manliness that would induce him to depose a royal despot would induce him to resist a vulgar tyrant.

We have seen that for Cooper a great protection against such vulgar domination had been a landed gentry. From Colonial days New York had been dotted with large manorial estates, of which the largest, Rensselaerwyck on the Hudson, comprised a million acres. Vast numbers of farmers rented small holdings on long leases from these great landlords, for which, in addition to their yearly rent, they often performed services that were feudal in character. During the 1840's agitation became widespread in the state to force large landowners to sell the farms outright to their tenants, and anti-rent societies that were formed had recourse to violence to prevent foreclosure and the collection of rents that had fallen in arrears.

Cooper wrote the Littlepage trilogy in defense of the landed gentry among whom he had grown up. After the Leatherstocking Tales, it is one of Cooper's most interesting achievements. These three novels, *Satanstoe*, *The Chainbearer*, and *The Redskins*, were all published in 1845 and 1846. They carry the story of the Littlepage family from Colonial times, through three generations living on their landed estates or sometimes in Europe, down to Cooper's own day, when such holdings were threatened by mob violence and by state law. For once Cooper had misjudged the situation. Whatever abuses the anti-rent agitators had been guilty of, the land laws against which they were rebelling established wealth and poverty on a permanent basis. If the old system guaranteed that the great estates and the incomes deriving from them should be handed on from father to son, they guaranteed no less the continuity of poverty on the small, often stony and infertile holdings. Tenants frequently were able to escape from the terms of their leases only into absolute and hopeless poverty. Nor were the great landowners whom Cooper supported so bravely any longer the chivalric natural aristocracy whom he seemed to remember from his youth. A fusion had already taken place between the great speculators and businessmen among the Whigs and the landed gentry of an earlier period. But Cooper was desperate in the middle 'forties to hold back that tidal wave of leveling influences which he saw sweeping everything before it. "The secret of this change among ourselves," he wrote in *The Redskins*, "is the innate dislike which is growing up in the country to see any man distinguished from the mass around him in anything, even though it should be in merit." Property appeared to be the last defense, and Cooper was ready to champion it, even on the most feudal of terms. "It is pretended that durable leases are feudal in their nature," he wrote. "We do not conceive this to be true; but, admitting it to be so, it would only prove that feudality to this extent, is a part of the institutions of the state." It was an unfortunate position for a man of Cooper's liberal instincts and intelligence to find himself in, but in the total context of his thought it was understandable and forgivable. In any event, he was championing a lost cause. Nevertheless, the Littlepage trilogy remains a solid achievement. Only *The Redskins*, written when the anti-rent movement was reaching its peak, is violently propagandistic. *Satanstoe*, taking its title from the name of the Littlepage estate in Westchester, is an indispensable book for any student of Cooper. It is mainly concerned with giving us a pastoral picture of Colonial New York when the great estates had only recently been acquired. The title of *The Chainbearer* has reference to the surveyor's chains, with the aid of which land is surveyed, boundaries are laid out, and property rights are guaranteed. These chains are symbolic of order and inheritance; but despite excellent parts, the argument of *The Chainbearer* begins to grow heavy. Each successive generation of the Littlepages, even if they do not admit it, finds it more difficult to reconcile the claims of democracy and aristocracy.

Cooper died in 1851, on the eve of his sixty-second birthday. His life, so energetically lived, had been all of a piece, dedicated passionately to certain principles and ideals from which he never deviated for a moment in the face of that public opinion which he held in such contempt as the source of American weakness. It has been impossible to relate here the long history of Cooper's successful libel suits against the Whig newspaper editors of his day, who liked nothing more than to slander an important and articulate Jacksonian Democrat. He reduced them to glowering silence in the end, and made it clear to all that a man and a writer of integrity, at least if he were Cooper, had means of redress against the Steadfast Dodges of the time, even if they were newspaper editors. Cooper is a major artist in the American literary tradition, but not the least of his value to us today is that he was, and remains, a mirror of the American conscience.

III

THE LEATHERSTOCKING TALES were written over a period of eighteen years, from 1823, when *The Pioneers* was published, to 1841, when *The Deerslayer* appeared. Nevertheless, an unusual consistency of tone and intention informs these five novels. This arises mainly from the character of Natty Bumppo, who also goes under the names of Deerslayer, Hawkeye, Pathfinder, and Leatherstocking. The creation of Leatherstocking is probably the most significant thing that happened in American literature during its first half-century of national history. Leatherstocking belongs to that small group of fictional characters which includes Melville's Ishmael and Ahab, Huckleberry Finn, and perhaps Jay Gatsby, who seem to be related in some special way to the deepest meaning of the American experience itself. Critics have sometimes described these characters as "mythic," and for Leatherstocking they have sometimes added the word "epic." D. H. Lawrence was among them when he said that the Leatherstocking books formed "a sort of American Odyssey, with Natty Bumppo for Odysseus." The "epic" quality of these novels is almost too obvious for comment. They create for us the primeval American wilderness as no art will ever be able to create it again. It is not, certainly, the wilderness as it ever existed, but a wilderness heroically imagined, belonging to a kind of American Golden Age. There is something undeniably Homeric about this faraway world of forest solitudes and more than life-size figures engaged in mortal combat: of Indians who have the bearing of ancient kings and can speak in poetry that would do no discredit to J. M. Synge's Irish peasants. It is a world of great but uncomplicated contrasts between cruelty and nobility, between the silence of endless woods and the sudden tumult of Indian ambuscade. All but one of the Leatherstocking Tales, *The Pioneers*, are concerned with bloody conflict, yet the fighting is always interpolated with passages of quiet beauty when that yet unspoiled American world glows on Cooper's pages like an earthly paradise.

By counterpointing his pattern of conflict and violence with scenes of forest loveliness, Cooper is not merely taking time out from action for descriptive detail. He is a master of pace and timing, and he disposes these blocks of prose in such a way as to achieve the maximum of effect. The bloodcurdling cries of his savages are the more terrifying because he first creates with great artistry the awful stillness of the woods. Scenes of violence and bloodshed in Cooper are regularly followed by interludes in which the calmness of the natural world is reasserted, when the claims of battle and death give way for a time before the regenerative forces of life. It is Cooper's wonderful ability to handle these shifts of tone and viewpoint that is responsible for the sustained intensity of his actions through many chapters, and for the sense of universality he imparts so often to his incidents of forest warfare.

Cooper has a splendidly pictorial imagination that was fostered by his interest in painting. He has a habit of framing his scenes as if they were enclosed in a picture space, circumscribing the action on a visually composed stage with concentrated effect, and intensifying emotion by accents of color and skillfully deployed areas of light and shadow. Here is a night scene of an Indian encampment from *The Deerslayer* (1841) that Natty views from the safety of an offshore canoe which is concealed by darkness from the Indians themselves:

> The canoe lay in front of a natural vista, not only through the bushes that lined the shore but of the trees also, that afforded a clear view of the camp. . . . In consequence of their recent change of ground, the Indians had not yet retired to their huts, but had been delayed by their preparations, which included lodging as well as food. A large fire had been made, as much to answer the purpose of torches, as for the use of their simple cookery, and at this precise moment it was blazing high and bright, having recently received a large supply of dried brush. The effect was to illuminate the arches of the forest, and to render the area occupied by the camp as light as if hundreds of tapers were burning. . . .
>
> Deerslayer saw at a glance that many of the warriors

were absent. His acquaintance, Rivenoak, however, was present, being seated in the foreground of a picture that Salvator Rosa would have delighted to draw, his swarthy features illuminated as much by pleasure as by the torchlike flame. . . . A boy was looking over his shoulder, in dull curiosity, completing the group. More in the background, eight or ten warriors lay recumbent on the ground, or sat with their backs inclining against trees, so many types of indolent repose. Their arms were near them, sometimes leaning against the same tree as themselves, or were lying across their bodies in indolent preparation.

Cooper handles this kind of composition almost plastically, and the result is not static, as one might fear. It confers on the action that occurs in such carefully composed scenes both tightness of form and an unforgettable theatricality. These novels are not meant to be realistic. Consider Chapter 30 from *The Deerslayer*, in which the ex-pirate's beautiful daughter, Judith Hutter, attempts to rescue Deerslayer from the torture stake by emerging from the surrounding forests into the Indian encampment dressed in a magnificently regal brocade gown, which Cooper has gone to great pains in the plot to place at her disposal. The Indians are almost, but not quite, awed into submission by this glittering vision of majestic beauty. It makes no difference that the incident as Cooper describes it could scarcely have happened. Cooper is not dealing in that kind of probability. It has an imaginative quality that is like some ballet of the American wilderness. One thinks, perhaps, of Dryden's heroic tragedies, but the high-colored extravagance matters even less with Cooper because not only is the whole action of the episode adequately imagined, but the moral stature of the hero is exalted enough, and of a character proper to sustain this kind of baroque stylization in the plotting. The scene is composed in the grand manner, and the accents of color are exactly right:

Objects became visible among the trees of the background, and a body of troops was seen advancing with measured tread. They came upon the charge, the scarlet of the king's livery shining among the bright green foliage of the forest.

On such occasions Cooper's colors, like his emotions, tend to be primary, and that is as it should be in writing of this kind. But the mastery with which Cooper controls the rapid action of the Leatherstocking Tales would not in itself be enough to ensure their pre-eminent status in American literature before the 1850's. The real source of their appeal and power lies in Natty Bumppo's character. It is as uncomplicated as the solitudes in which he dwells, as heroic as the actions he performs. Yet there is nothing primitive in his nature. Natty cannot read, but in contrast with this philosopher of the wilderness, the Effinghams themselves appear unsophisticated, even a little crude. Natty is never at a loss, for his wisdom seems as old as the continent, as enduring as the hills. At twenty-three in *The Deerslayer* he is as wise as he is in the *Prairie*, when he is in his eighties. In his extraordinary death scene in that novel we feel that we are in the presence of some hero of the ancient world about to be raised to the status of an immortal.

Deerslayer can catch a tomahawk in mid-air and return it to the sender, and his feats of marksmanship with Killdeer, his rifle, have never been equaled. But it is not on these feats that Cooper builds up the character's stature. Natty is a living incarnation of the natural moral law. Another character in *The Prairie* describes him in these terms:

"The man I speak of was of great simplicity of mind, but of sterling worth. Unlike those who live a border life, he united the better, instead of the worst, qualities of the two people. He was a man endowed with the choicest and perhaps rarest gift of nature, that of distinguishing good from evil."

It is not the least remarkable thing about the Leatherstocking Tales that, in the end, the reader actively and warmly shares this opinion of Natty. In attempting to present such a man, Cooper might have given us a prig and a bore; but, as D. H. Lawrence has said, Natty is a saint with a gun. His moralizing, without which he would not be Natty, is never offensive, and rarely tedious. There is nothing righteous about Leatherstocking, but—and this is something quite different—an aura of goodness seems to invest this aloof but talkative celibate of the wilderness. It has seemed ironical to some that Natty, who shows more concern for the sanctity of life than any other great character in our literature, should be responsible, as hunter and fighter, for so many deaths. But the irony is in the facts of existence, not in Leatherstocking, and Chapter 7 of *The Deerslayer*, in which Natty kills his first Indian, is an astonishing description of conscience struggling with brutal necessity. Natty's reverence for life is preserved through seas of blood, and the lifelong effort involved renders it for us in the concrete. We observe it as an integral part of Natty's character and behavior, even in the act of killing. The old hunter of *The Pioneers*, who is angered by the wanton slaughter of the pigeons, is in a direct line with the young Deerslayer of Chapter 7.

Related to this reverence for life is Leatherstocking's greatest gift, which is uniquely his among our greatest characters in fiction: a profound understanding, which goes deeper than generosity and tolerance, of the genius of race. Natty is always proud of his white "gifts," but by these he means nothing racist. He has an almost universal insight into those universal laws that ordain that each species, each race, shall exist according to its own nature, or as he calls it, its own "gifts." In his intuitive understanding and loving acceptance of "differences" that are according to nature, Natty's attitude is basically religious, though in a sense that looks towards the natural law rather than towards any specific theology. The friendship that exists between Natty and Ching-achgook is symbolic of this deep understanding of "differences." Like Ishmael and Queequeg, like Huck and Jim, it is one of the great friendships of literature, and it exists because of, not in despite of, their contrasting "gifts."

Natty is a kind of tutelary spirit of the American land. It is essential to his conception that he should stand aloof and detached, with no closer, more enduring relation than his friendship with Chingachgook, who himself represents the aboriginal life and culture of America. But if Cooper has created Natty in an almost "mythic" dimension, he also succeeds in imparting great warmth to him, and a capacity for emotion without which his virtues might seem a little forbidding. It would have done violence to Leatherstocking's conception of Leatherstocking to have given him a wife. There is something priestly about his role that domestic ties would have violated and rendered absurd. But in *The Pathfinder* (1840) Natty falls deeply and hopelessly in love. Cooper shows a sure control over his material here, for, so far from appearing out of character, Natty's moral nature grows in stature. The final effect is to add still greater weight to the wisdom he embodies by showing as its human source a nature that is no less passionately than nobly alive. Critics often say that American literature, at least until recently, has not attempted to treat seriously of love and the relation between the sexes, and the Leatherstocking Tales are sometimes mentioned as partial substantiation of the charge. The charge in general is probably true, but it should be said that Natty's interview with Mabel Dunham on the shores of Lake Ontario in Chapter 18 of *The Pathfinder* is the most impressive scene between a man and a woman in American literature until Hawthorne in *The Scarlet Letter* brings Hester Prynne and Dimmesdale together in the woods. Mabel Dunham is also a refutation, along with Judith Hutter, of the charge that Cooper is always hopeless in the creation of female character.

Poised between love of America and disillusionment with her course, Cooper was able to create in Leatherstocking a symbolic character who resolved artistically the tension he had come to feel in himself between patriotic devotion and disaffection. In his old age, Leatherstocking flees to the Western prairies to escape the advance of a civilization he distrusts as much as Cooper did. In words that sound like Cooper's own, the old man says:

> "What the world of America is coming to, and where the machinations of its people are to end, the Lord, He only, knows . . . towns and villages, farms and highways, churches and schools, in short all the inventions and deviltries of man, are spread across the region."

Cooper had become deeply discouraged, but with the creation of Leatherstocking—particularly as presented in the last three novels—he expressed his ultimate, his only, hope: that the wisdom of natural virtue, and a purifying love of the land and forests and water, might yet redeem the American from the selfishness of the settlements: by which he meant the greed for money and power that he felt was corrupting the Republic. Unlike the Effingham novels, the Leatherstocking Tales are not polemical. It is rather through poetry and discreetly symbolic action that they embody the complex tensions we have spoken of. And it is because they exist as art adequately realized that they remain, both below and above the levels of conscious argument, the best vindication we have in his work of Cooper's deepest convictions.

Leatherstocking is a richly original creation, but the originality resides in the fact that Cooper was able to realize his conception with such power, creating him from the inside out. Leatherstocking is no lay figure dressed in a green fringed hunting shirt and a fur cap, but, as we have already said, he gives tangible form to Cooper's searching quest for the meaning of American experience. He does not illustrate any set conclusions at which Cooper had already arrived when he began these novels. It would be more correct to say that Natty *is* Cooper's conclusion, by the time he writes *The Deerslayer*, about the American world, its limitations and its possibilities, and that he arrived at it *in the process* of composition. All of Cooper's hopes and fears about America, his love and his disgust, are realized in this one symbolic character, whose "great simplicity" is of that superlative kind that represents the resolution of opposed tensions in the transcendent unity of art. But it is essential to Leatherstocking's greatness that the final distillation of his wisdom be concerned with the lot of man in an inscrutable universe rather than with the lot of the American gentleman in the America of Cooper's time. In *The Prairie*, Leatherstocking says:

> "Here have I been a dweller on the earth for fourscore and six changes of the seasons, and all that time have I looked at the growing and the dying trees, and yet do I not know the reasons why the bud starts under the summer sun, or the leaf falls when it is pinched by the frosts. Your larning, though it is man's boast, is folly in the eyes of Him, who sits in the clouds, and looks down in sorrow at the pride and vanity of his creatures. Many is the hour I've passed, lying in the shades of the woods, or stretched upon the hills of these open fields, looking up into the blue skies, where I could fancy the Great One had taken his stand, and was solemnizing on the waywardness of man and brute below, as I myself had often looked at the ants tumbling over each other in their eagerness, though in a way and a fashion more suited to His mightiness and power. Knowledge! It is a plaything. Say, you who think it is so easy to climb into the judgment-seat above, can you tell me anything of the beginning and the end? . . . What is life, and what is death? Why does the eagle live so long, and why is the time of the butterfly so short?"

Cooper's unhappiness and concern with the specific American problems of his day are seen to be absorbed here into universal questions of the human situation itself. Leatherstocking thus becomes the means by which the problems of the narrowly national scene that agitated the Effinghams are refocused against the background of the eternal. This universalizing process is achieved largely through Leatherstocking's intimate communication with nature. In *The Deerslayer*, Cooper says of Natty:

> He loved the woods for their freshness, their sublime solitudes, their vastness, and the impress that they everywhere bore of the divine hand of their Creator. He rarely moved through them without pausing to dwell on some peculiar beauty that gave him pleasure, though seldom attempting to investigate the causes; and never did a day pass without his communing in spirit, and this, too, without the aid of forms or language, with the infinite Source of all he saw, felt, and beheld.

This passage illustrates not so much what is original in Leatherstocking as what he shares in common with the ideology of much American writing and art in Cooper's day. Compare this passage from *The Deerslayer* with the opening paragraph of William Cullen Bryant's "A Forest Hymn":

> *The groves were God's first temples. Ere man learned*
> *To hew the shaft, and lay the architrave,*
> *And spread the roof above them—ere he framed*
> *The lofty vault, to gather and roll back*
> *The sound of anthems; in the darkling wood,*
> *Amid the cool and silence, he knelt down,*
> *And offered to the Mightiest solemn thanks*
> *And supplication. For his simple heart*
> *Might not resist the sacred influence*
> *Which, from the stilly twilight of the place,*

And from the gray old trunks that high in heaven
Mingled their mossy boughs, and from the sound
Of the invisible breath that swayed at once
All their green tops, stole over him, and bowed
His spirit with the thought of boundless power
And inaccessible majesty. Ah, why
Should we, in the world's riper years, neglect
God's ancient sanctuaries, and adore
Only among the crowd, and under roofs
That our frail hands have raised? Let me, at least,
Here, in the shadow of this ancient wood,
Offer one hymn—thrice happy, if it find
Acceptance in His ear.

The attitudes towards nature in Cooper and Bryant appear nearly identical. Nature is the symbol of the Creator, the mighty Cause, the infinite Source. Nature, for Bryant, is a temple, and the metaphor is carried out in some detail. Nature should impart moral instruction, and it should elevate; but it should also be able to keep man suitably depressed on occasion, with its lessons of decay and death:

> *Written on thy works I read*
> *The lesson of thy own eternity.*
> *Lo! all grow old and die. . . .*

Natty repeatedly makes the most of this mutability theme, which he and Bryant share with their age:

". . . where are you to find your shades and laughing springs, and leaping brooks, and vinerable trees, a thousand years old, in a clearin'? You don't find *them*, but you find their disabled trunks, marking the 'arth like headstones in a graveyard. It seems to me that the people who live in such places must be always thinkin' of their own inds, and of universal decay; and that, too, not of the decay that is brought about by time and

253

natur', but the decay that follows waste and violence. They call 'em the temples of the Lord; but, Judith, the whole 'arth is a temple of the Lord to such as have the right mind."

But if Cooper and Bryant share certain attitudes in common, Cooper was not, like Bryant, the editor of an influential New Yorker newspaper. He had no editorial outlet through which to express his political convictions or assuage his feelings about America. His only recourse was to pour those convictions and feelings creatively into his novels. Even when Leatherstocking is expressing conventionally held views about mutability and the infinite Source which are indistinguishable from Bryant's in substance, we never confuse them. If Natty as a symbolic character is partly forged from certain current assumptions and ideas, they are metamorphosed by Cooper, in the process of creatively imagining Natty, into something original and new, and closely related to life. The Leatherstocking Tales grow directly out of Cooper's passionate concern with life; and where could he express that concern, being neither an active politician nor a newspaper editor, except in his art? On the other hand, Bryant tends to withdraw in his poems from the real field of his later interest, which is politics and journalism, into a genteel heaven of moral sublimity that is as unrelated to life as Bryant's daily editorial tasks were intimately a part of it. The result is that Cooper gives us major art, at least in the Leatherstocking Tales, and Bryant gives us conventional, rather bloodless verse.

THE LAND OF OZ:
AMERICA'S
GREAT GOOD PLACE

THE CONSIDERABLE imaginative achievement represented by the fourteen Oz books has been ignored for
well over half a century. Even those critics who have recognized their classic status have hesitated to approve their style;
but Baum was always a satisfactory writer, and at his best his
prose reflects themes and tensions that characterize the central tradition of American literature. Since he wished to
create in Oz a specifically American fairyland, or Utopia, it is
not particularly surprising that at first his writing was influenced by the comparatively new school of realists and natu-
ralists. The description of the grimly impoverished Kansas
farm of Dorothy Gale's aunt and uncle with which *The
Wonderful Wizard of Oz* (1900) begins is a very good
example of writing in this genre:

> When Dorothy stood in the doorway and looked
> around, she could see nothing but the great gray prairie
> on every side. Not a tree nor a house broke the broad

sweep of flat country that reached the edge of the sky in all directions. The sun had baked the plowed land into a gray mass, with little cracks running through it. Even the grass was not green, for the sun had burned the tops of the long blades until they were the same gray color to be seen everywhere. Once the house had been painted, but the sun blistered the paint and the rains washed it away, and now the house was as dull and gray as everything else.

When Aunt Em came there to live she was a young, pretty wife. The sun and wind had changed her, too. They had taken the sparkle from her eyes and left them a sober gray; they had taken the red from her cheeks and lips, and they were gray also. She was thin and gaunt, and never smiled, now. When Dorothy, who was an orphan, first came to her, Aunt Em had been so startled by the child's laughter that she would scream and press her hand upon her heart whenever Dorothy's merry voice reached her ears; and she still looked at the little girl with wonder that she could find anything to laugh at.

But Baum soon moved on to more distinguished models in the same mode, and in at least one instance, surprising as it may seem, he appears to have been strongly influenced by Stephen Crane.

Stephen Crane is a writer of great ability, but during the past fifteen or twenty years extravagant claims have been made for his work. His short story "The Open Boat," published in 1897, has been described by more than one eminent critic as the best short story in English up to the time of its publication, which is nonsense of course. In 1907 Baum published his third Oz book, *Ozma of Oz*. The opening chapter of this book, "The Girl in the Chicken-Coop," is so close to Crane's story in theme, imagery, and technique that it is impossible to imagine, on comparing the two in detail, that the similarity is wholly, or even largely, accidental. Baum's narrative of how Dorothy, during a storm at sea, is blown from the ship's deck in a chicken-coop and rides out the gale is developed through images and themes that correspond closely with those employed by Crane in his account of how four men battle the elements in a ten-foot dinghy after their ship has foundered. Considerations of space make it impossible to demonstrate this similarity in a brief essay by parallel quotations, but as most readers who will have an edition of Stephen Crane on their shelves are not likely to have *Ozma of Oz* as conveniently to hand, here are a few excerpts from the opening chapter:

Dorothy decided she must go to him; so she made a dash forward, during a lull in the storm, to where a big square chicken-coop had been lashed to the deck with ropes. She reached this place in safety, but no sooner had she seized fast hold of the slats of the big box in which the chickens were kept than the wind . . . suddenly redoubled its fury. With a scream like that of an angry giant it tore away the ropes that held the coop and lifted it high into the air, with Dorothy still clinging to the slats. Around and around it whirled, this way and that, and a few moments later the chicken-coop dropped far away into the sea, where the big waves caught it and slid it up-hill to a foaming crest and then down-hill into a steep valley, as if it were nothing more than a plaything to keep them amused. . . .

She kept tight hold of the stout slats and as soon as she could get the water out of her eyes she saw that the wind had ripped the cover from the coop, and the poor chickens were fluttering away in every direction, being blown by the wind until they looked like feather dusters without handles. The bottom of the coop was made of thick boards, so Dorothy found she was clinging to a sort of raft, with sides of slats, which readily bore up her weight. After coughing the water out of her throat and getting her breath again, she managed to climb over the slats and stand upon the firm wooden bottom of the coop, which supported her easily enough. . . .

Down into a valley between the waves the coop swept her, and when she climbed another crest the ship looked like a toy boat, it was such a long way off. Soon it had entirely disappeared in the gloom. . . .

She was tossing on the bosom of a big ocean, with nothing to keep her afloat but a miserable wooden hen-coop that had a plank bottom and slatted sides, through which the water constantly splashed and wetted her through to the skin! And there was nothing to eat when she became hungry—as she was sure to do before long—and no fresh water to drink and no dry clothes to put on. . . .

As if to add to her troubles, the night was now creeping on, and the gray clouds overhead changed to inky blackness. But the wind, as if satisfied at last with its mischievous pranks, stopped blowing. . . .

By and by the black clouds rolled away and showed a blue sky overhead, with a silver moon shining sweetly in the middle of it and little stars winking merrily at Dorothy when she looked their way. The coop did not toss around any more, but rode the waves more gently—almost like a cradle rocking—so that the floor upon which Dorothy stood was no longer wet by water coming through the slats. Seeing this, and being quite exhausted by the excitement of the past few hours, the little girl decided that sleep would be the best thing to restore her strength and the easiest way in which she could pass the time. The floor was damp and she was herself wringing wet, but fortunately this was a warm climate, and she did not feel at all cold.

The similarities between Crane's story and Baum's chapter are not merely superficial, and it is both amusing and enlightening to read critical articles such as " 'The Open Boat,' an Existentialist Fiction," by Peter Buitenhuis in *Modern Fiction Studies* (Autumn, 1959), or Caroline Gordon's essay on "The Open Boat" in *The House of Fiction*, as if they were also an analysis of "The Girl in the Chicken-Coop." The double application, which works out remarkably well, might have the salutary effect of recalling children's librarians and partisan literary critics back into a balanced and sanative perspective in which measured justice could be done to both authors.

Perhaps it was the nature of the land whose history he was writing that drew Baum's style away from literary realism. At any rate, after several more books, one becomes aware of allegorical themes and attitudes that put one in mind of Hawthorne's short stories. In *The Scarecrow of Oz* Baum tells the story of a Princess whose heart was frozen by witchcraft so that she could no longer love:

> Trot saw the body of the Princess become transparent, so that her beating heart showed plainly. But now the heart turned from a vivid red to gray, and then to white. A layer of frost formed about it and tiny icicles clung to its surface. Then slowly the body of the girl became visible again and the heart was hidden from view.

It is possible that Jack Pumpkinhead was suggested to Baum by Hawthorne's "Feathertop: A Moralized Legend," but he draws nearest to Hawthorne in his treatment of certain themes that, without breaking the frame of a children's story, explore the heart and personality with a good deal of subtlety. In *The Tin Woodman of Oz* (1918) Baum searches into the ambiguities of identity and one's relation to one's own past in a remarkable episode. The Tin Woodman, whose man's body was gradually replaced by tin parts as his limbs, torso, and head were successively severed by an enchanted ax, sets out

in this book to recover his past and to rectify certain sins of
omission of which he had been guilty in his youth. In a
remote part of the Munchkin country he comes face to face
with his severed but still living head:

> The Tin Woodman had just noticed the cupboards and
> was curious to know what they contained, so he went to
> one of them and opened the door. There were shelves
> inside, and upon one of the shelves which was about on
> a level with his tin chin the Emperor discovered a Head
> —it looked like a doll's head, only it was larger, and he
> soon saw it was the Head of some person. It was facing
> the Tin Woodman and as the cupboard door swung
> back, the eyes of the Head slowly opened and looked at
> him. . . .
>
> "Dear me!" said the Tin Woodman, staring hard.
> "It seems as if I had met you somewhere, before. Good
> morning, sir!"
>
> "You have the advantage of me," replied the Head.
> "I never saw you before in my life."

A pilgrim in search of his own past, its recovery proves
impossible for the Tin Woodman, and he and his former head
remain strangers without a common ground of meeting. The
pilgrimage back through time to one's origins and source was
a favorite theme of many American writers—for example, of
Hawthorne in his last fragmentary novels, or of James in *The
Sense of the Past* or "A Passionate Pilgrim." Baum, who
handles the theme expertly enough on his own level, also finds
that the past cannot be repeated, or even rediscovered in any
satisfying way.

Probably Baum never tried to incorporate a consistent
meaning or set of values in his books, yet a significant pattern
of values does exist in them. We know, for example, that
General Jinjur, who captures the Emerald City with her
army of girls in *The Land of Oz* (1904), is an extended

satire on the suffragette movement; and Baum's deep affection for monarchy and the trappings of royalty that runs through all the books reflects a facet of sensibility shared by many nineteenth-century Americans. Baum created a land so rich in palaces, crowns, costume, heraldry, and pomp that he had no grounds for complaining, as James had done, of the poverty of the American environment in supplying the writer with material. Yet Oz remains unmistakably an *American* fairyland. In nothing is this more apparent than in the way Baum transforms magic into a glamorized version of technology and applied science.

A few years ago, in a book called *The Machine in the Garden*, Leo Marx analyzed nineteenth-century American literature in relation to technology. American society evolved under the stimulus and energy provided by a new age of industrialization and technical discoveries. The new attitudes characteristic of this era were superimposed on a largely pastoral ideal inherited from the eighteenth century and from Jeffersonian agrarianism. "Within the lifetime of a single generation," Marx writes, "a rustic and in large part wild landscape was transformed into the site of the world's most productive industrial machine." This process of transformation really began in earnest with the widespread application of steam power. In an incredibly short space of time, "this fresh, green breast of the new world" had been replaced by a man-made landscape. Describing the painting "American Landscape," by Charles Sheeler, Marx writes:

No trace of nature remains. Not a tree or a blade of grass in view. The water is enclosed by man-made banks, and the sky is filling with smoke. Like the reflection upon the water, every natural object represents some aspect of the collective enterprise. Technological power overwhelms the solitary man; the landscape convention calls for his presence to provide scale, but here the traditional figure acquires new meaning: in this mechanical environment he seems forlorn and powerless.

The second half of *The Machine in the Garden* is concerned with showing us just how the dialectic between the pastoral vision and technology, which is the destructive element, is a central theme in nineteenth-century American literature. Marx equates the pastoral dream with "the kingdom of love," and technology with "the kingdom of power," and he asserts that they have waged war in American literature endlessly since Hawthorne. Now, the tension between pastoralism and technology is one of the things the Oz books are about, whether Baum was conscious of it or not. In the American literature of which Marx writes, technology seems to triumph despite the resistance the authors offer to it. The locomotive turns the garden into a desert. It is a distinguishing mark of the Oz books that a satisfactory resolution of the tension is achieved in them, and the Munchkins on their small farms in the East continue down to the time that Baum wrote of them to exemplify an agrarian ideal.

The best description of the economic, social, and political conditions that go to make up the Oz way of life is to be found in Baum's sixth book on Oz, *The Emerald City of Oz* (1910):

[The Emerald City] has nine thousand, six hundred and fifty-four buildings, in which lived fifty-seven thousand, three hundred and eighteen people, up to the time my story opens.

All the surrounding country, extending to the borders of the desert which enclosed it upon every side, was full of pretty and comfortable farmhouses, in which resided those inhabitants of Oz who preferred country to city life.

Altogether there were more than half a million people

in the Land of Oz . . . and every inhabitant of the country was happy and prosperous.

No disease of any sort was ever known among the Ozites, and so no one ever died unless he met with an accident that prevented him from living. This happened very seldom indeed. There were no poor people in the Land of Oz, because there was no such thing as money, and all property of every sort belonged to the Ruler. The people were her children, and she cared for them. Each person was given freely by his neighbors whatever he required for his use, which is as much as anyone may reasonably desire. Some tilled the land and raised great crops of grain, which was divided equally among the entire population, so that all had enough. There were many tailors and dressmakers and shoemakers and the like, who made things that anyone who desired them might wear. Likewise there were jewelers who made ornaments for the person, which pleased and beautified the people, and these ornaments were also free to those who asked for them. Each man and woman, no matter what he or she produced for the good of the community, was supplied by the neighbors with food and clothing and a house and furniture and ornaments and games. If by chance the supply ever ran short, more was taken from the great storehouses of the Ruler, which were afterwards filled up again when there was more of any article than the people needed.

Everyone worked half the time and played half the time, and the people enjoyed the work as much as they did the play, because it is good to be occupied and to have something to do. There were no cruel overseers set to watch them, and no one to rebuke them or to find fault with them. So each one was proud to do all he could for his friends and neighbors, and was glad when they would accept the things he produced.

At first this seems a garden into which no machine is likely to intrude. But we have to remember that magic is the science or technology of Oz. In *Magic, Science, and Religion* Malinowski wrote:

> Magic is akin to science in that it always has a definite aim associated with human instincts, needs, and pursuits. . . . The magic art is directed towards the attainment of practical aims. Like the other arts and crafts, it is also governed by a theory of principles which dictate the manner in which the act has to be performed in order to be effective. . . . Thus both magic and science show certain similarities, and with Sir James Frazer, we can appropriately call magic a pseudo-science.

The Ozites were much aware of the scientific character of magic. Glinda the Good, who, subject to Princess Ozma, ruled the Quadling Country in the south, always retired to her laboratory to perform her magical experiments, and the Wizard of Oz carried a small black bag filled with his magical instruments in very much the fashion of a nineteenth-century country doctor. In *The Patchwork Girl of Oz* (1913) the Shaggy Man explicitly says in some verses that he recites: "I'll sing a song of Ozland . . . where magic is a science." In *Glinda of Oz* (1920) we are told of the island of the Skeezers, enclosed in a glass dome, which could be submerged for defensive purposes. The method by which this was accomplished clearly reveals the "scientific" character of Oz magic:

> "I now remember," returned Aujah, "that one of the arts we taught Coo-ee-oh was the way to expand steel, and I think that explains how the island is raised and lowered. I noticed in the basement a big steel pillar that passed through the floor and extended upward to this palace. . . . If the lower end of the steel pillar is firmly

embedded in the bottom of the lake, Coo-ee-oh could utter a magic word that would make the pillar expand, and so lift the entire island to the level of the water.

But there is no need to multiply instances of this magical technology. The Ozites understood the necessity of bringing this source of energy and power under the control of the central government, and only Glinda the Good, the Wizard, and Ozma herself were entitled to practice magic legally. By this prohibition, which placed government restrictions on promiscuous and uncontrolled "technological" experimentation, Oz retained her pastoral landscape and guaranteed her people's happiness. There were of course criminal practitioners of magic—particularly in the still wild Gillikin Country in the north—but one of the principal functions of government in Oz was to keep these enemies of order under control. There were machines in Oz, but as with Tik-Tok, the clockwork man, they tended to be thoroughly humanized. And where the Powder of Life could be used as a source of power and energy, the steam engine and the dynamo could scarcely be considered a serious threat to human happiness.

Marx writes that American literature has been concerned with the endless warfare between "the kingdom of love" and "the kingdom of power." For love, technology is a destructive element because it is dehumanizing. So far from liberating man's humanity by giving him control over nature, as the nineteenth century often believed, technology tends to approximate man to the level of the machine he creates. It is perhaps an awareness of this threat that led so many American writers in the nineteenth century to accept the ideal of a selfless love as the central value of their work. Fenimore Cooper's Natty Bumppo embodies this ideal of selflessness and service to others; virtually all of Hawthorne's stories and novels revolve around the theme of "the magnetic chain of humanity," by which he means unselfish and disinterested love of humanity, and this is also one of the principal subjects of Henry James's fictions. Selflessness and loving kindness constitute the very air of Oz. It is the only American territory in which the magnetic chain of humanity is rarely broken, and in which the selfless generosity of James's "American Princess," Milly Theale, would appear little more than normal behavior. In an introductory essay to *The Wonderful Wizard of Oz*, Russell B. Nye wrote in 1958:

> The First Law of Baum's Utopia of Oz, the rule that inspires its harmonious order, is Love. This theme, on which Baum played constant variations, binds all the Oz books together as a moral unit. Love in Oz is kindness, selflessness, friendliness—an inner check that makes one act decently towards human beings, animals, plants, machines, and even one's enemies.

One has to bear in mind that love in Oz is a value actively present in the stories, dramatized in the action, and realized in the characters. There is nothing self-conscious, sentimental, or priggish about it. It is the imaginative element in which Dorothy, Ozma, Glinda, the Tin Woodman, the Scarecrow, the Cowardly Lion, and all the rest exist and have their meaning. As Nye points out, the most evil character in all the Oz books is the ruler of the Phanfasms, whose title is the First and Foremost. That beautifully sinister title sums up the final meaning of Oz history. The aggrandizement of the individual and private self at the expense of others is the root of all evil.

Marx speaks of a "design of the classic American fables" which embodies "the idea of a redemptive journey away from society in the direction of nature." A number of Americans managed to make their way to Oz—from Kansas, Nebraska, Oklahoma, and, of course, California. To do so they had to cross the Deadly Desert. The way was arduous and the dangers great; but when these happy few arrived in Oz they were confronted by a pastoral world as unspoiled as that which once greeted the eyes of those Dutch sailors whom Scott Fitzgerald invokes at the close of *The Great Gatsby*. It was a world in which magical technology was strictly controlled, and in which perfect selflessness and love was the element of life. It was, in short, the Great Good Place.

I V

WALLACE STEVENS
AND EMERSON

O NE TAKES PLEASURE in reflecting that Wallace Stevens received, during the year or two before his death at the age of seventy-five, some of the visible honors that should have been accorded to one of the greatest of all American poets. But it is not a matter for complacency. The obituary in *The New York Times* was at such a loss for words that it could only reprint a more than usually unfortunate review of *Harmonium* by the poetry editor that had appeared in the pages of *The New York Times Book Review* many years before. One should not mistake recognition for comprehension. And yet the difficulty of Stevens' verse is of a kind that may leave readers of his poetry a century hence wondering where the difficulty was. "Is the man sane who can deliberately commit to print this fantastic nonsense?" a writer in *The North American Review* asked when Emerson published his volume of poems in 1847. For those who may still read Emerson's poetry, unintelligibility, or even difficulty, will not be found among its dominant characteristics.

Great poets are not required to have new meanings any

more than the seasons are. What they contribute is life and a
sense of organic relation between ourselves and the world.
There is nothing new in what Wallace Stevens had to say;
and yet in another sense it is all new, immersed in a vision, an
originality, as new as morning. I think it is possible to gain a
fresh insight into Stevens' poetry by considering him as an
American Transcendentalist poet. There are some serious
difficulties in the way, but there are also some rewards.
Viewed in this way, he is no longer a sport in the American
tradition, a rather dandified anomaly, but an explicable
phenomenon.

Traditional American Transcendentalism is hard to define,
but if it stood for anything as a movement, it was for the
capacity to apotheosize the soiled pragmatic world, to justify
the grubby fact in a higher realm of intuition. Such a transcending process is essentially a motion, a becoming. But it is
not necessarily a flight from material reality. It can be an
intenser apprehension of life—a kind of spiritual metabolism
by which the boundaries of the physical are canceled, its
subtance becoming a part of some ultimate, central vision
that is the highest life. For Stevens the exercise of the creative
vision was the means towards achieving this intenser state of
being. He never submitted this state to dogmatic definition,
but he celebrated it in a great many poems.

Part I of Stevens' late poem "Prologues to What Is Possible," is representative in this respect:

*There was an ease of mind that was like being alone in a
    boat at sea,*
*A boat carried forward by waves resembling the bright
    backs of rowers,*
*Gripping their oars, as if they were sure of the way to
    their destination,*
*Bending over and pulling themselves erect on the
    wooden handles,*

*Wet with water and sparkling in the one-ness of their
    motion.*
*The boat was built of stones that had lost their weight
    and being no longer heavy*
*Had left in them only a brilliance, of unaccustomed
    origin,*
*So that he stood up in the boat leaning and looking
    before him*
*Did not pass like someone voyaging out of and beyond
    the familiar.*
*He belonged to the far-foreign departure of his vessel
    and was part of it,*
*Part of the speculum of fire on its prow, its symbol,
    whatever it was,*
*Part of the glass-like sides on which it glides over the
    salt-stained water,*
*As he traveled alone, like a man lured on by a syllable
    without any meaning,*
A syllable of which he felt, with an appointed sureness,
*That it contained the meaning into which he wanted to
    enter,*
*A meaning which, as he entered it, would shatter the
    boat and leave the oarsmen quiet*
*As at a point of central arrival, an instant moment,
    much or little,*
*Removed from any shore, from any man or woman, and
    needing none.*

These lines are almost as capable as passages in Eliot's
Quartets of taking a Christian interpretation. They acquire a
certain beauty in such a reading, and it has its own validity.
But it is dangerous to put Stevens' poetry in a specifically
religious frame. It belongs rather to a realm in which spiritual aspiration and psychological process, fusing together,
become an end in themselves. There is a mystical element in

that state of being "where," as Stevens puts it in another poem, "he would be complete in an unexplained completion."

In a published lecture Stevens has written: "The imagination is the power of the mind over the possibilities of things; but if this constitutes a certain single characteristic, it is the source not of a single certain value but of as many values as reside in the possibilities of things." This is a slippery formulation, but it should make it clear that if the imagination governs things, things detain the imagination on too low a level to permit us to look with any confidence for anything beyond a natural explanation of the experience involved. But on another level, this relation between imagination and things which he has described explains the process by which he makes his poetry—the avenue of *things* down which his mind moves towards that centrality which, for him, is the end of the creative act, just as the creative act is the fulfillment of life. The last two stanzas of the poem from which I have already quoted illustrate Stevens' constant habit of metamorphosing nature and art into higher states of awareness or being:

What self, for example, did he contain that had not yet
    been loosed,
Snarling in him for discovery as his attentions
    spread,
As if all his hereditary lights were suddenly increased
As by an access of color, a new and unobserved, slight
    dithering,
The smallest lamp, which added to its puissant flick, to
    which he gave
A name and privilege over the ordinary of his
    commonplace—
A flick which added to what was real and its
    vocabulary,
The way some first thing coming into Northern trees

Adds to them the whole vocabulary of the South,
The way the earliest single light in the evening sky, in
spring,
Creates a fresh universe out of nothingness by adding
itself,
The way a look or a touch reveals its unexpected
magnitudes.

In many of Stevens' poems the creative mind climbs the ladder of things in this fashion towards some final, vibrant insight into, or possession of, being. The implications of this ultimate discovery of a higher self through the imagination are revealed clearly in the closing lines of another late poem, "Final Soliloquy of the Interior Paramour":

We say God and the imagination are one . . .
How high that highest candle lights the dark.
Out of this same light, out of the central mind,
We make a dwelling in the evening air,
In which being there together is enough.

Ultimately, the self which is discovered through the imagination is not unrelated to the cosmic "I" of Whitman's "Song of Myself." Essentially, in Stevens, the process is psychological, but it is constantly on the point of tipping into mysticism —and perhaps sometimes it does, in its own peculiar fashion. In his lecture "Effects of Analogy" Stevens said that the poet "comes to feel that his imagination is not wholly his own, but that it may be a part of a much larger, much more potent imagination, which it is his affair to get at."

One thinks of Emerson at once, but apparently Stevens did not like Emerson. One of his last poems is called "Looking Across the Fields and Watching the Birds Fly." If I read the poem correctly, Mr. Homburg is a witty and unkind epithet for Emerson, or at least for the popular conception of him, which Stevens seems to have shared:

Among the more irritating minor ideas
Of Mr. Homburg during his visits home
To Concord, at the edge of things, was this . . .
To think away the grass, the trees, the clouds . . .

The poem goes on to concern itself with the Over-Soul, defined as: "mechanical/ And slightly detestable *operandum*, free/ From man's ghost, and yet a little like." It is detestable because it is remote from man. It is

Not one of the masculine myths we used to make,
A transparency through which the swallow weaves,
Without any form or any sense of form,
What we know in what we see, what we feel in what
We hear, what we are, beyond mystic disputation,
In the tumult of integrations out of the sky . . .

But if this is Stevens' description of what Emerson's Over-Soul is not, it might serve equally well, with a minor cavil about the word "form," as Emerson's description of what it *was* to him. I imagine that Stevens would object that Emerson was insufficiently impressed by the physical world. Poem XV of "Esthétique du Mal" begins:

The greatest poverty is not to live
In a physical world. . . .

And Stevens' poetry is filled with lines like these from "Crude Foyer":

Thought is a false happiness; the idea . . .
That there lies at the end of thought
A foyer of the spirit in a landscape
Of the mind, in which we sit
And wear humanity's bleak crown.

But we already know that Stevens is not the rugged materialist such lines might imply. Verses such as these are really more typical and more central in his thought:

> *. . . It was a queen that made it seem*
> *By the illustrious nothing of her name.*
> *Her green mind made the world around her green.*
> *The queen is an example. . . . This green queen*
> *In the seeming of the summer of her sun*
> *By her own seeming made the summer change.*

This (from "Description Without Place") is typical Stevens, but the meaning, apart from technique, makes it also typical Emerson: "Poetry begins, or all becomes poetry, when we look from the center outward, and are using all as if the mind made it. That only can we see which we are, and which we make. The weaver sees gingham; the broker sees the stock-list; the politician, the ward and the county votes; the poet sees the horizon. . . ."

There is no more insistence on "thought" and its transmuting power in Emerson than in Stevens, nor is Stevens enamored of the physical world more than Emerson: "These roses under my window make no reference to former roses or to better ones; they are for what they are; they exist with God today; there is no time to them. There is simply the rose; it is perfect in every moment of its existence. Before a leaf-bud has burst, its whole life acts; in the full-blown flower there is no more; in the leafless root there is no less. Its nature is satisfied and it satisfies nature in all moments alike. But man postpones or remembers; he does not live in the present, but with reverted eye laments the past, or heedless of the riches that surround him, stands on tiptoe to foresee the future. He cannot be happy and strong until he too lives with nature in the present, above time."

For Emerson as for Stevens, the world as it passed through the creative mind underwent perpetual metamorphosis which led, or ought to have led, into a more exalted spiritual state—a state of intenser imaginative vision. As Emerson put it (and Stevens would not have dissented): "Thin or solid, everything is in flight . . . everything undressing and stealing

277

away from its old into new form. . . ."

Both Stevens and Emerson described this inner illumination in terms that are either frankly or approximately mystical. But at this point certain differences begin to show. As I have already suggested, if we try to rationalize a metaphysic out of Stevens' poetry we have the sense of a man lifting himself by his bootstraps towards some kind of spiritual apotheosis normally beyond his capacity. The source of power remains a little puzzling because Stevens will not confront the mystical element implicit in his idea or experience with the frankness Emerson resorted to, sometimes with gullible and irritating readiness.

I quoted Stevens as saying that the poet's imagination "may be part of a larger, much more potent imagination, which it is his affair to get at." The imagination when spoken of in these terms is not only unmistakably the Romantic imagination as it developed during the last years of the eighteenth century and the first quarter of the nineteenth—it also has strong affinities with Emerson's Over-Soul. It is clear I think that Stevens has not, except now and then, gone along with the implications of his statement which I just quoted. And indeed the Over-Soul may not impress many people today; but something of its kind (failing some species of religious orthodoxy) is still a necessary support for the kind of inner illumination both Emerson and Stevens wished to achieve.

Although this one difference is crucial enough to warrant our looking for an essential difference in the character of their respective goals, if we reread "Prologues to What Is Possible" and compare it with Emerson's talents of the soul, both poets seem to be talking about the same thing. Here is Emerson on the soul, which for thinkers like these two may also be called the imagination: "The soul circumscribes all things. As I have said, it contradicts all experience. The influence of the senses has in most men overpowered the mind to that degree that the walls of time and space have come to look real and insurmountable; and to speak with levity of these limits is, in the world, the sign of insanity. Yet time and space are but the inverse measures of the force of the soul."

In Emerson's thinking the soul has this creative and destroying power, in some considerable degree, from the outside. It is able to transcend its usual limitations because it has superior assistance; but Stevens usually sheers away from this conclusion, although it is really implicit in his poetry, as the "mystical" overtones of so much of the imagery, especially in his late verse, indicate. And ungenerously he calls Emerson Mr. Homburg. As I once pointed out in an earlier essay on Stevens, he is in love with hat imagery, and he uses it frequently with great brilliance to suggest a man's spiritual or mental state. If a man wears a sombrero with a flaring brim, he's all right; if he wears a broad-brimmed hat that droops over his eyes and shades him from the moonlight, or if he wears a homburg, he's either a bigot or a prig. For once Stevens' mastery with hat imagery fails him, because Emerson is no more Mr. Homburg (probably a good deal less so) than Stevens himself.

The similarities of thought between Stevens and Emerson are not less real for being somewhat concealed, and they lead directly into similar conceptions of the role of the poet and the power of the word. Emerson was probably the second greatest poet (after Whitman) that America produced in the nineteenth century. The compliment is modest enough. His ideas as they come to us both from his prose and his poetry were seminal. From William Carlos Williams' wistful cry in *Paterson*, "No ideas but in things," the symbolist faith in the ability of the word to incarnate reality stretches back across Whitman's *American Primer* to Emerson's *Nature*. For Emerson, Nature was the encompassing metaphor or symbol through which God manifested himself to men, and conceptual symbolism and language were the means by which reality became intelligible to, and a possession of, the mind:

"This relation between the mind and matter is not fancied by some poets, but stands in the will of God. . . . When in fortunate hours we ponder this miracle . . . the universe becomes transparent, and the light of higher laws than its own shines through." This miracle of metamorphosis and discovery could not be performed in dead language and symbol, but only by words and symbols as they are used by the creative mind making forays into new reality. Stevens has described this better than Emerson succeeded in doing in his own poems:

There it was, word for word,
The poem that took the place of a mountain.

He breathed its oxygen,
Even when the book lay turned in the dust of his table.

It reminded him of how he had needed
A place to go in his own direction,

How he had recomposed the pines,
Shifted the rocks and picked his way among the clouds,

For the outlook that would be right,
Where he could be complete in an unexplained
*   completion.*

My remarks here concerning the shortcomings of Stevens' metaphysics when one attempts to rationalize a "system" out of his poetry are not to be construed as a criticism of that poetry. Poetry is not metaphysics, and Stevens remains, in my opinion, the greatest twentieth-century American poet after Eliot. I doubt if Stevens would have welcomed the comparison with Emerson I have made here, but despite differences in outlook, the affinities I have pointed to (as well as the differences) seem to me to reveal a great deal about Stevens' poetry. Poetry is not metaphysics, but there is such a thing as a philosophical poet, and both Stevens and Emerson deserve this title for reasons that are very similar.

THE POETRY OF
ISAAC ROSENBERG

"Sudden the Lightning Flashed upon a Figure. . . ."

WHEN Isaac Rosenberg was buried in an unmarked grave in France in 1918, he left behind only a slender sheaf of poetry that can be regarded as really important. Despite his several inconspicuous appearances in print, he must have seemed as nearly anonymous as most of the hundreds of thousands who were killed that year. And in spite of his talent, and Gordon Bottomley's edition of his poems, brought out in 1922, the years that followed his death have done little to rectify that churlish neglect which had been their chief gift to him while alive.[1]

1. This essay was first published in *Commentary* in June, 1949. Several minor revisions have been made here. It does not seem to me that Rosenberg's reputation as a poet has radically altered since I wrote this article. D. W. Harding's essay, "The Poetry of Isaac Rosenberg," *Scrutiny*, March, 1935, remains a distinguished exception to the melancholy generalization made in my text, as does T. S. Eliot's mention of Isaac Rosenberg, in a Poetry Bookshop Chapbook, as a poet whose neglect was owing to the bad state of contemporary criticism. In 1963 Mr. Harding included his essay in a collection named *Experience into Words*.

There is, certainly, a confusing unevenness in the collected volume [2] as a whole, an occasional fragmentary quality that is superficially disengaging. His best efforts are contained in a handful of *Trench Poems* which must be set off against a considerably larger number of poems written at different stages in his creative immaturity. This period of artistic uncertainty and more or less conventional poetics was more than usually protracted in Rosenberg's case; and that for a number of reasons, most of which can be traced to the discouragements of poverty.

In view of all this, it is sad, but not surprising, that Rosenberg has been left to languish among the Georgians. He is, of course, entitled to that classification by virtue of his inclusion, by a single poem, in Edward Marsh's 1916–17 Georgian anthology. His most influential friends had been Georgians; his small correspondence includes letters to Gordon Bottomley, Edward Marsh, Lascelles Abercrombie, and R. C. Trevelyan—all of them names that made Georgian literary history, and have been long out of fashion. But Rosenberg developed into something else, and left the suburbanized garden plots of Georgian poetry far behind him.

Before the war Rosenberg had served a hard apprenticeship in poverty; his life was short and sad, and looking back over it, an early sentence of his acquires a tragic significance: "What purpose was there in such wasted striving—and supposing success did come, would it be sufficient recompense for the wasted life and youth, the starved years . . . ?"

Isaac Rosenberg was born in Bristol, England, on November 25, 1890. His father, Barnett Rosenberg, had come from Lithuania; his mother, Chasa Davidoff, had been born in Latvia. He had seven brothers and sisters, and although his luck was generally bad, he was fortunate in preserving warm and sympathetic relationships with all his family until his

2. *The Collected Poems of Isaac Rosenberg*, edited by Gordon Bottomley and D. W. Harding, Schocken Books, New York, 1949.

death. His parents spoke Yiddish, and Rosenberg was sent to Hebrew school in his early childhood. The atmosphere of his home influenced him so strongly that by the time he was ten he was writing poetry on Jewish religious history.

His eldest sister, who was the first to recognize his talent, sought advice about her little brother from the local librarian, but the latter was only able to recommend that the child read "The Charge of the Light Brigade" often. Beth Zion Lask, in an article on Rosenberg which appeared in *Reflex* some years ago, maintains that the Rosenberg family was "poor in a Jewish way," which is something "totally different from non-Jewish poverty." Praise of poverty in any form is always unconvincing; and there is nothing in the tone of Rosenberg's early letters, where he refers to his own poverty as a "fiendish mangling machine," that leads one to suppose he reacted to it any differently from any other sensitive, highly talented young man struggling for an education.

His family had moved to London when he was seven years old, settling near Whitechapel. He attended an elementary school, where he began to show a particular interest in drawing; but when he was fourteen it became necessary for him to leave school and go to work. He worked for a firm of art engravers in Fleet Street as an apprentice, and although he hated the work he managed to go to night classes at the art school of Birbeck College. In view of the little time he had at his own disposal, he read a great deal, and always with enthusiasm; but he never quite lost a sense of educational deficiency. "You mustn't forget," he wrote years later, "the circumstances I have been brought up in, the little education I have had. Nobody ever told me what to read, or ever put poetry in my way."

In 1911 he rashly gave up his job, but after a few exhilarating weeks of freedom lapsed into nervous melancholy. Things seemed to brighten a little when three Jewish ladies gave him money to attend the Slade School of Art from

October 1911 until March 1914. At the Slade he had a successful student's career, won prizes, competed for the Prix de Rome, and exhibited some paintings at the Whitechapel Gallery. From available descriptions of Rosenberg's paintings one surmises they were strongly romantic, even pre-Raphaelite. But turning to the several reproductions of portraits and drawings in *The Complete Works*, one is surprised by their freshness and vigor, and one begins to have a faith in his capacity for painting, a faith that is strengthened by reading a rather sketchy, formless lecture called simply "Art," which he delivered while in Cape Town, and which was later published in a periodical named *South African Women in Council*. The lecture contains many insights which were far ahead of English art criticism of the day.

But actually these years of study at the Slade were not happy ones. Occasionally one glimpses humiliations imposed on him by at least one of his patronesses. "I am very sorry I have disappointed you," Rosenberg writes to her. "If you tell me what was expected of me I shall at least have the satisfaction of knowing by how much I have erred. You were disappointed by my picture for its unfinished state—I have no wish to defend myself—or I might ask you what you mean by finish. . . . I cannot conceive who gave you the idea that I had such big notions of myself, are you sure the people you enquired of know me, and meant me . . . ? I am not very inquisitive naturally, but I think it concerns me to know what you mean by poses and mannerisms—and whose advice do I not take who are in a position to give—and what more healthy style of work do you wish me to adopt?"

It is grim to learn from another letter that Rosenberg was dependent on this patroness at the time even for money to have his shoes repaired.

After three years of this kind of benevolence, his health gave way. It was thought that he had tuberculosis, and that he would be benefited by a trip to Cape Town, where one of his married sisters was living. One hears of difficulty in scraping together the twelve pounds passage money; and then his letters give a few pictures of him after his arrival: meeting Olive Schreiner, who liked him and admired some drawings of Kaffirs he made; visiting a wealthy family, and writing home with the enthusiasm of a really poor young man about "wonderful breakfasts—the unimaginable lunches—delicious teas, and colossal dinners." But South Africa seemed worse than tuberculosis, and he eagerly returned to England the following year, apparently improved in health. At home, he published at his own expense a pamphlet of sixteen short poems called *Youth*. These form a marked advance over the somewhat Keatsian pamphlet, *Night and Day*, which he had published in the same manner in 1912. But if Rosenberg's real genius is faintly heralded in *Youth*—perhaps at one or two points more than faintly—the moment of his poetic self-discovery was by no means at hand.

Meanwhile, the 1914 war came along. Whether sick or well, Rosenberg measured up to the army's physical requirements; and so, greatly discouraged, he anticipated the inevitable and enlisted, although he hated the whole war machine. "Believe me," he wrote, "the army is the most detestable invention on earth, and nobody but a private knows what it is to be a slave." His army letters are characteristically restrained, but they reveal the real horror of army life—the oversized shoes and ulcerated feet, the insolent stupidity of officers, the damp beds and the head colds, the filthy clothes, the endless obscenity—better than any war letters that spring to mind immediately; and yet they are the briefest scrawls, mere snippets of his experience. It is astonishing to consider that it was under these conditions that he began and carried on his most significant period of productivity.

In 1916, after a term of training in England, he was sent to France in the King's Own Royal Lancasters. Before going, he managed to have his one-act play *Moses* printed privately,

together with seven short poems, including the savage poem
"God." This last poem is best understood in the light of
Rosenberg's whole development, but inasmuch as some critics have complained about its theological improprieties, it had
better be said that the God of the poem is a very special, if not
very rare one, created by the middle classes out of their
"imaginative indolence" and preached by the recruiting
clergy of Rosenberg's day. It is a sociological, not a theological, god.

Trench Poems was composed between the publication of
Moses and Rosenberg's death on April 1, 1918, when his
twenty-eighth birthday was still half a year away.

Rosenberg belongs to that small group of poets who had
sensed how essentially different the war that began in 1914
was from all others. Their greater awareness was not merely
rational but intuitive, and their poetry is an attempt to explore and analyze the monstrous experience. In their hands
war poetry came to mean something different from what it
had commonly meant before. For them war no longer comprised a fragment of experience, but its totality. They no
longer tried to evaluate it in the perspective of peacetime
assumptions, to accept the apology of official slogans, or
absorb the war's effect on the individual by dreaming of an
imminent return to the status quo. They understood that, for
them at any rate, the tyranny was absolute.

The rift between the experiences of war and the experiences of civilization had widened so much by the twentieth
century that it was nearly impassable, with the experiences of
war becoming dominant for a large and ever increasing portion of the world's population. If war poetry were to have any
claims as valid artistic expression, it could no longer exist as a
specialized department of verse. It could no longer be merely
a rousing hunting song, nor was the ode of pure patriotism
any longer very pure.

Most of the poets who won recognition during World War

I developed a protective subjectivity like Alan Seeger, or, like that truly typical Georgian, Rupert Brooke, continued to experience the war in the cracked molds of old attitudes, and under the colors of a faded glamor. When mentioning the few names that one can positively bring forward, names like Edward Thomas, Wilfred Owen, and Isaac Rosenberg, one must remember that their profound perception of the nature of the crisis represented, necessarily, only a partial understanding, and that their insights were more personal than social. And so it is difficult to generalize, even about a group of three. But they did begin and end with this in common (and this they shared with a few others, such as Siegfried Sassoon): equally, they hated the sham and hypocrisy of the war, and they saw through it with a surprisingly radical vision.

Charles Sorley, another young poet who was killed early in the war, spoke for them all when he wrote: "England—I am sick of the sound of the word. In training to fight for England, I am training to fight for that deliberate hypocrisy, that terrible middle-class sloth of outlook and appalling 'imaginative indolence' that has marked us from generation to generation."

And yet these young men voluntarily went to war, and almost all were killed. This apparent contradiction ("Nothing can justify war," Rosenberg wrote at the time he appeared to submit most to its claims) sprang from no wavering resolution, but from a perception that naturally embraced expiatory suffering as the only way out. This perception may often have been greater than their poetry—the practical difficulties of writing at all were only short of insuperable—but ultimately it was the life of it. In time the poetry of Rosenberg would almost certainly have assumed proportions commensurate with the full reality it was trying to express. But I do not wish to make the mistake of dwelling on Rosenberg's "promise"; his achievement is evident enough.

For every person who has read a poem of Rosenberg's, a few hundred must have read something of Wilfred Owen's. And yet Rosenberg is the greater poet. Both men were rather like unguilty angels who had fallen with the rout into pandemonium, and their verse is an attempt to survey creatively their new midnight universe. Owen may have carried a little more of the old heaven with him, but Rosenberg understood better the brutal anonymity of the war, and the true dimensions of the tragedy. Owen never quite became more than a good Georgian, and while it would be rash to speculate about the course of his literary career had he lived, his work has none of that rampant, impatient eagerness to reach beyond itself which is so frequently startling in the other poet's work. There was something Wordsworthian about the Georgians, but it was a Wordsworth stripped of stature; and it is stature that one never quite discovers in Owen's own poems. His hatred of war is too exclusively a hatred of its physical effects on the lives of the young Englishmen under his command.

One cannot help feeling that Owen is caught and held back by the sight of all the suffering—which, after all, is only one anguished corner of the whole intolerable picture. Owen seems little concerned with any reality that is not to be penetrated by pity alone. He seems to converge his perspective lines towards the hospital cot rather than to unfold them from that terminus of pity. The vision he offers is poignant but incomplete, and too regretful to be great. It is a picture made up of many moving accidents—so many that the form of the tragedy is sometimes obscured.

Rosenberg's poetry does not stop short of the pity and tenderness in Owen's, but passes beyond it into something new. He is aware that the suffering of war is too great to be comforted, and he cannot mistake pity for succor; in his poetry, suffering achieves something like classical composure. Details are lost in bold simplicity of form, and his victims have a heroic moral strength, a stoicism which invites the

mind not to the frustrating pity of helplessness, but to something like the re-creative pity of the ancient stage.

As an example of this attitude one may look at a short
passage from "Dead Man's Dump," one of the greatest
poems of World War I. It is directly, even starkly, concerned
with suffering, and yet its terrible picture of agony never
hinders the poise, the freedom of inquiry that is maintained
throughout. In this poem, so impersonal and detached in
comparison with much of Owen's poetry, there is a hard,
almost shocking, concreteness and immediacy of imagery that
makes Owen seem vague and general by contrast:

> *A man's brains splattered on*
> *A stretcher-bearer's face;*
> *His shook shoulders slipped their load,*
> *But when they bent to look again*
> *The drowning soul was sunk too deep for human*
> > *tenderness.*
> *They left the dead with the older dead,*
> *Stretched at the cross roads.*
>
> *Burnt black with strange decay*
> *Their sinister faces lie,*
> *The lid over each eye,*
> *The grass and coloured clay*
> *More motion have than they*
> *Joined to the great sunk silences.*

One is not so much aware of the single, the private, death
here, as one is aware of the representative and universal
quality in the death which is described. All "the older dead"
and all who will die seem to participate symbolically in this
one soldier's death. The ineffectual resentment we might
otherwise feel is guarded against by very carefully handled
suggestions of inevitability, and, even as we watch, the action
reaches and seems to continue beyond that point where
human tenderness can follow, down into an antique, stoic

underworld of "great sunk silences." This soldier is less a private person than a point at which the fate of men in war becomes for a moment visible.

And it is significant that no facile, gratuitous commentary on that fate is offered in the whole eighty-six lines of "Dead Man's Dump." The poem's strength lies in the composure it maintains when faced by human pain, in its refusal to indulge an easy grief or extend an invitation to tears. It shows a sure control of words moving through dangerous emotions at disciplined speeds and leading the reader, by their very restraint and poise, into a fuller understanding of human dignity.

But Rosenberg did not pass from writing derivative poetry in civilian life to verse of this stature in a single day. One may arrive at a better understanding of the peculiar impersonality of *Trench Poems* if one looks first at the play *Moses*. Its strength is not the strength of the later poems, but it is a necessary step towards them and in some respects nothing Rosenberg wrote later exceeds it in interest.

Rosenberg wanted to find some intelligible correlation between the private agony and the tremendous destructive energy released in modern war, some way of imparting full weight to the unknown lives being snuffed out in pain and hence some way of guaranteeing his own identity against destruction. He sought, therefore, to create in Moses the idea of a human consciousness and will great and energetic enough to oppose war successfully. This conception of energy and power became an integral part of Rosenberg's imagination. It not only provided him with a theme and symbols: more important, it helped to strengthen the texture of his writing.

Rosenberg's concept of power has obvious affiliations with his Jewish background, and its genesis goes back far into his own life—back into those dreary years of poverty and sickness. One can trace its development in several disguises in his earlier work and letters. But Rosenberg never attempted to exploit the compensatory comforts of art, and he never developed his notion of power, such as it was, as an anodyne for the pains of experience.

Indeed, one sees how deliberately he exposed himself to the full horror of the war experience from a letter he wrote to Edward Marsh in 1916: "I am determined that this war, with all its powers for devastation, shall not master my poeting. . . . I will not leave a corner of my consciousness covered, but saturate myself with the strange and extraordinary new conditions of this life, and it will all refine itself into poetry later on." There were to be no shadowy places in his brain for retreat, no secret corners for weeping. Thus it was that the first impact of the war on Rosenberg conferred a universal significance on what had been merely private struggle before, and gave new scope and depth to his writing.

Moses was the first fruit of this enlarged frame of mind. Yet as things stand, the conception with which Rosenberg struggles in the play remains a little inchoate. Moses emerges as a figure of great force, but lacks a proportionate moral definition. Had Rosenberg lived longer, his conception of power would undoubtedly have gained in form as he successively invested it in other, and possibly more tractable, characters of Jewish history. Rosenberg wished to write a play about Judas Maccabaeus. He felt that in Maccabaeus he might be able to subdue the aggressiveness with which he had endowed his first hero, and add the note of magnanimity to power. But the chance never came.

For all its violence of language, the action of *Moses* is static. This is not necessarily a defect, for it is undeniably a play to be read. It is inconceivable on the stage. The play is in two scenes, and occurs at that point in Moses' career when he has not yet disclaimed Pharaoh but is about to do so. Moses is seen throughout as more god than man—a source of energy to all who come in contact with him. A young Hebrew describes him in hyperbolic terms:

He spoke! Since yesterday
Am I not larger grown?
I've seen men hugely shapen in soul
Of such unhuman shaggy male turbulence
They tower in foam miles from our neck-strained sight.
And to their shop only heroes come.
But all were cripples to this speed
Constrained to the stables of flesh.
I say there is a famine in ripe harvest
When hungry giants come as guests.
Come knead the hills and ocean into food.
There is none for him.

Moses was written when Rosenberg was twenty-six. There are certainly arresting qualities in the poetry of the above passage, but we are more aware of promise than of full achievement. For one thing, the verse is straining too hard to be Shakespearean, and naturally it comes off badly in the comparison. Place beside the young Hebrew's speech just quoted Cleopatra's eulogy of Antony, Act V. sc.ii:

> *His legs bestrid the ocean: his rear'd arm*
> *Crested the world. . . .*
>
>   *For his bounty,*
> *There was no winter in't; an autumn 'twas*
> *That grew the more by reaping.*

The young Hebrew appears to be speaking so far above and beyond himself that his ambition of elevation diverts our attention from the dramatic situation to his skillful but risky struggle with rhetoric and metaphor. The magnified image of Antony shines in the luminous medium of Cleopatra's language; Moses is all but buried from sight under the young Hebrew's hyperboles. Still, if these lines are not wholly successful, they by no means wholly fail. They may not persuade us to accept Moses at the young slave's evaluation, but they do hum with an authentic sound of power, and on occasion Rosenberg already knew how to harness that power.

In the beginning Moses is not aware of his own potential power. He is still a victim of Egyptian sensuality and indolence. The consciousness of what he can be awakens slowly in him, but when it comes it is a tremendous spiritual revelation:

> *I am rough now, and new, and will have no tailor.*
> *Startlingly,*
> *As a mountain-side*
> *Wakes aware of its other side*
> *When from a cave a leopard comes,*
> *On its heels the same red sand,*
> *Springing with acquainted air,*
> *Sprang an intelligence*
> *Coloured as a whim of mine,*
> *Showed to my dull outer eyes*
> *The living eyes underneath.*
> *Did I not shrivel up and take the place of air,*
> *Secret as those eyes were,*
> *And those strong eyes call up a giant frame?*
> *And I am that now.*

But Rosenberg's conception of power begins to reach towards its real complexity only in the long final speech of *Moses*, in which Moses reveals that he will exert his power on the Hebrews to

> *. . . grandly fashion these rude elements*
> *Into some newer nature, a consciousness*
> *Like naked light seizing the all-eyed soul,*
> *Oppressing with its gorgeous tyranny*
> *Until they take it thus—or die.*

Moses is Rosenberg's largest attempt to educe creatively the idea of a new kind of consciousness which would characteristically express itself in (the words are his) "virility" and "original action." This conception is available to the reader through a prose paraphrase of the play; it is far more important that the effects of this idea are felt in many passages as the strength of the verse itself.

However much the action flags, Rosenberg's verse has a dramatic quality locally that calls for special elucidation. Here is a short speech from the first scene:

> Moses: *Fine! Fine!*
> *See in my brain*
> *What madmen have rushed through,*
> *And like a tornado*
> *Torn up the tight roots*
> *Of some dead universe.*
> *The old clay is broken*
> *For a power to soak in and knit*
> *It all into tougher tissues*
> *To hold life,*
> *Pricking my nerves till the brain might crack*
> *It boils to my finger tips,*
> *Till my hands ache to grip*
> *The hammer—the lone hammer*
> *That breaks lives into a road*
> *Through which my genius drives.*

This passage contains the whole idea of the play in germ: an awakening sense of power, and the determination to grasp it. It is characteristic of this play that each speech has a tendency to become a microcosm reflecting the central conception in its full breadth and vigor. In this passage one remarks the strength of the verbs, which are not only violent but operate with kinesthetic effect: tight roots are torn up by a tornado, the hands ache to grip the hammer, nerves are pricked, the brain threatens to crack, and so on—figures full of tensions and resistances. As Moses symbolizes the desire for (in Rosenberg's own phrase) "original action," it is impressive that this desire should so tangibly incarnate itself here in a series of kinesthetic verb operations. These power images actually seem to release an energy within the verse which stands in apposition to the formally articulate desire. Furthermore, one notes that while the response one brings to the imagistic series is cumulative in effect, there is a rising curve of intensity, as towards a dramatic catastrophe. The first two images—the madmen and the tornado—clear the stage (carefully localized to the arena of the brain) for the influx of the new vision of power. The image of the broken clay is transitional and leads into the fully developed power image, the hammer which breaks lives into a road, and serves as climax to this particular sequence. Then, the ultimate image of regality closes the sequence—genius out-Pharaohing Pharaoh in a procession down a royal highway.

It is part of Rosenberg's high status as a poet that the power concept which he developed in *Moses* did not constitute a settlement that fostered the delusion of permanence, an investment whose dividends might be drawn on at leisure. He believed in energy as a bowstring might: taut, he was a singing resistant thing; but relaxed, he was abject and useless. Nevertheless, there was always the temptation to accept an easier solution, a reconciliation with the past, with what Charles Sorley had called "imaginative indolence," rather than to preserve the perpetual tension demanded by the exacting kind of consciousness Rosenberg sought. Shortly before he died he described the temptation explicitly in a fragment of a play called *The Amulet:*

> *In all our textures are loosed*
> *Pulses straining against strictness*
> *Because an easy issue lies therefrom.*

His poem "Returning We Hear the Larks" represents his tireless resistance against what appear to him to be temptations to capitulate. It is his best known poem, and Beth Zion Lask correctly says, "Had he written nothing else, this one poem could have stood to serve his fame." Since it is quite short it may be quoted in full:

> *Sombre the night is,*
> *And though we have our lives, we know*
> *What sinister threat lurks there.*
>
> *Dragging these anguished limbs, we only know*
> *This poison-blasted track opens on our camp—*
> *On a little safe sleep.*
>
> *But hark joy—joy—strange joy.*
> *Lo! heights of night ringing with unseen larks.*
> *Music showering on our upturned list'ning faces.*
>
> *Death could drop from the dark*
> *As easily as song—*
> *But song only dropped,*
>
> *Like a blind man's dreams on the sand*
> *By dangerous tides,*
> *Like a girl's dark hair, for she dreams no ruin lies there,*
> *Or her kisses where a serpent hides.*

The very first word of the poem is like a gong whose portentous reverberations carry through to the seventh line, at which point, with the interjection, the gloom is suddenly shattered. The opening situation is a stark statement of human insecurity, but the sudden burst of song which, after an initial moment of terror, the soldiers endure with joy, is, within the compass of the poem, something in the nature of a spiritual experience. The line which carries the main burden of that experience, "Joy—joy—strange joy," curiously resembles one of the ejaculatory lines in a secret memorandum of Pascal's commemorating an intense mystical experience: under the heading FIRE he had written "Joy, joy, joy, tears of joy." The two following lines in Rosenberg's poem confirm the mystical nature of the experience. There is the religious intonation of the interjection "Lo!," the ecstatic, evocative shrillness of "heights of night," the solemn mystery of the "unseen larks." Finally, in the following line, there are the beneficent suggestions of music, rain, and prayer.

From the viewpoint of their poetic integrity these lines present the experience as a valid one, certainly nothing to mistrust or regret. Nevertheless, a moment after the larks cease singing, a moment after the experience has passed, Rosenberg does question its validity in the last seven lines, which he marshals against the first part of the poem. Rosenberg seems almost to have preferred death, which might have dropped from the heavens, to the song that did, and he accuses it, in two closing similes, of concealed treacheries.

He had once written before the war: "It is all *experience;* but good God! It is *all* experience, and nothing else." During the war he had finally achieved a kind of organization of that experience, and gained a measure of control over it by informing his consciousness with a new energy and confidence. Once the immediate exultation of the larks' song had passed, everything the music meant to Rosenberg—and perhaps it had better be left vague—represented a temptation from the past to slacken his hold, to subside into "that terrible middle-class sloth of outlook and appalling 'imaginative indolence.'" At the beginning of the war, confronted with its first sights of injustice, he had asked in his poem "God," "Who rests in God's mean flattery now?" Certainly he did not wish to be guilty of doing so himself.

And yet one cannot help noting that the final seven lines of the poem do not carry the conviction poetically that the first part does. They lack the spontaneous immediacy of the opening. There is a profound poignancy about "The Larks" which arises from an ambiguity of which Rosenberg himself was not yet wholly aware. Do the siren larks sing from a past which Rosenberg is courageous enough to resist, inviting him to a spiritual surrender? Or are they ministers of a grace which still seems beyond the reach of his powers, which so far he has neither the courage nor the means of attaining? Probably both answers are partly true. At any rate, Rosenberg's poised indecision in this poem constitutes a brilliant examination of the bases of the spiritual security he was endeavoring to construct for himself.

Although one can occasionally trace an ironic inflection in *Moses*, irony was not a favorite instrument of Rosenberg's genius. His mind lacked the cynicism necessary for a mocking mode of expression. But one of his *Trench Poems*, "Break of Day in the Trenches," owes its success to the presence of something at its center approximating irony. Even here, however, the irony is without sarcasm, and almost without bitterness. There is a pervading stillness in the poem, an accomplished nervelessness. In some ways this is the saddest and most human of all his poems. It contains two points of consciousness: the poet who speaks, and who no longer seems to have any intense reaction to what he undergoes, and a rat who is credited with a personal and critical outlook:

> *Droll rat, they would shoot you if they knew*
> *Your cosmopolitan sympathies.*
> *Now you have touched this English hand*
> *You will do the same to a German—*

The positions of men and rats have been quietly exchanged. It is the rat who has become civilized (and for that reason only is "droll"). And it is the rat who has become the judge of men who appeal to him for knowledge of themselves:

> *What do you see in our eyes*
> *At the shrieking iron and flame*
> *Hurled through still heavens?*

Some particular mention should also be made of the poem "Louse Hunting." In twenty-five short lines it describes a delirious episode in a barracks at night. Naked soldiers, driven to frenzy by the biting of the lice, leap into a wild vermin-hunting dance by candlelight. Rosenberg invests the scene with Gothic depth, evoking the terror and fascination of a Walpurgisnacht. The first sentence is like a sculptured narration of lost souls from a church porch:

> *Nudes—stark and glistening,*
> *Yelling in lurid glee.*

There is the oblique sensuality of:

> *See gargantuan hooked fingers*
> *Pluck in supreme flesh*
> *To smutch supreme littleness.*

The weird orgy comes to an end abruptly with five lines whose sweetness reminds one of morning bells tolling the darkness underground:

> *. . . some wizard vermin*
> *Charmed from the quiet this revel*
> *When our ears were half lulled*
> *By the dark music*
> *Blown from Sleep's trumpet.*

After the metaphorical richness of *Moses*, the hard spareness of the images in *Trench Poems* may come as a surprise. Continued contact with the war inevitably led Rosenberg's poetry from the somewhat ideal experience of *Moses* into the harder realm of actual endurance. Some of the color and music fades to be replaced by steel, but there is a close relationship, nonetheless, between the earlier play and the later poems. And several of the *Trench Poems* reproduce with some directness the argument of *Moses*.

In "Soldier: Twentieth Century," Rosenberg returns to his conception of a "great new Titan" strong enough to subdue the forces which an evil world has raised against him:

Cruel men are made immortal,
Out of your pain born.
They have stolen the sun's power
With their feet on your shoulders worn.

Let them shrink from your girth,
That has outgrown the pallid days,
When you slept like Circe's swine,
Or a word in the brain's ways.

When Rosenberg's concept of power is stated as directly as here and in *Moses*, there is a certain ambivalence in its meaning. If, indeed, the saving power of the individual which he would oppose to the destructive force of war is primarily an affair of the consciousness, a kind of inviolable spiritual integrity, why is it expressed so predominantly in physical terms?

Part of the answer is involved in Rosenberg's sense of race, and his strong attraction towards those men in Jewish history who were deliverers from both spiritual and physical tyranny. Redemption from the apathy of life and the horror of war was hardly imaginable to him as possible under one aspect only. It was natural that a sensibility deeply impressed by Moses and Maccabaeus should find, when confronted with crisis, a militant, even a fierce symbolism and imagery congenial. But no rifles flowered in Rosenberg's poetry, and the conquest he envisaged always remained essentially a spiritual one.

Rosenberg's very last poems show how deeply he was coming to rely on the traditions of the Jews when he died. One of these poems deals with the burning of the Temple, another with the destruction of Jerusalem by the Babylonians, and the last poem included in the volume deals with the Jewish persistent sense of exile. It is clear that in dealing with Old Testament themes he discovered a norm of reference and a moral security he could find nowhere else. He reveals in his last poem his growing insistence on Jewish positives:

Through these pale cold days
What dark faces burn
Out of three thousand years,
And their wild eyes yearn,

While underneath their brows
Like waifs their spirits grope
For the pools of Hebron again—
For Lebanon's summer slope.

They leave these blond still days
In dust behind their tread
They see with living eyes
How long they have been dead.

The Semitic faces in the first quatrain look out across the following lines towards the sources of Hebraic tradition and life, only to discover that their long separation from them has brought spiritual death. It was in a return to these sources, what in *Moses* he had called "the roots' hid secrecy," that Rosenberg looked for the authority to reject the sterility of modern life, of which war was only the most hideous expression.

The probable course of Rosenberg's literary career, and what its influence on the literature of the 'twenties would have been had he lived may be an amusing form of speculation to anyone who admires his poetry, but that sort of game cannot substantially help a reputation that must, after all, rest on work done. In *The Complete Works* we do have an emphatic assertion of really great talent. One cannot help applying to him some lines of his own from "The Unicorn":

Sudden the lightning flashed upon a figure
Moving as a man moves in the slipping mud
But singing not as a man sings, through the storm
Which could not drown his sounds.

ELIOT, POUND, AND HISTORY

E LIOT'S AND POUND'S names are properly linked together, like Wordsworth's and Coleridge's, because in spite of the temperamental and philosophic differences that separated them, they shared what was most central and crucial in their period. What they shared together they shared of course with the best among their contemporaries. Perhaps neither of them ever phrased it more concisely or beautifully than Wallace Stevens when he spoke of the

Blessed rage for order . . .
The maker's rage to order words of the sea.

For all three, the sea was chaotic or disordered reality, and for Pound and Eliot at least, the rage was more than poetic inspiration, the order sought for, more than literary form. What Eliot, Pound, and in his own way, Stevens, shared, was a sensitivity to the peculiar forms of spiritual deprivation developed during the nineteenth and twentieth centuries. Stevens, perhaps the most "French" of the three in his literary derivations, was also the most Arnoldian in his solutions, and if he ultimately misses first rank it will be because order and form for him do not finally seem to transcend esthetic order and form.

Stevens was deficient in one prerequisite for greatness which Eliot possessed magnificently, and for which Pound has striven desperately in all his poetry: a sense of history. History must of course be understood here in its widest meaning, as incorporating all cultural tradition. Through history Eliot discovered order, and Pound took a lifetime's voyage of discovery across history, seeking order. By ignoring history, Stevens' poems are magnificent islands, sometimes quite paradisal, but from them there is no ready access to a mainland. "Sunday Morning" is one of the most beautiful poems, or sequence of poems, in English: but if for a moment it becomes almost electrically aware of history in its mythic and religious guises, it is only to deny its efficacy in the interests of a divinized moment.

Despite radical divergences in their understanding of the meaning and function of history, both Eliot and Pound are historical poets in a special sense. It is this more than anything else that pairs them together in the mind. If Pound is more obviously the historical poet by way of the *Cantos* than Eliot, he is far less successful in dealing with it. It remains a category of knowledge in his verse, whereas for Eliot it becomes a perspective capable, as in his greatest poem, "Little Gidding," of leading towards a final transcendence. The role history plays in Eliot's poetry reminds one of Virgil's farewell words to Dante in the *Purgatorio*—words which Eliot quotes at the end of his essay *What Is a Classic?*:

> *Son, the temporal fire and the eternal, hast*
> *thou seen, and art come to a place where I,*
> *of myself, discern no further.*

But for Pound, despite his widely advertised rejection of generalized ideas abstracted from the living moment, the concrete situation, history is essentially didactic and moralizing, not dramatic, and whatever his intention may be in the *Cantos*, his habit of *framing* moments from the past makes it episodic, discontinuous and inorganic. The simultaneity of historical experience that he seeks to achieve by juxtaposing episodic material from widely scattered periods in time is finally self-defeating and meaningless. Where past and present are so easily leveled, each loses its intrinsic significance, and where temporal sequence has been destroyed—as Pound has destroyed it in his poetry—a significant sense of contemporaneity with the past (a virtue which has sometimes been attributed to Pound) becomes an impossibility. Although Donald Davie has remarked that in "Pound's career as a whole the wish to transcend history is more powerful than the wish to act in history," by destroying time he has imprisoned himself in it. As Eliot so well knew, "Only through time time is conquered."

There are of course critics of Pound who would deny that the *Cantos* fail in this particular respect. Clark Emery, in his *Ideas into Action*, a study of the *Cantos* published in 1958, not only sees them filled with religious meaning, centering on something he refers to as the "Permanent," but with the *Rock-Drill* and *Thrones* sections of the *Cantos*, he believes transcendence has been realized. "In Canto 90," writes Emery, "Paradise is achieved—by the reader who has followed on the heels of the poet, and by the poet himself, who has been elevated 'from under the rubble heap.'" Pound himself long ago drew an analogy between the structure he premeditated for the *Cantos* and *The Divine Comedy*, and no doubt he would agree with Emery; but in an excellent recent book on Pound, *Poet in Exile*, Noel Stock offers what seems to me a more persuasive and sobering verdict, and one which appears to be essentially in agreement with Donald Davie's. Because of the importance of the point, the passage deserves to be quoted at length:

By the time Pound wrote the *Thrones* section, between about 1954 and 1959, he was no longer able to hold the work together; not so much because of any deterioration in the writing, but for the reason that the meaning which he had hoped would emerge as the poem moved towards its end, did not in fact appear. As a result he was driven to impose a patently false "theology" and "meaning" upon some of the *Rock-Drill* Cantos and the whole of *Thrones*, a "theology" and "meaning" made up of shreds derived from Catholic theology, Chinese philosophers, pagan writers like Philostratus, the works of Del Mar and L. A. Waddell, and fragments remembered from his early reading. Under this pressure to find some way of making the poem into a whole he returned to his earlier view of the pagan gods and miracles—which he had abandoned after the false start to the Cantos in 1917; he returned to this method or convention, and began to treat them as realities in the actual world. One can sympathize with Pound in his predicament, but not with the result.

Pound had begun the *Cantos* by attaching an almost superstitious, certainly a nominalist, importance to the separate "moments" which provided so much of the actual material for his poem. Harold H. Watts, in his book *Ezra Pound and the Cantos*, published in 1952, provided us with an excellent description of the kind of value Pound has always attached to these "moments":

Special events in human history and special facets of past culture remain potentially sovereign for our current ills so long as our handling of history and past culture allows the import of a special event to remain firmly attached to the moment in which it first occurred. The special event must be kept firmly localized, crusted over with all in the way of the peculiar and grotesque that being localized offers as opposition to the facile operations of a generalizing or abstracting realism.

305

Pound's refusal or inability to accept or break through to a transcendent meaning in history—a meaning which in a religious perspective would be eschatological—leaves him imprisoned in just such moments as Watts has described. Pound of course has seen his position as a liberation of man's creative energies from stereotyped and abstract ideas, but it has proved an arid and static one. In *An Essay on Man* Ernst Cassirer wrote that while history must work with the fixed and petrified shapes of human culture, "nevertheless it detects the original dynamic impulses. It is the gift of the great historian to reduce all mere facts to their *fieri*, all products to processes, all static things or institutions to their creative energies."

Such a conception of history bears an obvious analogy with Coleridge's description of the imaginative power, which he concludes by saying that "it is essentially *vital*, even as all objects (*as* objects) are essentially fixed and dead." But it is essentially *as* objects that Pound treats the successive separate moments of history in his *Cantos*. A passage like the great closing fifth section of "Little Gidding" is as beyond his power as his desire.

While Eliot's view of history is ultimately Christian, in its essentials it was fully developed long before his conversion to Anglo-Catholicism. *Four Quartets* merely completes and fulfills the view that was already present in *The Waste Land*, and which perhaps received its fullest expression as early as "Tradition and the Individual Talent." I believe it was Hugh Kenner who first pointed out in *The Invisible Poet* that Eliot's sense of history was indebted to the philosophy of Francis Herbert Bradley, on whom he had written his doctoral dissertation at Harvard. Kenner writes: "It follows from Bradley's denial of any separation 'of feeling from the felt, or of the desired from desire, or of what is thought from thinking,' that our attempt to separate the past from our knowledge of it, what really happened from the way we

306

imagine things to have been, is ultimately meaningless." In this view, history is really a creative function of the mind, a mode of perception by which the experience of the past is available to the poet as something quite different from documents or the evidence of monuments.

The classic passage in which Eliot's doctrine of the historic sense is developed occurs in "Tradition and the Individual Talent":

> Tradition cannot be inherited, and if you want it you must obtain it by great labor. It involves, in the first place, the historical sense . . . ; and the historical sense involves a perception, not only of the pastness of the past, but of its presence; the historical sense compels a man to write not merely with his own generation in his bones, but with a feeling that the whole of the literature of Europe from Homer and with it the whole of the literature of his own country has a simultaneous existence and composes a simultaneous order.

Although Eliot's formulation of the historical sense is highly distinguished, the attitude it describes was not an original discovery of his, even for the English tradition, and for reasons pertinent to this discussion it may be worthwhile examining an earlier instance in which this view was anticipated in practice. Among the English Romantic poets, Keats was the only one for whom Eliot ever evinced any great partiality, and in Keats we find an attitude explicitly developed in his poetry that approaches closely to Eliot's historical sense as an element in creativity. In Keats there is an attempt to define this position or attitude in more or less symbolic action and allegoric description as early as the second book of *Endymion*, but here we need only look at the more satisfactory statement that Keats achieved in "Hyperion," a poem about which Eliot once professed himself "not happy."

In its fragmentary third book we encounter the young

Apollo, who is shortly to displace Hyperion, the Titan sun god. He has not yet come into the fullness of his godhead, and he is wandering alone, afflicted with a profound and unexplained sadness. Apollo is the god of poetry, and the inexplicable suffering he is undergoing may be interpreted as the anguish or yearning of a poet who has not yet entered into the mastery of his powers. It represents the pain arising from an irresistible instinct that is frustrated in its exercise. Apollo encounters Mnemosyne, the goddess of memory and the mother of the Muses. As she stands before him, her arms upraised in prophetic gesture, Apollo with a shriek of agony enters fully into his godhead. Keats makes Apollo's elevation to this new dimension a matter of knowledge. The "knowledge" as Keats describes it in the following passage is precisely the kind of knowledge that Eliot associates with the acquisition of the historical sense in "Tradition and the Individual Talent":

> *"Knowledge enormous makes a God of me.*
> *Names, deeds, grey legends, dire events, rebellions,*
> *Majesties, sovran voices, agonies,*
> *Creations and destroyings, all at once*
> *Pour into the wide hollows of my brain,*
> *And deify me, as if some blithe wine*
> *Or bright elixir peerless I had drunk,*
> *And so become immortal."*

On no count can Keats be called a Christian poet, and he helps to make perfectly clear that while Eliot's conception of history is finally completed by his religious faith, notably in "Little Gidding," which relies so strongly on Christian eschatology, the historical sense as he has understood it is by no means the exclusive property of Christian poets. This historical sense as we see it in both Keats and Eliot is the cultivation of a particular mode of consciousness which insists on the *internality* of reality. In the "Hyperion" passage, history and

knowledge are externally communicated from the mind of
Mnemosyne to Apollo's by way of formal instruction, although of course what occurs would, in the natural order,
depend upon the *fact* of such communication. As Mnemosyne
is memory, she symbolizes a function *within* the poet's mind
itself, and these further lines, following close upon the passage just quoted, indicate through rebirth imagery the internality of the essentially creative process by which the individual apprehends the perspectives of past and future between
which he lives, and in terms of which he possesses his individuality:

Soon wild commotions shook him, and made flush
All the immortal fairness of his limbs;
Most like the struggle at the gate of death;
Or like still to one who should take leave
Of pale immortal death, and with a pang
As hot as death's is chill, with fierce convulse
Die into life.

This note of the internality of reality, of which history is a
part, clearly appears to be an important predication of the
historical sense, and it characterizes Eliot's poetry from the
first. It is a mark of "The Love Song of J. Alfred Prufrock,"
while the events of *The Waste Land*, with all the history that
lives in that poem, are conceived of as existing *within* the
inclusive consciousness of Tiresias. It is, indeed, the converg-
ence of the past, of history, on the consciousness of the
individual that constitutes his uniqueness. This particular
kind of impersonality, in which the mind is the medium in
which the past takes form, and by so doing appears to form
the mind that experiences it, Eliot found described in Keats's
letters, though not perhaps so early as "Tradition and the
Individual Talent," in which Eliot expresses this idea most
explicitly. In *The Use of Poetry and the Use of Criticism*

Eliot quotes the following passage from Keats with immense approval:

> In passing, however, I must say one thing that has pressed upon me lately, and increased my Humility and capability of submission—and that is this truth—Men of Genius are great as certain ethereal chemicals operating on the Mass of neutral intellect—but they have not any individuality, and determined character—I would call the top and head of those who have a proper self Men of Power.

Whatever other influences may have pointed Eliot in this direction, the philosophy of F. H. Bradley was certainly one, as the quotation from *Appearance and Reality* that Eliot includes among his *Notes to The Waste Land* makes clear:

> My external sensations are no less private to myself than are my thoughts or my feelings. In either case my experience falls within my own circle, a circle closed on the outside; and, with all its elements alike, every sphere is opaque to the others which surround it. . . . In brief, regarded as an existence which appears in a soul, the whole world for each is peculiar and private to that end.

The radical internality of each man's world, in such a view, necessarily makes every facet of it continuous with the whole, and such a situation inevitably leads to a symbolic mode of thinking in which any factor of experience is potentially capable of transecting the universe as it is present to one's consciousness. It is impossible to think of a better position for a poet to be in, for there is always the chance that his next word or metaphor may achieve apocalypse, and that universal illumination may be switched on by a trope.

But confronted with such prodigal possibilities, the poet may well have more occasion to rejoice than the critic who is faced with the task of analyzing and evaluating the poet's achievement. Criticism of Eliot has often, in the past, exhibited embarrassment when reminded of such published lectures as *The Idea of a Christian Society* or *After Strange Gods.* "If Eliot's poetry illuminates a universe," the critics have often seemed to ask, "do such lectures constitute a prose description of it?" Rather than admit they did (and the vestryman's tone in such lectures was always the reverse of conciliatory to a secular audience) the critics have often preferred to forget the larger shape of his thought as it developed during the 'thirties and 'forties and content themselves with explicating literary and historical allusions in the verse, or perhaps with talking about Sir James Frazer and Jessie L. Weston.

In *Approach to the Purpose,* Father Genesius Jones has broken through this barrier that so often seemed to confine earlier critics of Eliot to a myopic and partial scrutiny of his verse. He has succeeded in doing so, not because he is a priest and therefore sympathetic to Eliot's theology, but because he has been able to discover a critical strategy that enables him to trace out and describe in illuminating detail the extraordinarily complex morphology of Eliot's closed world of experience. While Father Jones sees this world (as it *must* be seen) in a Christian light, it is not towards any focus in orthodoxy that his discussion moves. Although he does not mention F. H. Bradley in his book, he bases his critical interpretation of the poems on the note of internality in Eliot's view of experience, and he has hit upon the happy expedient of doing so by way of Ernst Cassirer's cultural philosophy of symbolic forms.

It is by no means Father Jones's point that Eliot was directly influenced by Cassirer:

To be sure, I am unaware that Mr. Eliot has ever read Cassirer's books—indeed all of them were published after *The Waste Land* appeared. But there is quite a deal to show that Mr. Eliot was familiar with the research out of which *Das Mythische Denken* arose; and so, by a not too facile transition, with the outline which Cassirer's morphology of myth owes to the researchers. . . . And since Mr. Eliot is a poet and critic rather than a philosopher, there is much to show in his writings on Dante and some others, that he received lasting impressions not only from the religious, historical, linguistic, artistic, scientific and mythical strains of their work, but from its presentation of the "harmony in contrariety" of the human spirit. And so one may suggest that, from their different starting points, Cassirer and Mr. Eliot have, at the one time, woven different courses over the same ground.

The six categories of Eliot's interests that Father Jones enumerates in this passage are of course the six categories of symbolic forms isolated by Cassirer in his cultural philosophy. Cassirer describes the function of these forms very clearly near the beginning of his *Essay on Man:*

No longer in a merely physical universe, man lives in a symbolic universe. Language, myth, art, and religion are parts of this universe. They are the varied threads which weave the symbolic net, the tangled web of human experience. All human progress in thought and experience refines upon and strengthens this net. No longer can man confront reality immediately; he cannot see it, as it were, face to face. Physical reality seems to recede in proportion as man's symbolic activity advances. Instead of dealing with the things themselves man is in a sense constantly conversing with himself. He has so enveloped himself in linguistic forms, in artistic images, in mythical symbols or religious rites that he cannot see or know anything except by the interposition of this artificial medium.

This is a radical assertion of the essential *internality* of the world in which man lives, of which he is conscious; and

312

Eliot's definition of the historical sense may be seen as a natural consequence of some such view of reality. There is nothing at odds with Christian faith here because the nature of the ground behind the symbols is left open: and as Father Jones recognizes, "From the beginning . . . the final cause in Mr. Eliot's poetry is the attraction towards God. And the constant presence of this final cause changes the object of our contemplation."

It seems to me that this is the best book that has been written on Eliot's poetry. It not only incorporates (always with full acknowledgment) most of the best insights of earlier critics, but it manages to do so in a way that gives them new relevance and dimension. It is, in fact, a very original book on a subject in which originality has become extremely difficult to achieve in recent years. Father Jones's method necessarily involves some repetition, for he examines and reexamines most of the poems under each of Cassirer's symbolic categories; but by what may appear an uneconomic procedure he is able to show the simultaneous existence of meanings contributed by each of the forms within a controlling mythic structure. Thereby he illuminates depths and centers in these poems that earlier analysis had not quite reached, and most of all he shows the organic unity inhering in a lifetime's work. His skillful application of these forms to literary analysis and criticism constitutes in itself a significant contribution to method. The strategy is one that might profitably be used with other poets: perhaps the English Romantics in particular, certainly with Keats. Even a brief review of Keats's poetry in the light of the symbolic categories will reveal in an unprecedented degree the astonishing growth and organic unity of his work, and the continuous deepening of meaning, from "I Stood Tip-Toe" to "The Fall of Hyperion."

Father Jones has, then, written an important book: one that not only deals brilliantly with Eliot, but which demonstrates a method capable of enriching our sense of other poets as well. The "approach" he has used here is one that is superbly equipped to reveal the hidden morphology of meaning in poetry, of which metaphor and symbol are functions.

The objectivity of dramatic form and characterization would place difficulties, though not insuperable ones, in the way of analyzing Eliot's plays in terms of the symbolic categories, and Father Jones has refrained from doing so. But an examination of the plays has been undertaken from a closely related point of view in Carol H. Smith's *T. S. Eliot's Dramatic Theory and Practice*. The "Blessed rage for order" which, it was earlier suggested, was Eliot's compulsive motivation from the very beginning, is here studied in a historical perspective that leads Eliot the playwright, by way of Gilbert Murray, Francis Cornford, Jane Harrison, and the School of Classical Anthropology at Cambridge, straight back to the ritual origins of Greek drama. Eliot, as he himself has made abundantly clear, was much influenced by Cornford's *The Origin of Attic Comedy*, and Mrs. Smith, in her lucid and convincing analysis of the plays in their chronological order, demonstrates that the ideas that Murray and Cornford contributed to Eliot's conception of dramatic structure were comparable (though this is not a point she makes) to Jessie L. Weston's influence on the organization of *The Waste Land*.

Mrs. Smith's discussion of the plays shares in, if it does not repeat, the "approach" of Father Jones to the poetry. The meaning of Eliot's dramas and their structure as dramatic art are finally apprehensible only in terms of myth, religion, and history, which, playing against the contrarieties of contemporary spiritual experience, compose a dialectical unity in which the problems and the solution of the spiritual life are revealed to be as timeless as the symbolic categories which Eliot has used to define them.

Mrs. Smith describes the ingredients of an Eliot play in the following passage, and her illuminating discussions of them reveal how each in its way adheres to the design:

They included, first of all, a structure patterned on the model Eliot believed to be beneath both comedy and tragedy—the ritual drama with its agon, its pathos or sacrificial death, and finally its "discovery or recognition of the slain and mutilated Daimon, followed by his Resurrection or Apotheosis or, in some sense, his Epiphany in glory." His theme was to be based on the deeper religious meanings of that pattern, which could be suggested by creating situations based on those in later Greek drama which emphasized ritual themes. Finally the dramatic surface was to be stylized by creating flat characters and patterned actions which would provide entertainment and action to beguile the audience while at the same time suggesting, by their lack of realism and by the presence of serio-comic references to religious meanings, the symbolic dimension beneath the surface, just as the phallic comedy of Greece had.

"History," wrote Father Jones, "is an explicit theme of almost every poem which Mr. Eliot has published." We have already seen that it claims an even more obvious prominence in much of Pound's poetry, but with him it has none of the subtlety of form or fluidity of relation that we associate with a symbolist mode of thinking and feeling. This is not surprising, because in essential respects Pound has remained an imagist, devoted to hard and sharp outlines. Pound's poetry would prove utterly resistant to an approach through symbolic categories such as we have looked at here.

Although the *Cantos* provide the obvious point at which to begin an examination of Pound's use of history, his translations perhaps offer a more interesting, albeit somewhat oblique, commentary on his historical motives. Donald Davie has argued persuasively in his book on Pound that one of Pound's greatest works, *Homage to Sextus Propertius*, should not be considered a translation in any sense whatsoever. But this cannot be said of the Confucian Odes of the

Classic Anthology, which, however great the latitude Pound may have permitted himself as translator, are meant to be faithful after their own fashion to the 305 poems composing the *Shih Ching*, which Confucius is supposed to have selected and arranged in order in the fifth century B.C.

In view of Pound's faith in poetry's function of maintaining order and health, not only in the life of the individual but in the life of the state as well, it is not difficult to understand why the Confucian viewpoint seemed to coincide perfectly with his own. Pound does not translate the two prefaces which were added to the *Shih Ching* at an early date, but a good deal in the Great Preface sounds like a sweet and pure version of Pound's ideology:

> Therefore, correctly to set forth the successes and failures of government, to move Heaven and Earth, and to excite spiritual Beings to action, there is no readier instrument than poetry.
>
> The former kings by this regulated the duties of husband and wife, effectually inculcated filial obedience and reverence, secured attention to all the relations of society, adorned the transforming influence of instruction, and transformed manners and customs.

While most of the poems in the *Shih Ching* are extremely simple in themselves, the principles and purpose according to which the selection was originally made from a mass of older and mostly anonymous poems, were complicated, and the interpretations brought to the poems by Confucian scholars followed the intentions of the anthologist rather than of the original poets. The Sinologue H. G. Creel writes: "Very early this poetry was 'interpreted,' which means that it was often understood to mean what it did not mean at all. Thus the most obvious love poems were supposed to have deep philosophical meaning."

316

It is not altogether clear from his translations whether Pound wishes primarily to reproduce a document of Confucian orthodoxy, or to recreate the poems in the spirit in which they were originally written. From the freshness, beauty, and immediacy he often achieves in the translations, one would guess the second motive. But his insistence on translating all 305 poems—a genuinely formidable task—strongly suggests the first: for, as the distinguished nineteenth-century Sinologue James Legge wrote: "The collection as a whole is not worth the trouble of versifying"—a sentiment later echoed by Arthur Waley.

S. L. Dembo has recently published a scholarly and sensitive appraisal of these translations in an essay of one hundred pages, *The Confucian Odes of Ezra Pound*. Dembo devotes a good deal of detailed attention to Pound's suspect method of translating the Chinese ideogram. Pound's method, taken over from Fenollosa, has frequently been passed under unfavorable review. Several years ago, in *The Art of Chinese Poetry*, James J. Y. Liu summarized the fallacy of Pound's procedure in a more succinctly quotable description than Dembo provides. Pointing to Pound's and Fenollosa's tendency to exaggerate the pictorial qualities and etymological associations of Chinese characters, he wrote:

> Suffice it to say that this split-character method is at best like insisting that one must always think of "philosophy" and "telephone" as, respectively, "love of wisdom" and "far sound.". . . While one has no wish to deny the additional aesthetic enjoyment afforded by the form of the characters in Chinese poetry, the fact remains that a line of poetry written in Chinese characters is not a mere sequence of images like a film in slow motion, as Fenollosa thought, but a highly complex organic development of sense and sound (like poetry in any other language), with not a little suggestion, but

little more than a *suggestion*, of the visual aspect of what is being described.

A number of Dembo's best pages are devoted to showing how Pound achieves some of his most vivid images by translating not the dictionary meaning of the ideogram, but the etymological components of which it is formed, some of which may be present only for phonetic purposes. But, to resort to Liu again: "One need no more think of Shantung as 'East of the Mountain' than one would think of Oxford as a river crossing for cattle."

Fine as Dembo's discussions of the translations are from this point of view, in the present context one is more interested in what he says about the way in which Pound's theory of translation is a natural consequence of his view of history. At the beginning of his essay Dembo characterizes Pound's conception of history in an exact and clear formulation:

> . . . history is a chronicle of the achievement of an ideal Kultur (or paideuma) by the natural or good forces, and its corruption by the perverted or evil forces of the society. In regard to translation, the poet is inspired by direct empathy with the mind of the original author, in a sense his alter-ego, who voices the Kultur of his own epoch and therefore speaks to all epochs.

This is a fair and sympathetic statement of Pound's theory of history and translation. On the face of it there would appear to be little to object to in the conception, but it carries certain implicit assumptions that become apparent immediately when Dembo turns his attention to Pound's translation of Ode 16:

> The word "equivalent," seemingly innocuous, is in truth the foundation of his technique, and its ramifications become apparent when we find such renderings as "Don't chop that pear tree, / Don't spoil that shade; Thaar's where old Marse Shao used to

318

sit, / Lord, how I wish he was judgin' yet." There is more than whimsy in this kind of thing: the feelings of a Chinese peasant toward a benevolent lord are rendered by the equivalent of, ostensibly, an American Negro slave's feelings toward a benevolent master, in a language which Pound takes to be "living" dialect. It is more than a matter, here, of there being certain similarities between the two; the most scrupulous historian could concede the point without dishonor. But what has happened is that Pound has destroyed all sense of the differences. In seeking his "equivalent" he has in fact found perfect identity and has transcended all chronological barriers convinced that his rendering is an illumination reflecting the Truth of China and the Reality of history, even though to the Sinologue the reading is absurd.

This passage confirms that we have already observed: in Pound's poetry there is no feeling of historic process, no desire, in Cassirer's words that have been quoted, "to reduce all mere facts to their *fieri*, all products to processes, all static things or institutions to their creative energies." Rather, we have a pattern of repetition, of that cyclic recurrence in history that is transcended in Eliot's poetry. Although in the instance cited by Dembo, past and present are leveled in a common undifferentiated vulgarity, even more characteristically—and perhaps to better purpose—Pound may choose the alternative strategy, as in the *Cantos*, of "overlayering" selected periods and cultures. The word is Donald Davie's, who goes ahead to say: ". . . the layers remain, and are meant to remain, distinct. What is intended is a sort of lamination, by no means a compounding or fusing of distinct historical phases into an undifferentiated amalgam."

The two alternative procedures cited by Dembo and Davie are by no means as distinct as they appear to be. As they both place history in a static perspective they are equally destructive of any idea of tradition in Eliot's sense, which is not recurrence but continuity thought of in terms of organic change, growth, development.

I have already quoted from Noel Stock's book *Poet in Exile*. While its examination of Pound's poetry, personality, and thought is based on a rigorous critical examination of his writings, the method it follows is, on the whole, one of expository discussion rather than of practical critical analysis, which is the method of Donald Davie's book *Ezra Pound: Poet as Sculptor*. Both critics are in essential agreement in their respective evaluations of Pound and his poetry, and as each book to some extent supports the other's argument from a different point of view there is some value in considering them together.

A critical consensus appears to consider that Pound's greatest contribution to English poetry has consisted in the new flexibility and strength he brought to the verse line—a technical achievement that may have been made possible in part by Pound's long devotion to music. One of Stock's more interesting chapters is "Words and Music," in which he considers in some detail the application of Pound's musical studies to his renovation of verbal cadence in his poetry. But while Stock handles this theme with tact and insight, musical analogies in an investigation of prosody present peculiar difficulties, even when the poet, as Pound does, deliberately invites such an approach. Most readers will therefore find Davie's performance on the same ground more useful. Although he recognizes, as Stock did in greater detail, that a poet like Campion had already broken the pentameter line of English verse into smaller rhythmical components for the sake of setting the poem to music, Davie's discussion presses no musical analogies, but analyzes Pound's rhythms in terms of syntactical rather than of metrical structure. Davie offers prosodic analyses of a number of Pound's shorter poems from *Ripostes*, *Lustra* and *Cathay* that provide an excellent demonstration of the way in which Pound broke down the basic iambic pattern of traditional English verse: "To break the pentameter, that was the first heave" (Canto 81). Davie shows how Pound did this in his fine analysis of "Provincia Deserta" from *Lustra*, perhaps the most useful discussion of a single poem of Pound I have read. Pound's visual patterning of the poem on the page—so important for the *Cantos*—is effectively analyzed here.

It has seemed essential to speak of this particular aspect of Pound's work by which he achieved a revitalization of the language of English poetry in the earlier years of this century. It is undoubtedly in this area that his reputation will securely rest, and both Stock and Davie do it justice, though it is in the nature of Davie's critical method that it falls particularly within his scope and province.

On the more ambitious aspirations of the *Cantos*, both critics are again in essential agreement, and both are severe. Some admirers of the *Cantos* have been much impressed by Pound's Neo-Platonism, the recurrent light imagery, and so on, and have professed to see a mystical quality in the poem moving towards transcendence with the *Rock-Drill* section. Stock's second chapter, "The Pagan Mystery Religions," in revealing the extravagantly syncretistic nature of any faith Pound may have, would render it difficult to attach much importance to the religious element in the *Cantos*, even if one were inclined to do so. The failure of the religious aspect of the *Cantos*, if it may be said to exist, is intimately associated with the failure of Pound's historical sense in the poem, as Stock shows:

Pound has consistently failed to see or admit that Christianity—the truth or otherwise of which has no bearing on what I am about to say—coincides with a great change in human sensibility. Something was already happening in Virgil's time which that sensitive soul

321

perceived; with the establishment of Christianity some three centuries later that something was manifest. It was no less than the death of the old gods of the hearth and the city and the tribe—Eleusis, it should be remembered, was only a local religion—and their replacement by the conception of one God for all men. . . .

But that above all else which casts serious doubts about Pound's treatment of religion is his silence about Christ and the central Christian dogmas in a poem which purports to deal with human history over a great span of time. The closest he gets to the person of Christ is a tentative identification of Him, in Canto 98, with the Chinese barley god, Je tzu.

Eliot was able to use the ancient vegetation gods to magnificent purpose in *The Waste Land*. In his historical imagination they not only became precursory exemplars of the cosmic drama of death and resurrection that is at last absolutely enacted in Christian eschatology, but the vegetation cults provided him with a defined pattern of cyclic recurrence that made possible, on the stage of his poetry, the ultimate act of religious transcendence towards which his whole vision of history tended. But Pound's predilection for polytheism, and his nominalist mode of thinking, rendered any such solution for the *Cantos* as undesirable as it was impossible.

Both Stock and Davie treat Pound's failures as a historian at detailed length: the inadequacy of his historical researching, his eagerness to draw far-reaching conclusions from insufficient and selected evidence, his failure to deal with the documents incorporated into the text of the *Cantos* in any significant or vital way. But more fatal than these faults is simply the basic theory on which the *Cantos* proceeds: "The whole plan of them," writes Davie, "is absurdly, even insanely, presumptuous; there is simply too much recorded history available for any one to offer to speak of it with such confidence as Pound does." And Davie proceeds in his conclusion to as devastating a judgment on Pound the historian-poet as one is likely to encounter in contemporary criticism:

> Whatever more long-term effect Pound's disastrous career may have on American and British poetry, it seems inevitable that it will rule out (has ruled out already, for serious writers) any idea that poetry can or should operate in the dimension of history, trying to make sense of the recorded past by redressing our historical perspectives. The poet may one day be honored again as a seer. Within the time span of the individual life, his insights may be considered as not just beautiful but also true; and so they may, when they operate in the eschatological time-span of religion, or even in the millennia of the archeologist and the geographer. But the poet's vision of the centuries of recorded time has been invalidated by the *Cantos* in a way that invalidates much writing by Pound's contemporaries. History, from now on, may be transcended in poetry, or it may be evaded there; but poetry is not the place where it may be understood.

For a time it began to appear that the general unreadability and formlessness of the *Cantos* might encourage certain admiring writers to becloud the poem with a mystique. Happily, that danger now seems to have been averted, and Pound will no doubt be the gainer. He is, after all, one of the greatest poets of his time, if by no means the peer of Eliot. It is worth noting that in many respects these critical estimates show a good deal in common with the distinguished evaluations offered in the early thirties by F. R. Leavis and R. P. Blackmur. One might well feel, on closing these books, that the end of all our exploring has been to arrive where we started and know the place for the first time.

HART CRANE'S LAST POEM

THERE is a literary superstition to the effect that the last work of a good artist is likely to show a deeper insight or wisdom, a last gathering of forces, as death comes on. There is enough corroborative evidence offered by the late work of artists who will immediately spring to mind to suggest that the legend is sometimes true. The manuscript of "The Broken Tower" is dated March 25, 1932. As Hart Crane's death occurred on April 27, it is almost certainly his last poem. Brom Weber wrote of it: "This poem is as personal as any poem could be; it is unquestionably one of Crane's most magnificent pieces." His judgment, if more enthusiastically expressed, echoes the general opinion. Unfortunately, its magnificence seems to have been blinding enough to have prevented anyone from looking very closely at it, for I am not aware that the poem has ever been commented on sufficiently to give more than the barest indication of its meaning. It is one of the most difficult poems Crane ever wrote, and the general response to it has been one of bafflement. Yet, paradoxically, it is one of the most logically organized and coherent among Crane's more difficult pieces, and the statement it makes is more central to Crane's life and his view of poetry than any other title in *The Collected Poems*. But its images come to life only when we realize that they are the sheerest verbal integument for a meaning that perfectly informs every word and metaphor in the ten quatrains. To understand that meaning verse by verse is to revive the piety that, at the end, a poet may have a deeper intuition of the meaning of his own creative effort and his life than he ever had before.

If "The Broken Tower" is a deeply personal poem, it is also an objective and deliberately thought out expression of Crane's literary faith in his last months, and it expresses what he had learned of his own limitations by writing *The Bridge*. But it expresses most of all the anguish of that discovery, and it is from this center of pain that the poetry germinates. There is a letter that Crane wrote to Allen Tate acknowledging the latter's review of *The Bridge* in which he says:

So many true things have a way of coming out all the better without the strain to sum up the universe in one impressive little pellet. I admit that I don't answer the requirements. My vision of poetry is too personal to "answer the call." And if I ever write any more verse it will probably be at least as personal as the idiom of *White Buildings* whether anyone cares to look at it or not.

Crane's early recognition (which is recurrent in his *Letters*) that *The Bridge* failed is behind this statement to Tate, for we find no such modesty in the notorious letter to Otto Kahn of September 12, 1927, outlining the design of his epic. After its publication, Crane's physical and moral decline allowed him little opportunity for serious composition. We have only "The Broken Tower" that merits serious attention, and if it is magnificent, it is also a little anomalous.

The best external clue to the meaning of the poem is Leslie

Simpson's letter to the *New English Weekly*, which Philip
Horton quotes in his biography of Crane:

> I was with Hart Crane in Taxco, Mexico, the morn-
> ing of January 27, this year, when he first conceived the
> idea of "The Broken Tower." The night before, being
> troubled with insomnia, he had risen before daybreak
> and walked down to the village square. It so happened
> that one of the innumerable Indian fiestas was to be
> celebrated that day, and Hart met the old Indian bell-
> ringer who was on his way down to the Church. He and
> Hart were old friends, and he brought Hart up into the
> tower with him to help ring the bells. As Hart was
> swinging the clapper of the great bell, half drunk with
> its mighty music, the swift tropical dawn broke over the
> mountains. The sublimity of the scene and the thunder
> of the bells woke in Hart one of those gusts of joy of
> which only he was capable. He came striding up the hill
> afterwards in a sort of frenzy, refused his breakfast, and
> paced up and down the porch impatiently waiting for
> me to finish my coffee. Then he seized my arm and bore
> me off to the plaza, where we sat in the shadow of the
> Church, Hart the while pouring out a magnificent cas-
> cade of words. It was a Hart Crane I had never known
> and an experience I shall never forget.

If the experience which began the chain of subjective
associations was an intensely personal one, the final meaning
which the reader should take from the poem is far more
public than the imagery in which it is expressed, and which
seems at first so inscrutably private, as if only meant for the
eyes of initiated illuminati.

While "The Broken Tower" is self-contained as a poem, it
will aid understanding if it is read with *The Bridge*, and
particularly with "For the Marriage of Faustus and Helen,"
freshly in mind. In some ways "The Broken Tower" is a

return on Crane's part, after the grandiose aspiration of *The Bridge*, to the more modest intention of the earlier sequence of three poems that composes "Faustus." In the earlier sequence Crane asserts that in the interaction between the abstract ideal and the degrading encroachments of the world that seek to destroy it, the life of the imagination is necessarily condemned to death. Part III ends:

> *Distinctly praise the years, whose volatile*
> *Blamed bleeding hands extend and thresh the height*
> *The imagination spans beyond despair,*
> *Outpacing bargain, vocable, and prayer.*

But if the imagination persists beyond despair, its final victory is not a complete triumph. "Faustus and Helen" has shown us the ideal of beauty, symbolized by the Helen of Part I, swaying to jazz tunes and exposed to modern lust in the skyscraper roof garden of Part II. Finally, in Part III, the imaginative life and the ideal world towards which it aspires seem utterly destroyed by the catastrophe of the First World War, which Crane unsuccessfully attempts to merge with images of the Trojan siege. But always Anchises escapes to the sea and founds a new city. The imaginative ideal cannot, perhaps, be achieved in a permanent form, but the transient intimations it gives us are all we have of life:

> *A goose, tobacco and cologne—*
> *Three-winged and gold-shod prophecies of heaven,*
> *The lavish heart shall always have to leaven*
> *And spread with bells and voices, and atone*
> *The abating shadows of our conscript dust.*

These lines are damaged a little poetically by the awkward obscurity of the opening trio of images, but they express an attitude basically more mature than the mystagogic, self-induced levitation that is attempted in the "Atlantis" section of *The Bridge*. The creative imagination struggles against odds in the world, but it carries an implicit promise with it that makes life endurable. When we look at a goose we are much aware of the part the duck plays in its ancestry, but it also has a good deal of the swan. The reference to tobacco as a prophecy of heaven is unfortunate because it merely suggests the daydreaming escape of the tobacco trance, while the introduction of cologne is too private a reference to deserve discussion. As human beings, we are concripted to the dust; our spiritual and emotional stature lessens in secular shadow, but the word of the poet, ringing out like a bell, prevents the ultimate encroachment of despair.

It was to this attitude that Crane returned in "The Broken Tower," but he was able to express it in his last poem with far greater concision; and the ordeal of having composed *The Bridge*, in which he tried to transcend his "conscript dust" towards some vaguely conceived cosmic consciousness, gives this poem the weight of a felt, a suffered, experience. It is coherent and emotionally realized in a degree that "Faustus and Helen" is not, but a similarity of imagery indicates the relation between the two pieces.

The first four stanzas of "The Broken Tower" comprise a movement that may be considered as a unit:

> *The bell-rope that gathers God at dawn*
> *Dispatches me as though I dropped down the knell*
> *Of a spent day—to wander the cathedral lawn*
> *From pit to crucifix, feet chill on steps from hell.*
>
> *Have you not heard, have you not seen that corps*
> *Of shadows in the tower, whose shoulders sway*
> *Antiphonal carillons launched before*
> *The stars are caught and hived in the sun's ray?*
>
> *The bells, I say, the bells break down their tower;*
> *And swing I know not where. Their tongues engrave*
> *Membrane through marrow, my long-scattered score*
> *Of broken intervals. . . . And I, their sexton slave!*

Oval encyclicals in canyons heaping
The impasse high with choir. Banked voices slain!
Pagodas, campaniles with reveilles outleaping—
O terraced echoes prostrate on the plain!

In my last quotation from "Faustus and Helen" Crane gives us a hint of the meaning of the bells and the tower. And there is Leslie Simpson's letter. Bells had already been established in his consciousness as the poet's voice, carrying, as we gather from the "Faustus" passage cited and from Simpson's account of the genesis of the poem, an insistent religious connotation. Such a connotation would be agreeable to Crane as the disciple of Whitman, for whom the poet was prophet and priest. If this is the meaning of the bells, then the tower that supports them must necessarily be the poet's vision. Helen of Part I stood for such a faith or vision in the earlier poem. It adds little to the grace of one's reading at this point to suggest that the bell-rope of the first line is the creative impulse of the poet: but that is what it is. Just as the rope of a great bell tyrannically exacts the coordinated response of its ringer's whole body, so are the exactions of the creative impulse on the poet equally tyrannical. And as a church bell calls worshipers to prayer, and rings out divine praises, so the poet endeavors to celebrate his imaginative vision in song. But for the poet of imperfectly realized vision, poetic creation is as much of a struggle as bell-ringing is for the sexton who does not understand the life and rhythm of his bell. So, momentarily relinquishing his grasp, the poet wanders disconsolately between the hell of creative sterility and the heaven of imaginative fulfillment in his art.

In the second verse, the shadows in the tower of vision are the poet's imperfect efforts to create. They recall "The abating shadows of our conscript dust" in "Faustus and Helen," and they suggest the shades of the dead. The sun in Apollo, the god of poetry and music, who enters appropriately here after the dawn image of the poem's opening line. Although the god is not named in the poem, the reference to "that tribunal monarch of the air / Whose thigh embronzes earth" leaves us in no doubt. Moreover, the complex metaphorical development that so closely attends the unfolding argument makes the identification inevitable. The shadow-songs in the poet's tower have been created in darkness, not under the patronage of Apollo, and they are imperfect. In Part II of "Faustus and Helen" Crane spoke of "the siren of the springs of guilty song," and these songs, swaying their shoulders as if in dance, invoke the siren, not the god. They are the songs of lust and darkness that (to quote "Faustus" once more) lead only to

> *metallic paradises*
> *Where cuckoos clucked to finches*
> *Above the deft catastrophe of drums.*

In one of Crane's most impressive metaphors they are contrasted with the light and sweetness that poetry is capable of achieving. In *The Bridge*, stars were employed as a symbol of vision on the point of realization. To take a single instance, one might cite the seventh verse of "The Dance." The protagonist, before leaving his canoe near the headwaters of the river up which he has made his excursion backward in time to achieve mystic identification with the Indian heritage of the past, sees the morning star fading into light. It is not necessary to believe that Crane realized his vision in "The Dance" to recognize the symbolic role the morning star is called upon to play. It is the herald of that mystical immersion in his vision that follows almost immediately in the ritual dance and death. In "The Broken Tower" the stars that fade into the light of morning represent perfect poems that are totally assimilated in the vision they express. Their light is absorbed by the sun, the god of perfect poetry, and in one of his finest lines Crane implements the star imagery with a suggestion of bees returning laden with sweetness to a great Platonic hive of absolute song. Perhaps it is worth remarking that Crane speaks of them in the second verse in terms of a hypothetical future, and, in any case, as beyond his reach. His tower is still inhabited with shadows.

In the third verse Crane gives us the poet's grapple with meaning. The torturing urgency to express what may even be inexpressible sometimes comes near to destroying the vision altogether:

> *The bells, I say, the bells break down their tower.*

This had happened, or had come dangerously near to happening, in Crane's own case when he wrote *The Bridge*. But even among the fragments of a vision no longer intact, the creative urgency of the poet continues. The bells swing, surrealistically, even without a supporting faith. This constitutes agony for the poet, and recalls his earlier lines,

> *There is the world dimensional for*
> *those untwisted by the love of things*
> *Irreconcilable . . .*

The commonplace dimensional world of things is only for those who accept its conventional boundaries; it cannot be for the poet, even when his vision is broken. His poetry may be imperfect, but he must continue to make it.

But imperfect or not, there is a sanctity about poems. They are the poet's encyclicals. They are described as oval because, since the metaphor is that of bells, sound radiates outward from its source in circles; and because, since they attempt to embody the poet's vision of the ideal and perfect, they suggest the circle of perfection, yet are imperfectly circular in themselves. Life is an enclosed and low-lying place from which the poet cannot free himself, and by the walls of which his vision is cut off. In the first verse the poet had been "dropped down the knell of a spent day," just as in the

"Proem" of *The Bridge* elevators had dropped him from the skyscraper tower of his vision into the city streets where cinemas invite humankind to the pursuit of appearance rather than reality. The poet who seeks an absolute, as Crane had done in *The Bridge*, becomes more than ever aware of the shadow-filled impasse of this "world dimensional." The struggle to escape from its denials towards vision is across a battlefield scattered with the evidences of creative defeat— "Banked voices slain!" But it is a holy struggle, and the voices are a choir's.

The "Atlantis" section of *The Bridge* celebrated high buildings and towers, which became a symbol of aspiration and achieved vision. Returning to this imagery in pagodas and campaniles, eastern temples and bell towers for churches, Crane continues to insist on the religious and aspiring nature of poetry by the introduction here of religious architecture in a surrealistic scene that faintly recalls the "Falling towers" passage in "What the Thunder Said." As the reveille (continuing the battlefield imagery of the preceding lines) is a summons to rise, the word emphasizes here, in a line of frenzied excitement bordering on delirium, the desperate quality of the poet's aspiration. It was a desperation Crane had learned in his struggle with *The Bridge*, seeing the vision elude him and its promises turn to ashes.

But if his vision was fragmentary, it was all he had of life; it was both his love and his hell:

And so it was I entered the broken world
To trace the visionary company of love, its voice
An instant in the wind (I know not whither hurled)
But not for long to hold each desperate choice.

My word I poured I poured. But was it cognate, scored
Of that tribunal monarch of the air
Whose thigh embronzes earth, strikes crystal Word
In wounds pledged once to hope—cleft to despair?

There is a reference here to the lovers Paolo and Francesca, hurled aimlessly in infernal winds, clasped in each others arms. The cruelty of the line

But not for long to hold each desperate choice

exists in Crane's growing belief that he had betrayed his vision and his powers. What seemed to him his creative inconstancy is expressed here in imagery that wells up from the growing frustration, in his last years, of his increasingly aimless sexual encounters. He envied the lovers the eternity of their embrace, even in hell.

The sixth verse gives us what are possibly the most moving lines of the poem. Crane handles the dual Christian and pagan implications of his verse with much skill. "My word I poured." "Word" here has a theological significance that is almost immediately developed. The "tribunal monarch," as I have already said, is Apollo. Were his poems, Crane asks, embodiments of that vitality or life force of the sun, suggested here in the reference to Apollo's embronzing thigh? Then, capitalizing Word, he shifts it to its Christian meaning, associating, in a fine act of compression, the word of the poet with the creative fiat of God. As the wounds of Christ brought hope, must the ordeal of the poet be hopeless? Is it (returning to Apollo in the musical term) "cleft to despair"?

The last four verses are technically the most original, as they are also the most difficult and the most personal. They provide us with Crane's final comment and judgment on his own practice as a poet, and on the possibilities of vision:

The steep encroachments of my blood left me
No answer (could blood hold such a lofty tower
As flings the question true?) —or is it she
Whose sweet mortality stirs latent power?—

And through whose pulse I hear, counting the strokes
My veins recall and add, revived and sure

The angelus of wars my chest evokes:
What I hold healed, original now, and pure . . .

And builds, within, a tower that is not stone
(Not stone can jacket heaven) — but slip
Of pebbles — visible wings of silence sown
In azure circles, widening as they dip

The matrix of the heart, lift down the eye
That shrines the quiet lake and swells a tower . . .
The commodious, tall decorum of that sky
Unseals her earth, and lifts love in its shower.

To recapitulate briefly: the poet, dedicated to an absolute, a Platonic vision, must necessarily fail to achieve it in his art. Crane had learned that the tower of absolute vision was much too lofty for him to climb in his poetry, and he realized this with peculiar clairvoyance at the close of his life when he seemed to be running down in a frenzy of neurotic debauchery. The steep encroachments of his blood seemed to be not only qualifying but destroying his poetic vision. Crane turns, therefore, from Apollo, whose fierce exactions he cannot satisfy, to the instruction of a lowlier, more human, guide, "she /Whose sweet mortality stirs latent power." This woman is not merely an abstract personification like the Pocahontas of *The Bridge*, she is a gracious evocation from the very center of Crane's own being, and she beckons him back to an acceptance of those creative limitations no poet can escape, but which *The Bridge* had desperately tried to deny. Crane is intimately aware of her in ways that suggest she is not, indeed, physically separable from Crane himself, but is an emblematic concentration of the feminine qualities of submission and humility in his own nature. Crane counts the beats of her pulse, but it is important to observe that the throbbing is in his own veins. She faintly recalls, in her identification with Crane, the nostalgic, nameless yearning he had expressed in "Southern Cross" and embodied in his picture of

homeless Eve,
Unwedded, stumbling gardenless, to grieve
Windswept guitars on lonely decks forever.

This rather exceptional Eve, unwedded and an outcast (Crane's own condition), he describes as "docile, alas, from many arms/ . . . wraith of my unloved seed!" She is less the object of his desire than his feminine counterpart and (in the guitar image) the burden of his songs. In what Brom Weber has called Crane's "womanless life," this focusing of the female elements in his nature—acceptance, passivity, acquiescence, humility—in terms of a symbolic woman is an astonishingly original way of encompassing the full circle of human experience which is necessary to achieve the final vision towards which the poem is directed, and which is explicitly described in the tenth verse. Crane's technical achievement here is more startling and original than Eliot's invention of using the male-female consciousness of Tiresias in *The Waste Land* to attain a somewhat similar goal.

The woman of "The Broken Tower" is differentiated at once from the swaying shadows of the second verse. Her "sweet mortality" relates to the bee and honey imagery of perfect song, but simultaneously qualifies the reference by the idea of limit implicit in "mortality." The presence of the qualities she represents provides a regenerating influence on Crane's vision: "What I hold healed, original now, and pure." The agony he has endured so long subsides before the Angelus, which teaches submission to the creative Word: "Be it done unto me." This is the lesson that he can only learn from woman, and the sweet lady of his poem suddenly looks towards him in the guise of the Virgin.

From this new feeling of wholeness and integrity the poet builds a new vision in which there is an interaction between heaven and earth—a vision in which both the Apollo of absolute song and the lady of "sweet mortality" play their parts. The Angelus, prayer of prophecy and submission, rings the

335

key of the last two stanzas, and they are verses composed of humilities and quiet acceptances. A slip is a pier to which ships come for docking and unloading. The word suggests here Crane's willingness to accept what his vision brings to his poetry without the frenetic attempt to force his experience, as he had done for so long. It is worth noting that the circling wings of the ninth verse recall the circling gull of the "Proem," which was a metaphorically successful prophecy of vision in *The Bridge* before that vision collapsed. In a sense Crane has returned in almost the last lines he ever wrote to a new beginning and a better vision than the old.

There are two aspects to poetry, then: its godlike aspiration, symbolized by the sun imagery, and its human limitations, embodied in the evoked lady of the seventh and eighth verses. Neither aspect can exist successfully without the other. The last verse deals in opposites which, in the imagery, live harmoniously together. Thus, "lift down" represents a poised balance between the two directions and tendencies. The "eye" is both the eye of the poet and the eye of heaven, the sun. Now that Crane understands that absolute vision can be approached only through the limiting and perhaps distorting perspectives of mortal vision, he draws closer to the possibility of genuine vision than he had ever been before, and one word does service both for the poet's eye and for the sun. This eye, or symbol of vision, shrines a lake—feminine symbol of acquiescence and passivity; but it also swells a tower—a masculine, aggressive symbol. Both symbols are sexual and implicitly contain the images of the god and the earth-bound lady, between whom union is now seen as possible. The blending of these constitutes the resolution, and the heaven of the poet's imagination. The last two lines show the interaction once again of the two tendencies, but it is the god imagery, the sky and the sun, which remains the stronger, though only complete in its acceptance of earth and limitation.

* * *

There is something oddly unsatisfactory about the state of Crane criticism today. Crane is readily accorded the rank of "major" American poet, but, the accolade having been given, usually in the most general terms, the talk then continues to anatomize the structural defects of *The Bridge*, the threadbareness of Crane's intellectual tradition, the inadequacy of his myth, or the occult obscurity of his imagery. One wonders how anyone dare call such a fellow, whom everyone is engaged in showing up, a "major" poet. The practical result has been that Crane is less read today than any other American poet of comparable importance. It is essential to understand the large defects of his poetry, and the critics who have outlined them have only performed their function in doing so. But on the positive side there is still a good deal to be said, and this is largely concerned with the complex beauty of Crane's best imagery, and the effectively original organization of his best poems. Yet on these points there has been comparative silence.

Crane himself is largely responsible for this state of affairs. His early admiration for P. D. Ouspensky and the higher consciousness, and his scattered remarks about a new dynamics of metaphor, and a use of symbols outside the rational order, have not encouraged a close scrutiny of what he was doing on the level of practice. Crane's poetry shows an unusually strong rational bias, which his blueprints for the structure of *The Bridge* should indicate, even if other evidence were lacking. Through most of his career it is probable that he misunderstood the nature of his own genius, for his theoretical statements on logic and metaphor sometimes seem to apply more aptly to *Ash Wednesday* or to Wallace Stevens' work than to his own, which is essentially different from either. The importance and beauty of "The Broken Tower" partly arise from the new depth of Crane's intuition into the creative process of his own mind, and from his willingness to accept it at last without forcing it into something larger than itself. It shows us Crane working his way into a new wisdom.

337

The organization of the poem clearly employs no new order of logic, no suprational use of symbols. It is an extremely difficult piece to cope with at first, but it gradually becomes clear that its difficulty is similar to what an early reader of Hopkins would have experienced. It is chiefly a matter of extraordinary verbal and syntactical compression, and the occasional elimination of nonessential words. In Hopkins' case such metaphorical compression has been called Shakespearean, and the term seems to me no less applicable to certain verses of this poem. Nor do I find a strained relationship between Crane's symbols and the reality they signify. The bells and the tower correspond at least as naturally and as tautly to the poet's voice and vision as Hopkins' windhover corresponds to Christ. Allen Tate has written: ". . . with a poetry which is near us in time, or contemporaneous, much of the difficulty that appears to be in the language as such, is actually in the unfamiliar focus of feeling, belief, and experience which directs the language from the concealed depths that we must laboriously try to enter." The difficulty of much of Crane's language is easily resolved by an application of those disciplines with which critics have been so ready and so adept in the case of Crane's contemporaries. Crane's poetry will not again have many readers until we cease to take Crane at his word and forget all that he said about the new dynamics of poetry and its new logic, its new use of symbols, and P. D. Ouspensky. These are will-o'-the-wisps, and only distract us from the more deeply traditional ways in which the originality of Crane's poetry, as its very best, enlarged and enriched the resources of language.

A NEW KIND OF POETRY?

R ELIEVED of all their former responsibilities, they [poets] can go about their business of making poems with words as pure as any scientist alone at his blackboard, solving theoretical problems that have absolutely no practical application at all." This quotation from John Thompson comes from a perceptive review of a group of new volumes of verse in which he describes one aspect of the current situation in poetry better than I have encountered elsewhere.[1] In the 1930's and '40's we heard a great deal from critics of the importance of the individual word or image in the context of the poem. "Every word can give an account of itself"—if I remember correctly, the statement comes from a discussion of Pope's poetry by F. R. Leavis, and in the ensuing analysis each word proceeded to do so. The account it gave was before the bar of the poet's total complex of creative motivations and intentions seen in the ambience of his ethos insofar as this could be apprehended by an intelligent, critically disciplined twentieth-century reader. There is no doubt that the American auxiliaries (if one may loosely and inaccurately call them so) of such English critics as Eliot, Leavis, Empson, and

1. *The New York Review of Books*, August 1, 1968.

Richards (who were independent critics and no "school") rapidly proceeded to Alexandrian excesses. Today it is customary to speak of a certain narrowness and constriction in their reading of poetry. If this is so in a short view, their criticism works ultimately towards a significant enlargement of the possibilities and precision of literary critical evaluation. Never before had the justified word been able to proclaim its election and assert its integrity so roundly and so proudly, and never before had the reader been able to understand the verbal-sense-rhythm morphology of a poem so well. These critics (both the English and the Americans) made a greater stride towards understanding *how* and *why* a poem is a success or a failure than any other critic or group of critics since Coleridge. But what I have to deal with here is not their success, but an unfortunate by-product of the excesses of the American auxiliaries.

The justified word, as these critics understood it, was a complex organism perfectly adjusted to the particular poetic environment in which it lived and fed and bred. Unfortunately, the Alexandrian critics of America were inclined to stop here, and they began to talk rather too much about the "autonomy" of a poem. But this was a conviction the English critics were not inclined to share. If they believed that the poem had to be read and evaluated in terms of its own verbal being, and not as a surrogate for social history, economic motives, archetypal patterns, or Freudian analysis, they continued to recognize that words and poems had responsibilities beyond themselves: responsibilities to meanings at many different levels—meanings *outside* the poem which were nevertheless relevant to the poem, as the poem was relevant to them; meanings to the poet who made the poem, to the reader who *remade* it in reading it, and was in turn altered by his reading; and meanings to the spirit of the age, which helped to make it, and which it helped to make. For the most part, English criticism resisted the Alexandrian concentration of focus and exclusiveness of purpose that the American critics of that day rejoiced in, and for whom the justified word had pretty much become the antinomian word which could do no evil.

With the advantages of hindsight it is easy to understand how this belief in the "autonomy" of the poem—indeed, of the word—gradually developed a *mystique* around it. If power corrupts, and absolute power corrupts absolutely, it is not astounding that the words in a poem, relishing their "autonomy" to the full, soon developed into god-emperors ready to renounce any and all responsibilities to anything save their own divinity.

Divinity is its own justification, and its name is I AM. The 1960's in America have seen the development of a kind of poetry whose strongest claim to being poetry is the fact that it is words on a page. Despite the fact that some of this poetry is written by young men teaching in important universities, it has become an axiom, frequently seen in print, that a formal literary training—especially if acquired in a university—disqualifies one from understanding these poets. If they really *are* poets, I agree.

In 1968 I received a review copy of a small book, *If Personal*, by Armand Schwerner, published by the Black Swallow Press. It contains what the author calls "window poems." Each page has a number of word sequences variously disposed across its surface, interspersed with small squares and rectangles that have been cut out of the paper. The pattern of open squares and rectangles varies on each page, and between each pair of pages there is a loose page of yellow paper that can be lifted out. By successively removing these loose pages, new words appear in each word sequence. On page 1:

> had striven, no,   striven
>   not Japan? not growing?

Removing the first loose yellow page, we have:

> *had striven, no, would had will ought striven*
> *not Japan? not growing?*

Removing the second yellow page, we have:

> *had striven, no, would had will ought striven*
> *orange ochre?*
> > *not Japan? not growing?*
> > *of the*
> > *surrender that*

Removing the third yellow page, we have:

> *had striven, no, would had will ought striven*
> *orange ochre?*
> > *not Japan? not growing?*
> > *of the*
> > *surrender that*
> > *on-&-on*

And so on.

From these four epiphanies it is clear that the words participating do not undervalue themselves *as words*. But what meaning or value is a mere mortal reader likely to discover in them? None, I am sure, unless he participates in that *mystique* which, as I suggested, has been growing up around the "autonomous" word as one of the unforeseen consequences of the worst excesses of the American New Criticism of the 1940's and the earlier '50's. The underlying assumption seems to be that words embody a unique reality that can be apprehended directly. This reality is a *thing-in-itself*, out of relation with other realities. The ultimate value of the word is neither descriptive nor significatory. What god's is? At this point proponents of this new attitude towards poetry grow a little vague. But there is usually the implication that the new poets—the liberated ones—are creating a new understanding of ontology, discovering some fresh dimension of, or perspective on, reality.

This is the general impression I have received over the past few years of a new kind of "poet" developing in America. The group is small but flourishing. I am the more convinced that my description of them is just because of a book that appeared several years ago, *Poets of Reality*, by J. Hillis Miller, a member of the faculty of Johns Hopkins University.

Miller is a learned and serious—indeed, solemn—critic and scholar, who has written this book to prove that a profound and radical shift has occurred, not only in the sensibility of the best poets writing in the twentieth century, but that it has occurred because they have learned to understand reality in an entirely different way from their predecessors. The relation existing between the word and reality for these writers is altogether more intimate, and essentially different in nature, than it was for traditional poets. Though this is surely not his intention, Miller in effect becomes the apologist for a large quantity of bad, shapeless poetry being written on these assumptions in America today.

Miller has little or nothing to say of the young poets who are writing now in the tradition he is so careful to describe and provide with a metaphysic, perhaps recognizing that the heirs would disgrace the founding fathers—or, at any rate, the poets whom he sees as the founding fathers. One of the founding fathers whom Miller postulates, however, seems to me richly worthy of his descendants. Miller gives us extended studies of six twentieth-century writers: Joseph Conrad, Yeats, Eliot, Dylan Thomas, Wallace Stevens, and William Carlos Williams. He is concerned to show how, under their almost extravagant differences, all of them have participated in what I suppose might be called a literary revision of the ontological assumptions of post-Cartesian, and especially Romantic, poets. His central argument begins with the plight of the nineteenth-century writer:

Writers of the middle nineteenth century . . . tend to accept the romantic dichotomy of subject and object, but are no longer able to experience God as both immanent and transcendent. . . . What was once a unity, gathering all together, has exploded into fragments. The isolated ego faces the other dimensions of existence across an empty space. Subject, objects, words, other minds, the supernatural—each of these realms is divorced from the others, and man finds himself one of the "poor fragments of a broken world."

The Victorians were unable to rectify this situation, largely because they persisted in a dualistic way of thinking and apprehending reality. God, the unifying ground of subject and object in the old system, had absconded, and not even Tennyson and Father Hopkins could call him back again. Nietzsche was more honest and announced that God was dead. Without God as the unifying ground, the foundation of everything, man turned inward for an alternative and made his consciousness the foundation of everything that existed. All objects became mental objects, and man found himself trapped in his own mind and in a universe which exists because his thoughts confer existence upon it. Of this situation Miller writes:

When God and creation become objects of consciousness, man becomes a nihilist. Nihilism is the nothingness of consciousness when consciousness becomes the foundation of everything. Man the murderer of God and drinker of the sea of creation wanders through the infinite nothingness of his own ego.

This kind of absolute subjectivism is like the descending spiral of a whirlpool rushing into the "eye" of its own annihilation. The only solution is for the artist somehow to escape into a real world which is more than a projection of his consciousness. But since the subjectivism of modern man has become the condition of his existence, escape is monstrously difficult. However, Miller believes that his chosen poets demonstrate there is still hope:

> The act by which man turns the world inside-out into his mind leads to nihilism. But this can be escaped only by a counterrevolution in which man turns himself inside out and steps, as Wallace Stevens puts it, "barefoot into reality.". . . To walk barefoot into reality means abandoning the independence of the ego. Instead of making everything an object for the self, the mind must efface itself before reality, or plunge into the density of an exterior world, dispersing itself in a milieu which exceeds it, and which it has not made.

The romantic conception of the self which voraciously draws the universe of objects into its vortex, remaking everything in its own image, Miller believes, is closely related to the world of modern technology, which also remakes the world in the images of man's ideas. While the domination both of the "subjective" self and of technology is so complete that man finds it hard to conceive of a different state, it was not always so. During the historical "imperialist" phase of technological expansion and development there were dark places on the earth where the primitive terror still lurked. Utilizing in art these peepholes into the buried darkness which is the substratum of all society and of personailty itself, Joseph Conrad was able to reveal the radical falsity of human action and of that collective effort we call civilization. This was essential in helping modern poetry escape its subjective prison, for: "Only if the nihilism latent in our culture would appear as nihilism would it be possible to go beyond it by understanding it."

Miller's chapter on Conrad serves as an approach to his five poets. One cannot help being distressed by his insistence on exploiting that very aspect of Conrad that has often drawn the fire of his better critics. Some years ago F. R. Leavis, regretting Conrad's "adjectival insistence upon inexpressible and incomprehensible mystery," went ahead to say: "He is intent on making a virtue of not knowing what he means. The vague and unrealizable, he asserts with a strained impressiveness, is the profoundly and tremendously significant." This element in Conrad not only enters into Miller's own argument but colors altogether too much of his prose, as in the following inscrutable passage:

> The heart of darkness is the truth, but it is a truth which makes ordinary human life impossible. It is the absorption of all forms in the shapeless night from which they have come. A man who reaches the truth is swallowed up by a force which invades his reason and destroys his awareness of his individuality. To know the darkness is to know the falsity of life, and to understand the leap into emptiness man made when he separated himself from the wild clamor of primitive life.

Miller, then, argues that Conrad's art, by revealing (in Conrad's own words) that "one's own personality is only a ridiculous and aimless masquerade of something hopelessly unknown," makes possible for later writers a retreat from darkness back into the light of an objective world.

Of the chapters which deal with the poets, the one on Eliot is the best. In the essay on Williams, Miller refers to Eliot as an example of "the academic mind, dry and abstract, imposing its dead forms on life," but if this is an expression of his real view the prejudice does not intrude into his study of Eliot's work.

Eliot's earlier poetry was written when he was deeply under the influence of F. H. Bradley. Although the monistic base of Bradley's philosophy might (one would have thought if there is truth in Miller's thesis) have provided an escape hatch from the extreme subjectivism of the modern writer, Bradley proved a peculiar case. For him, each individual (or finite center, to use Bradley's term) is completely enclosed within the opaque, impenetrable circle of his own consciousness. As Miller summarizes it: "Each man seems destined to remain enclosed in his separate sphere, unable to break out to external things, to other people, to an objective time and space, or to God. All these exist, but as qualifications of the inner world which is peculiar and private to the self."

The way in which this idea of the incommunicado ego, unable to communicate with others, influenced Eliot's early poetry is apparent at once. When one recognizes that Prufrock is a "finite center" one makes a significant critical perception about the poem, and simultaneously senses something of the horror concealed in Bradley's system. Eliot's problem from the first was to establish lines of communication between "finite centers," and this was a task in comparison with which interplanetary communication seems elementary. Miller's account of how Eliot managed to do this, evolving a complex theory of poetic creation in which emotive images were made to vibrate in resonance not only with the deepest centers of the buried self, but to command across the unfathomable gulfs sympathetic vibrations in the responses of others, constitutes a brilliant display of critical legerdemain. One can't really believe it, but one enjoys the illusion of belief.

The vibrating emotive images are only the first step in his description of the elaborate strategy developed in Eliot's earlier essays in which, to achieve universality within the closed circle of one's own consciousness, Eliot ingeniously turned his mind inside-out into a collective consciousness he labeled "the mind of Europe." It is impossible to follow Miller's unfolding of this process here, but at the moment of Eliot's apparent triumph in escaping from the subjective self, Miller draws us up sharply: "This triumph is really defeat. The quality of the mind of Europe is exactly the same as the experience of the solitary ego. Though Eliot has expanded his mind to include all history he is within the same prison, the prison of the absence of God. . . ."

In other words, at this mid-point in his career Eliot was still in the position of most nineteenth-century writers, for God remained an object of consciousness rather than its sustaining foundation. Eliot's conversion to Christianity occurred between *The Waste Land* and *Ash Wednesday*. With his conversion he accepted the idea of Incarnation. This acceptance of Incarnation is crucial in Miller's analysis of Eliot as a "poet of reality," for with this idea he necessarily rejected the idealism that had imprisoned him in a subjective world. Incarnation constitutes "a reversal which recognizes that time, nature, other people, and God are external to the self. . . . Only when he sees the emptiness of collective subjectivism can he find the humility to see that existence is outside himself and not the same as his understanding of it."

Several of the other essays contribute more heavily to the general sense of Miller's central thesis. Among these the one on Wallace Stevens is the most satisfactory. The one subject that Stevens took for his poetry, the relation between the imagination and reality, is at the very heart of Miller's argument. The essay demonstrates that the relative values Stevens attached to the imagination and reality were not constant, but shifted like light and color in his "Sea Surface Full of Clouds." "It is impossible to find a single systematic theory of poetry and life in Stevens," Miller writes, and herein, one suspects, resides the perpetual vitality of a large body of poems, every one of which is written on the same subject.

Miller is interesting on the relation between Stevens' poetry and modern painting, and on his rarefied but moving concern with being in his later poems. One is pleased that he singles out one of Stevens' finest but neglected poems, "Chocorua to Its Neighbor," for special recognition. But a note that has been faintly sounded from time to time begins to grow more insistent. To cite a single sentence that exemplifies it: "Poetry can take only one step farther into reality, and that is to make language itself into a substance." Naturally Miller knows this is impossible, but he begins to talk a little queerly whenever the subject comes up, no doubt as a means of preparing the reader for his final chapter on William Carlos Williams.

Stevens has a habit of speaking as if he regretted having to use words in his poems instead of the things signified by the words. There are a number of possible legitimate theories of esthetic reality behind Marianne Moore's famous reference to "imaginary gardens with real toads in them," but one knows that she never meant a poem is a vivarium. If Stevens had really wanted to make a poem out of, say, a primrose, an amethyst, a glass eye, and a coronet he would have become another Joseph Cornell and not one of the major users of words in this century. To maintain that a poet really resents the limitations of his medium is either to suggest that the man is no poet or that oneself subscribes to literary occultism. That poetry and language should be on the move towards the light and circulating air of objectivity is fine, and Miller gets the exodus from a subjective underworld off to a splendid start. But before his book is quite finished one has the impression that words are not expected to be words any longer, but should sprout feathers and fingernails.

Up to and including the chapter on Stevens, Miller's book has been illuminating, even though one may have made a number of reservations along the way. But what is meant to be the climactic essay on Williams impresses me as a disaster. Miller's thesis that modern poetry moves into and apprehends reality in a new way unquestionably possesses *some* validity, though precisely how much is not settled by this book. Discreetly employed, it is capable of contributing to an understanding of modern poetry, but it is also the kind of thesis that easily betrays the author into inflated statements and judgments.

We learn that at the age of twenty, by a deliberate decision which he mentioned in a letter to Marianne Moore, Williams deserted his private consciousness and resigned himself to objective existence, thereby bypassing the arduous labors of Eliot and Stevens and so getting virtually a lifetime's start on them in which to bring his genius to unprecedented perfection. Of this electric moment in and out of time Miller declares:

> The resignation to existence which makes Williams' poetry possible is the exact reverse of the Cartesian Cogito. Descartes puts everything in question in order to establish the existence of his separate self, an existence built on the power of detached thinking. Williams gives himself up in despair and establishes a self beyond personality, a self co-extensive with the universe. Words, things, people, and God vanish as separate entities and everything becomes a unit.

The lack of polarity described in this statement may explain what Miller calls in another place "a strange lack of tension in his work." In a vocabulary different from Miller's it may also explain why Williams is the dullest poet of any importance America has produced in this century. To justify the claims Miller makes for Williams, poetry would indeed have had to move into a different dimension of reality from the one I assume it still more or less occupies. But as it is precisely Miller's point that in Williams' poetry the transition into a new dimension has been accomplished, disagreement or discussion is perhaps futile.

Miller submits poem after poem to sustained technical analysis, the effect of which, for me at least, is only perversely to reveal the nullity of the work he is examining.

350

Miller once again wheels out that creaking old red wheelbarrow from "Spring and All," of which he writes:

> The wheelbarrow . . . does not stand for anything or
> mean anything. It is an object in space dissociated from
> the objects around it, without reference beyond itself. It
> is what it is. The aim of the poem is to make it stand
> there for the reader in its separateness, as the words of
> the poem stand on the page.

If the reader is inclined to ask why one shouldn't go out in
the chicken yard and look at the wheelbarrow itself, Miller is
not unaware of the difficulty, but his answer is singularly
hollow: "The poet must make use of the referential meaning
of words to relate them to physical objects as a springboard
from which they may leap into a realm of imagination carrying with them the things named in a new form." I do not
know what this means, or rather among several possible
meanings that occur to me I can discover none that is ever
likely to illuminate one's knowledge of a poem or enrich one's
response to it.

Many years ago the late R. P. Blackmur wrote of Williams' poetry: "Observation, of which any good novelist must
be constantly capable, here makes a solo appearance: the
advantage is the strength of isolation as an attention-caller to
the terrible persistance of the obvious, the unrelenting significance of the banal." That seems to me a critical judgment
substantial and durable enough to cast its shadow in any
dimension of reality, however new or strange.

I have by no means wished to imply that I think Miller's
argument is without some validity. What I object to are the
intimations of *cult* and *initiation* which he communicates to
the reader when he discusses such poets as Williams. Williams' decision, mentioned in his letter to Marianne Moore, to
desert his private consciousness and resign himself to objective existence is as absurd as Margaret Fuller's decision to

accept the universe. And it becomes doubly absurd in the inflated commentary on it which I have quoted. Williams and Fuller may have been speaking of somewhat different things, but in their pretentiousness and lack of humility they were like brother and sister. The Romantics may have wished to merge with the universe: I know of none who wanted to swallow it.

Of course Miller is correct when he argues that some younger poets are turning from a romantic and subjective perspective on reality to a more objective one. This, however, implies nothing more than a shift in sensibility where a relatively small group of writers is concerned. Nothing so radical as a revolution in metaphysics or psychology is required to explain it. Probably a good many of these writers really did take Williams' attempt to establish "a self beyond personality, a self co-extensive with the universe," as seriously as Miller. At any rate, a good many of them have succeeded in excluding individual personality from their poetry. What Miller conspicuously fails to observe is that, while some young poets are intent on walking "barefoot into reality," a larger number—and on the whole, I think, much better poets—are more subjective than ever before.

INDEX

353

MARIUS BEWLEY

Marius Bewley received his B.A. and Ph.D. degrees from Cambridge University, and was Professor of English at Rutgers University. He was the author of *The Complex Fate: Hawthorne, Henry James and Some Other American Writers; The Eccentric Design: Form in the Classic American Novel;* and *The English Romantic Poets: An Anthology with Commentaries.* He was also a member of the editorial board of *The Hudson Review* until his death in 1973.

Atheneum Paperbacks

LITERATURE AND THE ARTS

Atheneum Paperbacks

HISTORY—AMERICAN—BEFORE 1900

Atheneum Paperbacks

HISTORY—AMERICAN—1900 TO THE PRESENT

Atheneum Paperbacks

HISTORY

HISTORY—ASIA

Atheneum Paperbacks

Atheneum Paperbacks

THE WORLDS OF NATURE AND MAN

LIFE SCIENCES AND ANTHROPOLOGY

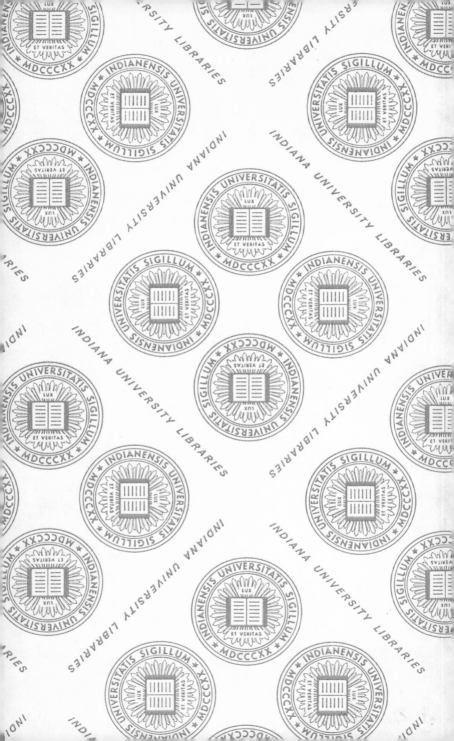